SHARED SERVICES

In an increasingly competitive world, it is quality of thinking that gives and edge. An idea that opens new doors, a technique that solves a problem, or an insight that simply helps make sense of it all.

We work with leading authors in the fields of management and finance to bring cutting-edge thinking and best learning practice to a global market.

Under a range of leading imprints, including *Financial Times Prentice Hall,* we create world-class print publications and electronic products giving readers knowledge and understanding which can then be applied, whether studying or at work.

To find out more about our business and professional products, you can visit us at **www.business-minds.com**

For other Pearson Education publications, visit **www.pearsoned-ema.com**

SHARED SERVICES

Mining for Corporate Gold

BARBARA QUINN

ROBERT COOKE

ANDREW KRIS

FINANCIAL TIMES
Prentice Hall

An imprint of PEARSON EDUCATION

Harlow, England · London · New York · Reading, Massachusetts · San Francisco · Toronto · Don Mills, Ontario · Sydney
Tokyo · Singapore · Hong Kong · Seoul · Taipei · Cape Town · Madrid · Mexico City · Amsterdam · Munich · Paris · Milan

PEARSON EDUCATION LIMITED

Head Office:
Edinburgh Gate
Harlow CM20 2JE
Tel: +44 (0) 1279 623623
Fax: +44 (0) 1279 431059

London Office:
128 Long Acre
London WC2E 9AN
Tel: +44 (0) 207 447 2000
Fax: +44 (0) 207 240 5771

Website www.business-minds.com

First published in Great Britain 2000

ISBN 0-273-64455-6

British Library Cataloguing in Publication Data
A catalogue record for this book is available from the British Library.

Library of Congress Cataloging in Publication Data
Applied for.

10 9 8 7 6 5 4 3 2

Typeset by Pantek Arts
Printed and bound in Great Britain by Biddles Ltd, Guildford & King's Lynn

The publishers' policy is to use paper manufactured from sustainable forests.

ABOUT THE AUTHORS

Barbara E. Quinn

Barbara is one of the founders and a managing partner with CAIL Consulting Group Inc., a company based in Canada with offices and strategic partners in the United States and the United Kingdom. CAIL Consulting Group Inc. specializes in helping internal staff groups position themselves as "supplier of choice." The group has helped numerous organizations design and successfully implement shared services. Barbara is a strong and outspoken advocate for retaining corporate staff groups in-house provided that they operate as a business and are completely client focused. She recently co-authored the immensely popular and much sought after professional journal *Adopting and Implementing Shared Services*. This work was commissioned by the Certified Management Accountants Society, AICPA, and the Australian Society of Certified Practising Accountants. Formerly the head of human resources for Levi Strauss and Company Canada, Barbara has a Masters Degree in Education, a Batchelor of Arts Honours Degree and an undergraduate certificate in Psychology. With her extensive shared services expertise, Barbara is a frequently sought-after conference presenter.

Robert S. Cooke

Robert is one of the founders and a managing partner with CAIL Consulting Group Inc., which works exclusively with corporate and internal staff groups on improving their effectiveness and profile within an organization. Robert has a reputation for creating provocative dialogue and for being relentless in his challenge for corporate staff functions to become a well-run business. He co-authored the professional journal *Adopting and Implementing Shared Services*. With extensive international corporate and consulting experience, combined with an MBA and Batchelor of Science Degree, Robert is a much sought-after chairman and conference presenter on the subject of designing and implementing shared services.

Andrew Kris

Andrew is a prominent commentator on the worldwide development of shared services and founder of The Shared Services Forum, the leading news, advice and information website on shared services. A Brussels, Belgium-based partner in Amrop International, Executive Search, Andrew's experience in leading and restructuring business units and internal services in The Dow Chemical Company is the foundation for his work as an international headhunter and shared services expert. Passionate about eliminating corporate bureaucracies and the liberating impact of internal enterprise, Andrew is a challenging and sought-after speaker in corporate boardrooms and at international conferences.

The authors have made every effort to contact all those who appear in
Shared Services: Mining for Corporate Gold. *They would like to thank the*
following people and organizations for their contribution to this book:
David Ulrich; David Maister; Richard Julien *of the Bank of Canada;*
Wayne Bester; Richard Ussery *of Total System Services Inc.; Dan*
Henderson *of Allied Signal Business Services; Jossey Bass Publishing Inc.*
(for permission to reproduce extracts from Leadership Practices, Boards
that Make a Difference, The Leader of the Future and Organizational
Culture and Leadership*); Dennis Wymore of Shell Services International;*
David Harrison and John Ashurst of BC Hydro; John O'Connor and Vipin
Suri of Ontario Hydro; Jack Welch and Steven Kerr of General Electric;
Bernie Kocanda of Kraft foods; Peter Adye of Procter and Gamble; Edgar
Schein; Bjarnie Anderson of Mobil Business Resources Corporation; Reg
Milley of Husky Oil; Steve Freeman of Whirlpool Europe; Bertil Wrethag of
the ABB Group; William Stavropoulos of the Dow Chemical Company;
Rory Colfer of KPMG; Andrew Tank of the Conference Board; Random
House (for permission to reproduce from Dangerous Company*); Bob*
Gunn of Gunn Partners; Fran Bengtson of Lockheed Martin; Sheila Reid
of Xerox Canada; Paula Farrell of Fidelity Investments; Rosabeth Moss
Kanter; Doug Massingill of J.D. Edwards; Larry Giammo of the
Corporate Leadership Council; Richard Hays; Gordon Shank of Levi
Strauss & Company; Waters Davis of Reliant Energy; Gelco Information
Network; David Kunkel of PSINet Inc.; John Cleghorn of Royal Bank
Financial Group; Tribune Company; Malcolm Kitchener of the Post
Office; David O'Sullivan of Whirlpool Europe; Joe Corry of Ashland
Services; Milan Kunz of SmithKline Beecham PLC; Jim Bryant and
Joseph W. Rahain of Ernst and Young; David Garrison of Aetna
Insurance; Lee Kercher of the California State Department of Information
Technology; Marianne Elliot; Harvard Business School Press (for repro-
ducing material from The Balanced Scorecard*); James Bryan Quinn;*
Simon & Schuster Inc. (for reproducing material from Intelligent
Enterprise *and* Managing the Professional Services Firm*); Tom Peters and*
Waterman; HarperCollins Publishers (for reproducing material from
In Search of Excellence *and* Built to Last*); Dr Leland Forst of The*
Amherst Group; Janet Faas of Ontario Government Shared Services
Bureau; Nate Oubre of Kaiser Permanente; Dun & Bradstreet; Dwight H.
Mills of Owens Corning; Ian Gordon; John Wiley & Sons (for reproducing
material from Relationship Marketing*); The Drucker Foundation; Chip*
Bell; Peter Block; Berrett Koehler Publishing (for reproducing material
from Customers as Partners and Stewardship*); Ricardo Semler; Warner*
Books Publishing (for reproducing material from Maverick*); IBM Global*
Services; Shell Services International Inc; Baxter International, Darcy
Volk of Unisys Shared Services Centre; Ralph Andretti of Amex;
Robert Clausen of Solutia Inc.; The Conference Board; Ashridge
Strategic Management; Informix; IDA; the Netherlands Development
Agency; Edward de Pasquale of Conemaugh Health Systems;
and TRW Automotive.

We thank Marc Besner for his encouragement and tenacity in urging us to write this book and for keeping us going before any of this mammoth project was even a process; to June Dagnall for her constant vision and excellent project management; to Les Ames of Meta Design Inc. for breathing life into our major models and artwork, to Colleen Causton for making our words come alive with her design; to Barbara Schultz-Jones for her insightful and wise comments on the content and structure.

CONTENTS

Chapter 1

THE SEARCH FOR GOLD

The lights dim, the theater crowd sits in expectant silence as the curtain goes up. The show is called "Mining for Corporate Gold" with a byline that reads "Staff functions are the key." There are some chief executive officers who can be seen to stifle their yawns discreetly while a few impatiently finger their program. A handful of chief financial officers are quietly chatting to their neighbours about the probable plot and storyline. Information technology executives are musing about the future, confident they will be a major player. Human resource executives are wondering what the chief executive officers are thinking about. Supply executives are still pondering how they ended up in the same room as these people, and marketing is wondering why anyone ever called this kind of work staff and overhead functions. Not a good branding move, they think to themselves. Many consultants and outsource suppliers are in the audience taking bets on how much of a starring role they will play in the movie. Over to one side of the theater is a group of senior government officials and a few heads of "not-for-profit" corporations, looking anxiously around at the corporate audience. They are quietly hoping the show will have some meaning for them, having been disappointed before at the difficulty of translating big business ideas to their unique environment. If you look carefully to one of the faintly lit exit signs, there is a handful of line managers looking ready for an early escape. They discuss their common love of action films, wishing they were at the theater next door.

The curtain slowly rises. A flickering image of an old prospector with a rumpled felt hat scratches on to the screen like an old black and white snapshot. The grainy background shows a rocky patch of terrain, a focused man bent over, hiking boots muddy and worn, two hands grasping a gold pan, tilting the pan in murky water and swirling it to concentrate the heaviest materials on the bottom. Before he lifts his face and before we know whether he will smile silently at the discovery of the elusive gold lying shyly at the bottom, the narrator's voiceover begins.

STAFF FUNCTIONS ARE BIG BUSINESS

Staff functions are big business. Worth billions of budget dollars, they represent the last frontier for major cost savings, they are the gold nuggets at the bottom of the pan. Organizations which have taken the time to concentrate on staff functions have found an amazing yield. Not only have they taken an easy 25–30% out of their operating budget, they have managed to increase service responsiveness to the operating and business units. Yet there are still organizations today where enormous duplication of effort spans countries, companies, divisions and business units. These organizations do not seem to notice that each business has a carbon copy staff function, doing basically the same thing with little unique refinement. Granted the core business might be different in each unit but staff work is staff work. In fact, staff people can get jobs from one sector to the next, moving from mining to insurance, demonstrating that the essential discipline is common even though the business or government is different. There is simply no longer an argument for staff duplication based on proprietary needs, culture, language or simple uniqueness. Pan-European shared service centers are working effectively today.

Organizations have been working hard over the past decade trimming and refining processes, weeding out unprofitable product lines, and seeking out strategic acquisition and growth opportunities to stay a winner in the game. Terms like downsizing, rightsizing, streamlining, re-engineering, process ownership, and value creation are all part of the current lexicon to describe the frantic search for cost savings. Up until recently, staff functions have generally not kept pace with their operational colleagues although exceptions are duly noted. In a way, corporate and internal staff groups are under siege since the war being waged against them is to dangle the Damocles sword of outsourcing over their heads. Fingers pointing squarely at staff groups, with a threat to shape up or they will be shipped out.

> *Outsourcers in the audience snap to attention, thinking to themselves, "See, I knew we would be featured." Some of the line managers in the audience are leaning forward.*

There is a growing view amongst business units and operating company heads that corporate functions such as finance, information technology, human resources, and supply are not doing enough, or in some cases not doing anything differently than they have in the past. In fact, in some cases, there is growing animosity and resentment over the costs these functions are incurring for providing what is perceived to be of nominal value. Public sector managers share the frustration with their private sector colleagues, angry at the fact that too much money is being siphoned away from the actual program areas and spent instead on administration and overheads. They want more money in education at the classroom level, in health services at the patient care level, and in social services at the street level, not in burgeoning staff groups in head-quarters or the regions.

The public sector and government is a huge arena for change where corporate staff functions represent big ticket items in an ever decreas-ing budget. The tax paying public are demanding increased accountability for spending wisely and simply are not prepared to keep funding the cost of government without any clear evidence of a major and fundamental move to decrease costs. This tax paying public is not expecting to have fewer services but rather expecting government to find ways of delivering those services at less cost. Government's typical method for decreasing costs is to universally make cuts across all pro-gram lines rather than take a focused look at the difference between internal corporate functions and the delivery of programs to the public. Cutting public services at the ground level will not be sufficient to assuage the growing animosity over high costs of government. We don't want the local licensing bureau to cut office hours and reduce the time the office is open; we want more accessible services for less cost and that means looking to staff areas.

Public sector executives in the audience lean forward, pleased to hear that they are part of this story. A few CEOs and public sector executives sit smugly knowing they have already discovered this gold.

These are the ones who have endorsed shared services which is the relatively simple practice of deciding to share common services between a group of companies, divisions or business units. A group of health care organizations decide to share common financial and human resource services rather than fund their own. A global manufacturer creates a common financial processing center dedicated to providing world-class services to operations located around the globe. A government decides it can no longer afford to support seventeen staff groups spread across eighteen ministries or state offices. These leaders have been busy think-ing. They know the value of staff work, its potential as valuable grease for the company wheels, but they have figured out how to lever and extract the potential from the resource.

Dan Henderson, vice president and general manager of Allied Signal Inc., is one of those executives. Five years ago, the 70,000 plus employee company decided on a mission to be a model of corporate effi-ciency and combined more than 75 functions into a shared service center spanning five functional areas. Today, about 1,100 employees provide services to the entire organization which has saved the com-pany $300 million during the last five years.[1] Gaurdie Banister, president of Shell Services International Inc. (USA), is also nodding at

The challenge of shared services is to reduce costs without compromising quality

the fact that the company has one of the largest shared service organizations in the world with approximately 5,000 employees and about $1 billion in sales. It has helped Shell Oil pare costs by 30–40% and have risen to the challenge of taking costs out without compromising quality. Darcy Volk, general manager of the Unisys Shared Services Center is another executive reflecting on the fact that they have helped the company to slash costs by about 50% and reduced the time needed to process financial transactions. Malcom Kitchener, managing director of the Post Office Services Group in the United Kingdom, has figured out the need to get the internal market strategy right. Janet Faas, the chief executive officer of the Shared Services Bureau for the Ontario Government of Canada, is thinking about how much of a challenge lies ahead to manage the successful change to shared services. They have taken a bold step to remove the duplication of staff functions across 17 ministries and formed one separate service entity.

Bertil Wrethag, the manager of Support Services for the ABB Group, also sits in this group knowing how wise shared services has been for them. Thirty-six shared service centers around the world, 3,000–4,000 people providing services in seventeen countries dedicated to the service vision of being competitive with external services both in quality and price and offering a 10% improvement in productivity and price year on year. Fran Bengtson, business development manager at Lockheed Martin, also sits there knowing that their shared service organization has pledged a commitment to take out 60% of the staff costs in the center while providing high quality service to sixty lines of business. Wayne Bester, the general manager of Amoco's Canadian Shared Services, thinks about how since 1995 their move to shared services has resulted in a $40 million reduction in total cost structure – a huge 30% of their operating expenses. Joe Corry, the director of shared services for the Ashland Company in Rotterdam, also thinks about their experience and is anxious for people to know that shared services is not only about costs. They have really worked at providing their internal customers with better services. Paula Farrell of Fidelity Investments acknowledges the powerful cost savings from shared services but admonishes staff groups which do not take the time to understand client expectations and how best to meet them. She likes to challenge shared service groups which only see cost as the issue with, "How arrogant for you to assume you know what your clients want." Bernie Kocanda, the director of shared services for Kraft Foods, thinks about the 200 people in their shared services center. They began in 1994 and know the benefits of dollar savings but also stress the need for a renewed service focus. These organizations are only a few of the many that have discovered the gold in shared services.

Other executives tune out since staff work has never and will never be what excites them. They reflect on the fact that costs have been cut before in these areas. These ones get a nudge from their chief financial officers in the audience with a whisper that the best is yet to come. The narrator continues.

Staff functions have a history of being a primary target in corporate cost cutting exercises and over the years have taken their fair share of budget slashing. The problem is that simple cost cutting is a short-term measure. The long-term answer for staff functions lays not only in numbers and dollars but in a much deeper and more fundamental exploration of what staff groups need to deliver and how best to deliver it.

A few executives from information technology, finance, and human resources sit fuming in the audience wondering why the film isn't showing the success stories. As if the narrator senses the tension, the next words soften the sting.

In some companies, the staff groups are seen as vital and strategic contributors to overall corporate performance. There are lots of success stories. Unfortunately, the negative comments tend to outweigh the positives in many cases. Staff groups are openly and sadly referred to as bloated bureaucracies which as one executive put it, "are woefully out of touch with reality and the real needs of the business!"

The business of staff business needs an overhaul. Smart staffers will not wait for the tap on the shoulder but will take a courageous stand to reinvent themselves. The pressure is mounting for staff groups to redefine themselves even if they are seen as relatively good today. It's true that outsourcing of staff groups is becoming a way to dump problems into someone else's backyard hoping third parties will find gold in the debris. This would make for a good action film. Companies rushing forward to take the plunge, not necessarily knowing why!

To understand the plunging phenomenon, we need to delve more deeply into the staff storyline, so we can figure out how to account for the fact that outsourcing is predicted to be a whopping $200 billion market by the year 2000.[2] We have to study the intricacies of staff functions, explore the underlying dilemmas that are inherent in the role disparagingly referred to simply as "corporate overhead." We need to discover the plot and sub-text, the discrete characteristics of staff work.

The top three plot elements:

✦ staff groups are monopolies and monopolies are always resented and reviled;

✦ decentralization is passé – line managers favor it even when it does not make any sense;

✦ staff roles suffer from wearing two hats: corporate enforcer and friendly service representative all rolled into one.

STAFF GROUPS AS MONOPOLIES

Staff groups typically operate in the privileged position of a monopoly supplier at a time when deregulation has virtually touched every traditional industry including the local telephone and electric light company. Few companies in the world today enjoy the privilege of an unregulated monopoly where customers are forced to buy their products and services at whatever price the company wants to charge. Monopoly behavior breeds arrogance. The phone company of the old days would primly inform you that it would take three weeks or two months to get an installation, or that there was one rate for long-distance calling, take it or leave it. The hidden sub-text was: "You don't like it, too bad for you." Organizations which have undergone deregulation will tell stories of how they underestimated to a factor of one hundred the challenge from having guaranteed customers to having to earn them one at a time. Old monopolies often delude themselves into considering themselves world class without any idea how hard it is to attract and retain customers who are no longer hostages. In one telephone company, executives did not really hear the continual plaintive cries for help from their internal sales group until one brave sales executive put an overhead up on the projector which showed an astounding 14,000 customers leaving weekly to go to competitors. The current vernacular for this kind of event is known as "a wake up call." They got the message!

Yet internal functions such as finance, information technology, human resources, marketing and supply are allowed to operate as internal monopolies where their internal clients are hostage to what comes from having the choice of only one supplier. Typically, there is no option to seek alternatives since the staff groups are in essence mandated services. When the quality of service does not meet expectations, there is no real recourse. For staff working in a monopoly, it is hard to service the customer. It is not as though staff people wake up in the morning and tell themselves not to care about service, it is just that no pressure to perform over time makes staff groups become inwardly focused. Staff groups often unwittingly start seeing their clients as an intrusion. One staff member actually said in a meeting, "We need to close our office down for a half a day every week because the clients keep interrupting us when we are trying to get our paperwork and records in order." The privilege of sole supplier often turns into a liability since it is difficult to establish a service-minded attitude when your game is the only one in town. Staff people unconsciously have a hard time shifting from an entitlement mode where work is guaranteed to a service mode where work and reputation are earned.

Any type of monopoly by definition establishes artificial supports that do not allow natural forces of supply and demand to determine destiny. Staff services are frequently subsidized today where products, programs and reports are produced that clients don't even want and certainly would not pay for if they had to. There is something about a monopoly environment that makes for a great deal

Having choice is a fundamental desire for consumers of any service

of resentment. After telephone companies became deregulated and there were choices, many consumers reported they left their old phone company simply because they could, not even because they had any deep and dark grudges against them. There is something powerful about choice. Applying the same logic to staff functions is long overdue. Good client relationships do not generally start out with a resentful attitude. It is time for staff groups to open themselves up as free agents.

DUPLICATION AND DECENTRALIZATION ARE PASSE

The luxury of having duplicate identical services in each business unit and operating company is a cost that most companies simply can no longer afford. For years, staff groups have vacillated between centralization and decentralization. Centralization is unarguably cheaper and more efficient but often suffers from its sordid history of a bureaucratic center with no idea of service or the real world. The corporate memory is long and fraught with real stories about deals lost, staff grievances and customers caught in the middle because of center staff insensitivity and incessant bad judgement. When line managers do not get what they need to run the business, they find other ways. In fairness, the proliferation of distributed or decentralized staff groups is usually due to a likely history of unacceptable service from a centralized group. Operations executives did not wake up one morning and say to themselves, "Hey ho, let's waste corporate money and duplicate services unnecessarily."

Imagine this duplication spread across twenty companies, fifty operating divisions, and the picture of redundancy becomes very clear.

Business units unhappy with the service they receive from the corporate center have been duplicating services and functionality, in some cases just to survive. So, corporations have ended up with multiple human resources, finance, and information technology functions (see Figure 1.1) which is costing the enterprise far more than it should be spending with little evidence of increased value. The myth of decentralization is that service must be better. Maybe and maybe not. A business case can often be made that clearly demonstrates improved service levels, not just reduced costs through a consolidated center. Faced with the facts, individual business units will still argue to retain control, which leads to a working theory that it must really be about control. Most organizations cannot sustain the duplication from distributed staff

FIGURE 1.1   Duplication of business units

Business Unit	Business Unit	Business Unit	Business Unit
Finance	Finance	Finance	Finance
HR	HR	HR	HR
IT	IT	IT	IT
Supply	Supply	Supply	Supply

groups. It is folly unless an organization has unlimited operating expenses. Operating companies believe they get better service from their own staff groups even though there is no economic rationale or demonstrated service improvement for the strategy.

Business is hard enough to run. Executives and managers in operating companies, divisions and business units should not be distracted with worrying about the accounts payable function. There are customers to service, operations to run and maintain, and people to manage without the need to divert the attention of managers who end up running a mini finance, information technology, human resources, and supply function at the same time. The concept of core business popularized by many management theorists means sticking to the very essence and focus of what you are in business to produce or sell or achieve. Although corporate functions such as information technology may argue passionately that they are a fundamental element to running a gas, oil, insurance or financial company, they are not the core business. The fact that technology is required to run any kind of sustainable enterprise today is irrefutable. There is a lot of built in redundancy when there are distributed or decentralized staff groups duplicated in each business unit or company. Beyond redundancy, one also has to question what the staff groups are actually doing.

Most staff functions spend a disproportionate amount of their time on routine and transactional activities such as paper processing and administration at a time when technology and opportunities to leverage volume and scale abound. This has been well studied in the finance function where it is well known that most financial groups spend as much as 65% of time and resources at the transactional processing level. Transactions are budget consuming when you consider the sheer volume of activities such as accounts payable, receivable, travel and expense reporting, payroll, credit and collections, general, and cost accounting. These transactional activities are often derogatorily referred to as low-value-added while risk management is seen as strategic and value-added. The issue for chief financial officers is rooted in the need to do both the transactional and the strategic functions very well. Transactional processing is key to a smooth running organization. Just see what happens when paychecks are not issued or suppliers are not paid on time! The domination of transactional processing applies equally to other staff functions such as human resources, information technology and the supply chain. When looking to the future, staff groups need to scrutinize closely how best to deliver at both the transactional and the strategic level. Consolidation of transactional processing is a minimum to capture benefits from economies of scale. The strategic role is a little more complex due to the paradox of wearing two hats.

THE SPLIT PERSONALITY OF STAFF ROLES: WEARING TWO HATS

In Latin America there is a saying that you can either have a successful business, or you can do business ethically.[3] Not to provoke discussion on unique customs and practices, but the fact of the matter is that Latin American businesses know they need to do both. Either/or is not an option. So too for staff groups which have two roles that are diametrically opposed to each other: one says service, and the other says policy and rules. You can either have service or you can have anarchy. Which one will it be? The fact is corporations have an inherent need for both roles: they need the services staff groups provide and they need a set of governing rules and policies to minimize liability and risk. Neither role is in dispute but what is subject to intense debate is the historical precedence for fusing the two roles together. One day staff groups are expected to provide stellar customer service, and the next day they must enforce corporate rules and standards. The people who set and enforce policies and standards are the same people who are supposed to help the business units or operating companies with their needs for human resources, systems and financial advice. Fundamentally these two roles are at odds. The idea is not to pit one role against the other and have service triumph over rules. In fact, both roles are critical. The policy role is needed for good governance, while the service role is needed to help businesses deliver the goods.

In finance, there is a legitimate need for a control role, hence the term controller. There is also a service role for things like financial advice, business case analysis, and investment guidance to name a few. The problem lies in the fact that on one given day, the finance person genuinely tries to help while the next day, he has to lay down the law. This is a fundamentally flawed design which is even more conspicuous when comparing internal professional services to external consulting services. Even though some staff executives are downright annoyed at being compared to the external consulting community, line managers do, in fact, make comparisons and more so today as fewer and fewer corporate groups are allowed the luxury of being the sole supplier of services.

The comparison is often detrimental for staff groups which are forced to carry the yoke of both roles. Corporate cops are generally not seen as role models for service reps of the year. When external consultants provide professional services, they are not burdened by the baggage of enforcement. They can instead position themselves as helping clients work within the constraints, keeping them out of corporate trouble. Staff groups often mistakenly think that they have to protect line managers from themselves, that line managers are out there just waiting to get into trouble. Some staff groups even love the police role, finding delight in catching managers in trouble. They think that external consultants will gladly help line managers break all the rules. Consultants who stay in business for the long term do not make a habit out of getting their clients fired but they are at liberty to help their clients work constructively within corporate policy dictums rather than feeling obliged to carry handcuffs to every meeting.

This duality of role is at the heart of fundamental dissatisfaction with staff groups. There is a word in German, *Weltanschauung,* which means how you see the world. Once people begin to think about the illogical nature of having two diametrically opposed roles merged into one, it becomes a "Weltanschauung"! There is no other way to see the world. The status quo is not an option. For many staff groups, this is one of those "eureka" moments because it explains much of the angst and frustration experienced when being forced to split themselves in two. When they serve two masters, they end up serving none. Corporations have to start seeing this new world where the fusion of policy and service does not form a workable framework, that it is deeply flawed on paper, let alone in practice.

These are some of the dilemmas at the heart of the problem with staff functions. The monopoly position that people love to hate, the fact that decentralization is passé for much of the staff work and finally the cop and service rep duality of role. New strategies have emerged to help organizations fix some of these fundamental dilemmas.

STRATEGIES FOR STAFF FUNCTIONS

There is no one right strategy. As lawyers are famous for saying, "It all depends." Figure 1.2 illustrates a range of strategies that smart staff groups are considering and working on in tandem. The only prescription is that companies should start with shared services before considering outsourcing.

| FIGURE 1.2 | Strategies for staff functions |

SOURCE: Barbara E. Quinn and Robert S. Cooke, 1998

Shared services

Shared services at a simple level refers to the practice of business units, operating companies and organizations deciding to share a common set of services rather than have a series of duplicated staff functions. Although no company has yet created one gigantic shared service center that provides services globally, there are companies which have this vision. On the surface, this kind of shared service looks like a centralized business model, which is nothing new. In practice, excellent shared service centers really work at building a service culture and do not see this strategy as a pure cost cutting exercise, although the cost improvements are phenomenal! This kind of service center typically offers mandated services where clients and operating companies have no choice due to the sunk costs and infrastructure. Payroll, travel expense reporting, and disbursement accounting would typically be found here.

Shared services is spreading rapidly. There are too many companies to include all, but Figure 1.3 indicates companies which have some form of shared services according to a recent publication and our own research.[4]

These companies, through their efforts, can demonstrate cost savings safely in the 25–30% range, but equally important is the idea that service to the business units has improved. According to Gunn Partners, 10% of shared service groups have reduced operating costs by an incredible 50%. One of the most compelling stories relating to savings comes from pioneer in shared services, Amoco, which saved $400 million through consolidation and an estimated $1 billion in value creation as a result of shared services. Value creation at Amoco is defined as reduced project cycle time, reduced total delivered costs for capital projects, systemic processes for sourcing decisions, and lowered delivered cost for operating expenses. The $400 million savings is amazing on its own, but

FIGURE 1.3   Companies that have discovered the gold of shared services

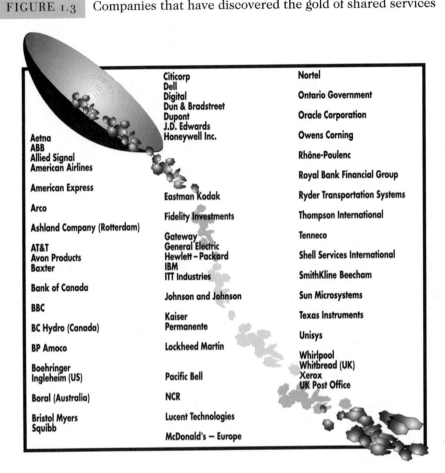

	Citicorp	Nortel
	Dell	
	Digital	Ontario Government
	Dun & Bradstreet	
	Dupont	Oracle Corporation
	J.D. Edwards	
Aetna	Honeywell Inc.	Owens Corning
ABB		
Allied Signal		Rhône-Poulenc
American Airlines		
		Royal Bank Financial Group
American Express		
	Eastman Kodak	Ryder Transportation Systems
Arco		
	Fidelity Investments	Thompson International
Ashland Company (Rotterdam)		
	Gateway	Tenneco
AT&T	General Electric	
Avon Products	Hewlett – Packard	Shell Services International
Baxter	IBM	
	ITT Industries	SmithKline Beecham
Bank of Canada		
	Johnson and Johnson	Sun Microsystems
BBC		
	Kaiser	Texas Instruments
BC Hydro (Canada)	Permanente	
		Unisys
BP Amoco	Lockheed Martin	
		Whirlpool
Boehringer		Whitbread (UK)
Ingleheim (US)	Pacific Bell	Xerox
		UK Post Office
Boral (Australia)	NCR	
Bristol Myers	Lucent Technologies	
Squibb		
	McDonald's – Europe	

the idea of $1 billion in value creation opportunities would attract the attention of most chief executive officers.

Groups of companies, especially in the health care industry, are also pursuing the sharing of services to minimize cost and avoid duplication (see Figure 1.4). A group of independent hospitals will decide to pool common shared services. This requires inordinate discipline and rigor on the part of the executives of the health authorities or health care organizations. To initiate it there has to be either a crisis in finances or a group of smart leaders who know that it makes sense to share common staff services and have the courage to do the right thing even though it means yielding control in the short term. This is the future! The argument for local service is weak. The old familiar whine of unique needs and markets is becoming tiresome. Consulting compa-

FIGURE 1.4 Shared services for the health care industry

nies and third party suppliers figure out how to understand numerous companies' idiosyncrasies and requirements. This is not all that difficult. Besides, there is a move to standardization to find the one good process that works. Why have ten hospitals following ten different processes for accounts payable?

Conferences on the topic of shared services are taking place around the world and although American in origin, the concept is rapidly taking root in Europe and beginning to surface in Australia, the Asia Pacific region and Latin America. Adopting a business strategy should not be done blindly just because others are doing it, but executives should be hard pressed by their boards to justify why they can't do it or shouldn't do it.

Some shared service organizations are really businesses within a business, where staff groups must earn the right to be a supplier. This is a disciplined but high risk strategy where internal staff functions put themselves on the line. It means ultimate choice for business units to go outside and hire suppliers if the internal staff groups are not living up to their expectations. Not for the faint of heart but exhilarating and profitable to those shared service groups that have succeeded in turning their bloated bureaucracies into successful enterprises.

Shared services can be true free enterprise models where staff functions must operate as business entities. In shared services, internal clients choose the type, level and quality of services they want from the staff groups, at the price they are willing to pay. Staff groups charge fully loaded costs for their services, like an external consulting organization: the finance department would charge the actual cost of producing a business case, including labor dollars, office equipment, lights, computers, telephone and office space charges. This means that internal clients pay the real cost just as if they had purchased the services outside. This forces a whole new relationship where internal staff functions must earn the right to do business. Nothing is inherited or free. This notion is at the heart of successful shared services. Staff groups, like outside suppliers, must prove themselves competent at meeting or exceeding client expectations. In true shared services, business units retain the right to go outside and purchase services externally if the internal groups cannot meet expectations.

Outsourcing: sleeping with the enemy

At minimum, organizations should consider a careful consolidation and move to shared services as an interim step before outsourcing. This enables the organization to at least get its hands around the function, understand the costs and issues, so meaningful performance standards can be created and a contract with a third party can be designed that will result in improved performance. Furthermore, it is likely that smart companies would select strategically the staff functions to be outsourced, rather than go to a wholesale move with a third party. With information technology, there is a compelling argument for companies with legacy systems to look for a third party rather than invest precious capital in developing technologies that have already been invented. The other good reason for moving to shared services prior to adopting an outsourcing strategy lies in the fact that outsourced functions require internal management. A shared service can still be a shared service even though the work is done outside by a third party. Some people see outsourcing as the hero, others see it as the villain, poised to destroy and conquer unsuspecting staff groups.

> *Heads of staff functions in the audience can be seen leaning forward in their seats watching to see how the story will unfold. The narrator continues.*

The lucrative business of staff outsourcing is estimated to be in the range of over $200 billion with a double-digit growth rate of 20% predicted over the next few years. Outsourcing part or all of staff functions is definitely a strategy to improve service and/or reduce costs. The problem is that companies have experienced both results: costs have been both lower and higher. Backsourcing is already a phenomenon whereby companies take back outsourced functions. It is probably true that many companies have simply hacked out a staff function due to sheer frustration with either poor service, exorbitant and spiraling costs, or both. The decision to outsource has to be deliberate and the move takes careful planning. Organizations which have dumped poorly performing staff functions will probably find at least as many problems as before and maybe even more. It doesn't make sense to take a big messy problem and dump it over the fence to a third party hoping they will somehow turn a rocky pile into shiny gold.

Outsourcing may or may not be good for the long term since companies are yielding control to outside forces which might be good for today but not sufficient for tomorrow. The experience for companies which have had to backsource functions for non-performance would suggest it is a task one would want to avoid. Hence the strategy of co-sourcing where organizations decide to form a joint alliance and actually create a joint capital venture for a certain shared service. The BBC in London created a joint venture with PricewaterhouseCoopers and EDS, to form a shared financial systems and service group. In Canada, the Royal Bank Financial Group, Bank of Montreal and Toronto Dominion Bank formed a shared document processing organization called Symcor.

Co-ventures offer organizations more direct control and say over how the services are performed and are likely to be a good long-term strategy to minimize the risk of turning over services wholly to a third party. This strategy is obviously a function of size and magnitude. The scale has to be present to justify the capital investment but is well worth considering since it offers up cost savings, leveraging economies of scale and still retaining a say in how the operation runs. In many ways, it offers the best of both worlds: world-class processes with a stake in the outcome.

Co-sourcing may offer the best of both worlds: world-class processes with a stake in the outcome

So outsourcing or co-sourcing are possible strategies, once the functions have been consolidated or in essence formed into a shared service.

Reengineering and technology – when is the right time?

It is critical to decide on and form shared services first, secondly investigate outsourcing and then investigate reengineering, streamlining processes or applying integrated technology systems. The actual form of shared services must take place first, with a leader and an organizational structure that will take accountability for improving processes, reducing costs and improving client satisfaction. Trying to reengineer before going to shared services is a recipe for failure. There is no power structure or motivation for disparate business units and organizations to agree on a single process or accept joint accountability for improvement. It is a waste of time and money to consider reengineering or streamlining of processes while the duplicate staff units remain in place. Sure, staff groups will all meet in some central location. North Americans pray it will be in one of their European locations! Picture all the companies and countries at one table with no other mandate than a lame attempt at reengineering. Who will be the first to offer up their process? It is like a set of bodies without a head – there is no single rallying or central force to make anything happen. There is no inherent motivation to get in line for the overall good of the enterprise. Who will be selfless enough to give up their own local process to adopt someone else's? Reengineering is not a pre-requisite to shared services, it has to happen after shared services is formed or during implementation.

Technology is usually one of the key enablers in the move to shared services. Most companies which are implementing shared services are simultaneously migrating to ERP (enterprise resource planning) software programs, like those available from SAP and Peoplesoft, to integrate critical processes and cost information. The integration of pension, benefits, compensation, and payroll information, for example, allows for significantly improved processing productivity.

Quality improvement

For some companies, there may be a sense that nothing is broken, that wholesale and radical change is not an option for the staff groups. Or it may be a timing issue. At least, corporate groups need to have a plan in place to ensure they are working to improve continually. This is a non-invasive strategy but should include client satisfaction data as an absolute minimum. It is frightening to imagine that there are still corporate staff groups which have no clear and articulate picture of how they are viewed by their clients. This is unacceptable and corporate executives should yell at the top of their lungs, "We are not going to take it any more." Can you imagine operating in a free floating world with no accountability to prove value for investment? Many staff groups are allowed to meander along without proving to their stakeholders that clients are satisfied, and whether their costs are within an acceptable benchmarked standard.

Quality improvement is about the ongoing search for better ways to meet client needs and to increase productivity. It is about never being satisfied with the status quo.

On the capability issue, staff groups need to invest regularly in the development of their people and to ensure that skills and capability are up to speed. One of the factors clients use to determine whether staff services are satisfactory is the perceived degree of credibility. In other words, clients will rate services depending on how much capability and credibility they find in the staff groups. Old skills wear thin. If organizations are not prepared to invest in helping staff groups to maintain high standards of excellence in capability, then they should consider outsourcing. It's not fair to expect staff groups to compete for credibility with one hand tied behind their back.

Ongoing evaluation

All staff groups need to put themselves under the microscope and subject their services to a rigorous evaluation. The only people qualified to evaluate staff work are the clients, the business units and users of the services. This feedback allows staff groups to improve their services and to change products to meet changing expectations.

Finally the time has come for organizations to step up to the plate. There is considerable gold to be mined and shared services is here to stay. Companies which have adopted shared services have amazing stories to tell. Watching a corporate staff bureaucracy transform itself into a business enterprise is quite a journey. Staff groups which feared that business would decrease once clients had choice over the level of services and the option to go outside, have, in fact, seen business grow. These same people know that they are in a much better position than ever before because no one has to tap them on the shoulder, they have already done it themselves.

The picture fades back in of the old prospector who lifts his head and grins openly out at the audience, the find obvious at the bottom of his mining plate, his future, if not secure, at least hopeful and optimistic.

NOTES

1 Greengard, 1999
2 Peter Pritchett and the Outsourcing Institute
3 Maverick, 1993
4 Schulman, Dunleavy, Harmer and Lusk, 1999

Chapter 2

KNOWING WHAT TO MINE

One hundred and fifty years ago, James Marshall reached down and picked up a piece of gold metal that was to change the United States for ever. Gold! Gold! It was the shout that was heard around the world and started the greatest single voluntary mass migration the world has ever known.

THE BIRTH OF SHARED SERVICES

Most of the corporate world is migrating towards shared services. So what is causing this migration and how did it all begin? The origin of the shared services term and concept is somewhat unclear, although General Electric in the US had a group called Client Business Services as early as 1986 which seemed to be the model for what we know today as shared services. Bob Gunn of the consulting firm Gunn Partners believes the term was coined when he led a best practice study at A.T. Kearney in 1990 that included companies such as Ford, Johnson and Johnson, IBM, AT&T, Nynex, Digital, Dupont, Hewlett-Packard, Alcoa and Shell. One common theme was companies with some kind of shared financial services operation in place. It would appear that consultants who were part of the A.T. Kearney study have a legitimate claim to discovering or at least naming the idea of shared services. It is in hot dispute as to who actually coined the phrase. Theories abound from someone who thought of it in the shower to more academic explanations as to how they strung the three words together. Dr. Leland Forst, CEO of the Amherst Group, is from the A.T. Kearney days, and sees himself as one of the founders of the shared services strategy.

Historically, we know only two things for sure: shared services was born in the United States and the finance function was its specific birthplace. Although finance is a key player in any organization, this is one of the few wider corporate and business strategies actually to come out of the finance area. The chief financial officer is frequently the starting point for the idea of shared services because of the immediate benefits through consolidation of financial transactional services such as accounts payable, accounts receivable, travel and expense processing, payroll and customer billing operations. The move to shared services has had a number of benefits for the finance function. In addition to cost savings it has provided the opportunity for finance to focus more of its efforts on providing higher level strategic support and financial analysis as the basic transactional work moves to the shared services center. Sharp financial officers see the need to shift the orientation of the finance function to more of an executive decision support function or to position themselves as experts in control and risk management. These are the high value creation activities that finance wants to put its stamp on. So, if the majority of the finance function is dominated by transactional processing, the possibilities of consolidation manage to kill two birds with one stone. Finance can reduce the costs of doing transactional work through consolidation while also freeing itself to work in the professional services area.

On the surface the move to shared services can look like simple consolidation or in some cases a return to centralization. To differentiate itself from these two historical strategies, shared services must look and feel different than what has occurred in the past. Two basic elements help differentiate shared services: it operates like a business, focused and obsessed with meeting client needs, and services are charged back to clients to recover costs. In more advanced models of shared services, clients have increased choice of which products and services they are willing to pay for. Corporate and internal functions have to provide products and services at a cost, quality and timeliness that are competitive with alternative suppliers, and are what clients want. The need to provide cost competitive options is what forces the internal service provider to understand what their true costs are in providing services and to benchmark their costs against best practices from other corporations, and competing external suppliers.

Shared services is a business

CLIENT FOCUSED   CHARGE BACK FOR SERVICES   **BUSINESS**

Focusing on what clients want means that no work is undertaken unless there is an identified and paying client. All too often internal functions try to position their products and services according to what they think the internal clients should want rather than providing services that the clients actually want at a price they are willing to pay.

WHEN STAFF GROUPS FAIL TO GIVE CLIENTS WHAT THEY WANT

In one organization we found a human resources function that considered itself quite knowledgeable on current trends. Contemporary literature on the future of human resources suggests a strategic partnership role with a move away from traditional services such as recruiting. This human resources function had worked on streamlining administrative processes and getting line managers to do their own recruiting. A year later the human resources department was experiencing difficulty in getting sponsorship for its strategic initiatives. It turned out that business units had quietly duplicated human resources. Naturally, they were politically smart enough not to call it human resources but instead called the position something bland and generic like business services. The business units, in fact, wanted services like screening resumes, campus recruiting, and selection interviewing. The good old "bread and butter work" we all used to call personnel.

In our experience working with shared services human resources functions, we have found that clients want recruiting as a service and are willing to pay for it. It is not that they do not value organizational development or that they are unsophisticated buyers, it is simply that recruiting is seen as an essential product for running their own plant, operation or business area. In shared services, the customers determine the product mix. As in the outside world, failure to provide products that customers want is generally not a good business decision. In shared services there are no rights or wrongs. Corporate and internal functions over time tend to develop a morally upright attitude to what should and should not be wanted by their internal clients. Clients are somehow seen as Neanderthal for wanting simple products such as recruiting. In a marketplace economy, clients are just clients. The example of human resources is intended to be illustrative since these fundamental principles apply to every other corporate and internal function.

Sad but true

One of the most poignant stories in our shared services experience comes out of the finance area. As part of the process, the finance group decided to work at really understanding its products and services, what it actually cost to produce the products and services, and the extent of satisfaction by the internal clients. They discovered some interesting facts. There was a lot of work being performed internally for which there was no actual customer. One report in particular which involved consolidation and roll-up of business unit, geographic location data was not seen as useful by any one of the clients. This document was not a corporate report required for audit purposes. Most business units simply filed the report or worse sent it to the trash. When the horrified finance group pressed the business units as to why they never provided feedback on the lack of utility of the report, the answer came back quite simply. Each one of the vice presidents thought that some other business unit used the report or that it was a necessary part of corporate reporting. The story is sad and memorable for the fact that the people in finance had faithfully set out to do good work. They had toiled and probably agonized over business units not getting their input data to

In shared services there is an accountability for only providing services that clients want and are willing to pay for

them on time. They had done what was right except that nobody cared. Compounding the problem is the fact that business units spent time and money creating the input data for no tangible result. This example shows that the finance report would not survive as a finance product since no client was willing to pay for it even though some vice presidents admitted it had marginal use.

WHY CHARGE-BACK IS FUNDAMENTAL

In our society, money is a measurement of value and when things are "free" they are not considered of value. Expressions abound within our value system. Free advice isn't worth the paper it is written on. There is no such thing as a free lunch or a free ride. Yet staff groups in essence offer free services in most organizations.

Charge-back creates a different mindset than free services. It

Charge-back forces line management and shared services staff to think about value for money

puts accountability on line management to think about the expenditure, to think about value for the money they are spending on the services. Within the shared services function it causes people to think about the costs of the services they are providing. Staff know that if the costs they are transferring to clients are too high,

clients will seek alternative suppliers.

There are organizations that are adamant in denying the concept of internal charge back for services. It is seen as unnecessary, as creating internal bureaucracy, as funny money and not worth the effort. The resistance to charging back for services is one of the factors that will convince global companies that shared services *The difference* really is a code word for centralization. How can *between running a* business units and operating companies run their *cost center and a* businesses, make decisions on what services they *business is a shift* need if they don't know what it costs to do their *from a billing to a* payroll or process their bills or run their reports? *pricing mentality* How can business units compare the internal ser- vices to what they could get on the street if they cannot compare the price part of the equation? Charge-back is a fundamental tool for accountability. Shared services centers have to account for their costs and deliberately work on streamlining and applying new technology to reduce the per unit costs of transactions. Productivity improvements are much more possible in a consolidated center than they are in a decentralized operation due to the degree of specialization and the speed that comes from working on one kind of process, on one kind of system. Corporate and functional people have trouble understanding the difference between running a cost center and running a business. The shift in mindset is from a billing to a pricing mentality. Some cor- porate groups claim to already operate like shared services. They talk about charging back to their clients. In most cases, this translates to some kind of arbitrary allocation system. If the human resources group in an organization takes its whole budget and then allocates it out to the businesses, it is not based on the actual consumption patterns of the businesses because it is guaranteed that each business will be charged. It will not differentiate that the marketing and sales group rarely used human resources services while the manufacturing opera- tions used human resources two-thirds of the time for recruiting, health and safety, and workers' compensation issues. These examples do get to the heart of the central theme in shared services which has corporate and internal functions operating as a business. It means clients understand what it costs to get certain services and they have choice over what and how much they want.

A CONTINUUM OF SHARED SERVICES MODELS

There are a number of approaches to shared services being adopted around the world (see Figure 2.1). They range from the most basic form of consolidation of transactional activities all the way to creating an independent business set up to provide shared services internally and to sell shared services externally to multiple clients. There are choices and decisions to be made and the models need to be seen as evolution- ary over time as the shared services organization has a chance to mature and evolve.

BASIC SHARED SERVICES: IT IS MORE THAN CONSOLIDATION

At its most basic, the move to shared services involves the consolidation of transactional processing and administrative work (see Figure 2.2). Services such as payroll and accounts payable are typically mandated services in that business units are not allowed to go out and source their own payroll for example. This trend to consolidation and away from decentralization is evident in global companies with multi-site operations. Technology has greatly assisted the move to consolidation with call centers springing up in the most unlikely locations. Call center technology has enabled a shift in thinking about geography and linguistic barriers since multi-lingual operators can easily provide service independent of where they actually sit. In basic shared services, the predominant drivers are cost reduction through economies of scale and the standardization of processes, as well as a focus on client service. What differentiates shared services from the simple consolidation of transactional services is the focus on the client. Shared services must start from a client vision; on what benefits will accrue to the client and what will satisfy them. The mission and objectives of any shared services center needs to include a strong client-centered vision. Even with mandated services, successful shared service leaders are working very hard to create a new mindset with clients at the core.

FIGURE 2.1   A continuum of shared services

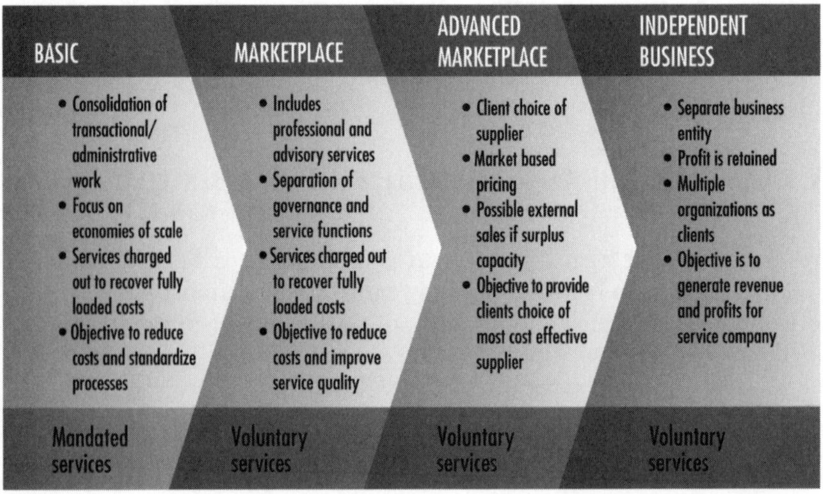

BASIC	MARKETPLACE	ADVANCED MARKETPLACE	INDEPENDENT BUSINESS
• Consolidation of transactional/ administrative work • Focus on economies of scale • Services charged out to recover fully loaded costs • Objective to reduce costs and standardize processes	• Includes professional and advisory services • Separation of governance and service functions • Services charged out to recover fully loaded costs • Objective to reduce costs and improve service quality	• Client choice of supplier • Market based pricing • Possible external sales if surplus capacity • Objective to provide clients choice of most cost effective supplier	• Separate business entity • Profit is retained • Multiple organizations as clients • Objective is to generate revenue and profits for service company
Mandated services	Voluntary services	Voluntary services	Voluntary services

FIGURE 2.2   A continuum of shared services: the basic model

BASIC	MARKETPLACE	ADVANCED MARKETPLACE	INDEPENDENT BUSINESS
• Consolidation of transactional/administrative work • Focus on economies of scale • Services charged out to recover fully loaded costs • Objective to reduce costs and standardize processes	• Includes professional and advisory services • Separation of governance and service functions • Services charged out to recover fully loaded costs • Objective to reduce costs and improve service quality	• Client choice of supplier • Market based pricing • Possible external sales if surplus capacity • Objective to provide clients choice of most cost effective supplier	• Separate business entity • Profit is retained • Multiple organizations as clients • Objective is to generate revenue and profits for service company
Mandated services	Voluntary services	Voluntary services	Voluntary services

The mission statement of Dun & Bradstreet's Shared Accounting group defines the need for superior quality services and meeting the needs of customers. While also emphasizing cost efficiencies, the priority order is quality, service level and then costs.

D&B SHARED ACCOUNTING MISSION STATEMENT

♦ The mission statement of Accounting Services at D&B is to provide timely, superior quality services and financial information to meet the changing needs of internal and external customers; to achieve best demonstrated cost efficiencies; to meet the fiduciary responsibilities of the Corporation.

♦ The development of Shared Accounting Services means realizing this mission through continually improving quality, service levels, and cost structures across D&B.

The Chicago based Tribune Company with 12,700 employees in 40 business units and $3 billion in revenue established a shared services center in 1992 to process financial and procurement related transactions. The mission statement of the center focuses not only on the goal of reducing costs but also on having more time to provide clients with decision support and giving managers better information for making decisions that will contribute to the overall strategic positions of the company.

The mission statement and objectives of the Tribune Company's financial shared services center go beyond the basic cost reductions that occur through consolidation. They include the qualitative benefits that come from being client-focused and providing increased value to the organization.

TRIBUNE COMPANY FINANCIAL SERVICE CENTER
MISSION STATEMENT

The Financial Service Center seeks to create value for Tribune through consolidated administration of financial and procuremnet tasks and processes.

✦ Streamlining these processes lowers costs and maximizes efficiency, leaving business unit managers more time for decision support.
✦ This will allow better managerial decisions at the business unit level, and improves Tribune Company's strategic position.

Another factor that differentiates shared services from the simple consolidation of transactional processing is giving clients the opportunity to choose service levels and customized products. The menu of products and services is in essence unbundled so that internal clients can choose the level of service they require. If a business unit in one country wants a payroll weekly, there is a different cost than if the payroll is done bi-weekly in the rest of the world. It is up to that one business unit in that country to make the choice as to what it needs. Since the real costs are different for weekly versus bi-weekly, a proportionate cost is charged accordingly. This puts the business unit or operating division in the driver's seat with the accountability to make the right choice for its own part of the business. This shift in control and accountability from the centralized functional group to the business unit client is one of the cornerstones of shared services. It is fundamentally different to centralization where it is the payroll function that would usually dictate the standards to the business units. Here there is choice and the opportunity for line management to make an informed decision based on real costs.

In the traditional model of centralization, standards for service are self-defined. Finance groups produce pay-checks every two weeks and the production of manual checks is discouraged since they are foreign to the regular rhythm. The definition of service levels is determined by what internal technology or functional professionals believe to be good service. Talk to centralized groups and they will swear up and down that they provide good service even when they have absolutely no client satisfaction data to prove it. Most internal functional groups have never asked their clients to evaluate their services since they do not consider them clients in the typical sense. So when corporate functions all around the world announce with great fanfare that they are going to consolidate all of the billing operations into one big consolidated center, it is no wonder that you can hear the sound of one hand clapping.

In practical terms, shared services is fundamentally different to simple consolidation or centralization. The following chart illustrates the differences between shared services and simple consolidation or centralization using accounts payable as an example.

This move to a basic model of shared services can create corporate gold on two fronts. The company gets lower operating costs and a positive hit to the bottom line. Secondly, corporate functions can reduce resources at the transactional end so they can invest their energy and resources in positioning themselves at the strategic finance level.

FIGURE 2.3   Why shared services is not centralization or just simple consolidation

Shared services	Centralization and consolidation
Role is to provide products and services at a cost, quality and timeliness that meets the need of internal clients	Role is to provide products and services at a reasonable cost, quality and timeliness that meets the "corporation's needs"
Shared services enables internal customers to select services and service levels based on what they want and are willing to pay for	Centralized corporate functions usually offer a universal set of products and services at a service level deemed reasonable
Example: clients could opt for checks in the normal production period at a certain price or they might decide they want rush checks cut which they would be willing to pay a premium for	Example: centralized functions would opt for a standard to be set and adhered to. Checks are cut every two weeks with a certain requirement for inputs
Shared services is accountable for providing products and services at the real fully loaded cost. If it costs three times as much to cut a rush check, the client is charged for that	Centralized functions usually operate on a cost plus basis; allocations are made on either a unit or transaction basis or apportioned out to business units and divisions as a percentage
Shared services has a role in ensuring that products and services are offered at competitive rates compared to the outside marketplace	Centralized groups have a role in ensuring that products and services are offered at competitive rates compared to the outside marketplace
Shared services does not typically or ideally enforce policy compliance	Centralized groups enforce policy compliance

THE MARKETPLACE MODEL

The next evolution in shared services is a move to the marketplace model. These services are essentially voluntary in that clients will eventually have choice in using them or not. In other words, they are not mandated. This is brand new thinking concerning corporate functions. The key differences between the basic model and the marketplace model are the inclusion of professional and advisory services and the need to separate governance related activities from the delivery of services to clients. In the marketplace model the delivery of professional and advisory services is consolidated and included in shared services along with the transactional processing that was discussed under the basic model. In the marketplace model, clients have increased choice over the products and services that they can buy from the shared services organization.

FIGURE 2.4   A continuum of shared services: the marketplace model

BASIC	MARKETPLACE	ADVANCED MARKETPLACE	INDEPENDENT BUSINESS
• Consolidation of transactional/ administrative work • Focus on economies of scale • Services charged out to recover fully loaded costs • Objective to reduce costs and standardize processes	• Includes professional and advisory services • Separation of governance and service functions • Services charged out to recover fully loaded costs • Objective to reduce costs and improve service quality	• Client choice of supplier • Market based pricing • Possible external sales if surplus capacity • Objective to provide clients choice of most cost effective supplier	• Separate business entity • Profit is retained • Multiple organizations as clients • Objective is to generate revenue and profits for service company
Mandated services	Voluntary services	Voluntary services	Voluntary services

In marketplace shared services, functions such as application development, desktop support and project management are typically included. We also find other professional advisory services such as human resources, legal, materials management, public affairs and financial and business analysis. These services operate on the principles of an internal consulting company, tailoring products and services to those that clients want to purchase and perceive as valuable.

The second major and most fundamental difference is the requirement to identify and separate out those activities that are governance related from those that are services to clients. Governance activities carried out by corporate functions include the development of corporate policies and standards and ensuring compliance with corporate direction. In the past, corporate functions established, owned and enforced policies while also providing services. For example, the information technology function would develop policies and standards around software and would monitor and ensure compliance at the same time as providing supposed help. In other words, information technology would deliver services while acting as a corporate law-enforcer.

Another example is in the facilities area where facility groups typically establish standards on furniture and space allowances according to the client's position and level within the hierarchy. In this historical scenario, the facilities group when asked for service on designing a "beyond standard" new office space would lead with its speech on how it did not meet corporate standards. This model was often referred to as "control through services."

While not typically an issue in the basic model of shared services, which is about consolidating transactional processing, once professional advisory services are included there is a need for clarity around real services to clients and the governance role. Governance activities are those carried out on behalf of the CEO and the board of directors; they are aimed upwards in the corporation.

The separation of governance activities from the delivery of services to clients is what enables the move to a real internal marketplace and what makes shared services a profoundly different strategy from what we have seen before. In the marketplace model, the same service providers are not accountable for policing adherence to policy. In the marketplace model accountability for adherence to policy rests firmly in the hands of line management. Once a policy or standard is approved by the corporate executive, it is owned by them and it is up to them to ensure compliance. This allows the services group to focus on the delivery of client-centered services. To see how the services change, here follows one example of the products and services divided between transactional, professional, and governance within the information technology function (see Table 2.1).

TABLE 2.1　The information technology function

Transactional	Professional	Governance – CIO role
✦ Data center operations	✦ Application development	✦ Enterprise wide standards
✦ Network services	✦ Application architecture	for software/hardware
✦ Maintenance	✦ Software/hardware	✦ Corporate purchasing
✦ Help desk	installation	policy
✦ Data support	✦ Strategy and training	✦ IT strategy
	✦ Telecommunications	✦ Infrastructure investment
		strategy

Information technology through the lens of shared services

The separation of governance activities from the delivery of services is the most controversial and provocative element distinguishing the marketplace model of shared services from the basic one. Corporate and internal functions typically must offer services on the one hand and police clients with the other when policy or standards are being violated. Expense account processing is a good example of this. An expense claim comes into a finance operation, the clerk checks it over, notes the signature on the bottom, nods appropriately that it is indeed the claimant's boss and then spies an item that is forbidden according to policy. In the public sector, this may amount to a lowly bottle of beer but nonetheless rules are rules. The clerk highlights the forbidden item and sends it back to the claimant for revision. In this scenario, the clerk is performing a service while also enforcing policy. Line management is not accountable for adherence to company policy. The boss either did not know the policy or chose to ignore it because, after all, the finance group looks after policy. The clerk receives the expense claim, sees the appropriate signature for authority and processes the claim. This shift away from policy enforcement causes considerable angst and grief and needs a long and well thought out transition. This is not a recipe for anarchy. The culture change of the processing people is huge and rightly so after spending years protecting the "corporation" from itself, where you were in essence the defender of the faith for righteousness. To make this transition away from the police state of corporate functions successfully, it is essential that policy and accountability are clearly transferred to line management. For control purposes periodic audits of policy compliance are essential but this is carried out by a governance or audit function, not by the service providers. For the marketplace model of shared services to work there is also a need for action following failure to comply with corporate policy.

In shared services, the clerk is not required to enforce policy

This liberation from policy is one of the most powerful elements for providing shared services groups with the opportunity to concentrate on what they should be doing, which is providing excellent products and services at competitive prices. This removal of the policy and control role is essential for groups engaged in a professional level of services such as property and facilities management, purchasing, human resources advisory services, financial analysis, application development and systems support. In shared services, it works best when the people who deliver services to clients are separate from those who develop, administer and ensure compliance with corporate policy and standards.

Freeing up staff groups from policy is essential

For example, in information technology it is necessary to have enterprise-wide standards for hardware and software. The board and the executive of the company want this to avoid excessive spending and to ensure system compatibility. However, 70–80% of any information technology shop is comprised of pure services, not policy and standards. This removal of the policy control role allows the services group to focus on what it does best, providing quality products and services to clients willing to pay for its services.

The removal of governance activities now enables the systems group to look like, feel like, and smell like a real business. When consulting firms make pitches and bids for systems development work, they are not in the unfortunate position of having to enforce corporate policy. For the information professional who have been groomed and conditioned to accept their role in enforcement, this move to pure services shakes their foundation and belief systems. The most frequent statement of resistance comes in the form of this question: "You mean we are now supposed to help clients get around policy and let them do whatever they want?"

The answer is yes and no. When a good external systems consulting firm is called into an organization, it makes a point of understanding the context and complexities. Good consulting firms don't make a business out of getting their clients into trouble by saying let me help you ignore company policy, let me help you burn all your bridges and engage in corporate illegal behavior and end up getting fired. In shared services, it is not the job of the systems group to enforce policy. It is not the system's policy. It is corporate policy and line management's policy. The difference is in the conversation.

A tongue in cheek look would go as follows:

Before shared services with governance and service role	**In shared services with seperation of governance and service role**
"I'm sorry, you can't have the system because it does not meet our enterprise-wide standards.	"Yes, we could help you install the system. However, it doesn't meet corporate standards.
Now then, is there anything else I can do for you today?"	Maybe I could help you to do a business case if it is worth your effort to get executive approval."

"no, we won't let you." VS. "yes, if you can get approval."

This dramatizes the essential difference between a centralized systems function and the new world of shared services. It is for this reason that shared services is not a retread of previous thinking. This separation of policy and governance is truly a distinguishing feature and represents fundamentally new thinking about how to look at corporate and internal functions.

In any given corporate function, the majority of products and services are purely services. The governance role however is absolutely essential. The strategic chief information officer (CIO) role means having a small team of resources dedicated to ensuring appropriate controls are in place for long-term strategic IT investment and operations. Their role is to scan the marketplace and ensure that the right technology is brought to bear on the business. They need to help the executive and board articulate an appropriate IT strategy and investment plan to ensure the value of the IT assets are maintained and will facilitate increased shareholder value. The enterprise-wide standards that are developed and institutionalized are for the good of the ultimate shareholder. Policies are designed by nature to place constraints. That is the policy job and good governance ensures that controls exist to avoid risk and liability that comes from the absence of constraint. In the marketplace model, people physically are transferred into a governance department. This may be in head-quarters or in the holding company entity but the people who do policy and governance for a living do not get to sit side by side with the professional IT consultants who deliver IT services. Most emphatically, they are not the same people.

In the basic model of shared services most service offerings consist of "required" services over which clients have no choice of supplier and minimal choice over the nature of services they pay for. In the marketplace model clients have increased choice over what services they want, especially those related to professional and advisory services. Hence the term *voluntary*! Professional and advisory services must be customized to meet the specific needs of clients or they may choose not to buy. In the past corporate functional groups typically decided what products clients needed and that was what they delivered. The move to shared services means that clients have the ultimate choice as to what products or services they choose to pay for and which ones they do not want.

So far we have discussed the elements that differentiate the marketplace model of shared services from the basic model. These are the inclusion of professional services, the separation of governance from services and increased client choice of products and services. Like the basic model, services are charged out to recover fully loaded costs. The financial target is to arrive at zero since this is not a profit model where the shared services group is expected to bring in a return. Services are charged out either on a basis of daily rates similar to IT consulting houses for professional services, or on a volume basis, or on an annual kind of service contract for items such as help desk support. The move to a pricing model means that the corporate functions understand what the various products and services cost to deliver. You need to know how much a joint application development process costs versus a rapid prototyping process so you can charge the client based on true cost.

Whereas the objective with the basic model is mainly cost savings and service quality related to the delivery of consolidated transactional services, the marketplace model is about a competitive model of high quality professional advisory services. Service quality goes up in the eyes of the internal clients when professional service groups are given the chance to offer service unfettered by the governance role and the clients, rather than the central group, determine the level, service and type of services wanted Organizations which adopt a marketplace model of shared services are putting themselves in an excellent position for the future. The rigor of operating like a business makes them tough and resilient. They know what their value is because their clients tell them with their feet and their wallets. Reports don't get tossed in the garbage when clients choose them and pay for them. When organizations select the marketplace model, they are usually aware of the long-term goal to move to a more advanced model offering choice over supplier and where prices are market-based.

One key dilemma: mandated versus voluntary services

One of the key decisions that will arise during a discussion of marketplace shared services is the judgement as to which services will be open to marketplace rules and which ones will not. Typically, transactional services are not optional, they are usually mandated. Countries and companies are not given the choice of any old payroll or disbursement system, they must use the shared service. During implementation, there will be a great battle for staff groups to try to load as many services as possible into the mandated category. This is an attempt at safety and security since there is real fear about opening up and providing clients with choice.

THE ADVANCED MARKETPLACE MODEL

In the advanced marketplace model clients have the opportunity to influence who supplies their services. Clients who are dissatisfied with the services or service quality can make the case to purchase their services from external providers. As discussed earlier, this does not mean that individual managers can decide whether to use the shared services payroll group or whether to go to a local bank for their service. The decision to purchase services from an external vendor, or to outsource the service, is made at a very high level whereby executives decide collectively if the payroll function should be outsourced. There may be control issues and stringent processes for going outside to purchase services such as legal or information technology as an example. This is not a model of anarchy but it does mean that failure to get business from internal clients will result in layoffs.

In this model, internal services are charged back at marketplace rates. If there is an internal consulting group of some kind offering advisory services at say $1,500 per day, which is market based pricing, clients would be able to choose between internal and external providers. In other words, external consultants of similar quality, offering similar services, would charge $1,500 per day so that clients could make a comparison and decide which service to choose based on their perception of value for money.

In the advanced marketplace model, we see the internal marketplace economy at full speed (see figure 2.5). The prices for internal services are based on market rates whether the internal group costs less than or more than the market prices. If the costs of delivering the internal services are more than market pricing because internal costs are higher, this will be a problem over time and needs to be rectified. One of the greatest fears of internal service providers is that they will never be able to compete with the costs of external providers. Either internal service groups find a way to reduce their costs to compete with external providers or their clients will take steps to purchase their services elsewhere.

A major debate for executives

An additional feature of the advanced marketplace model is the move towards the commercialization of internal services where the shared services group can in effect market its services externally. Some shared services groups have reduced their costs and increased their service quality to the point where they compare very favorably with external providers of similar services. These groups become focused on selling their services to other organizations, acting like a real business and gen-

FIGURE 2.5   A continuum of shared services: the advanced marketplace model

BASIC	MARKETPLACE	ADVANCED MARKETPLACE	INDEPENDENT BUSINESS
• Consolidation of transactional/ administrative work • Focus on economies of scale • Services charged out to recover fully loaded costs • Objective to reduce costs and standardize processes	• Includes professional and advisory services • Separation of governance and service functions • Services charged out to recover fully loaded costs • Objective to reduce costs and improve service quality	• Client choice of supplier • Market based pricing • Possible external sales if surplus capacity • Objective to provide clients choice of most cost effective supplier	• Separate business entity • Profit is retained • Multiple organizations as clients • Objective is to generate revenue and profits for service company
Mandated services	Voluntary services	Voluntary services	Voluntary services

erating real dollars from the sale of their services. Some shared services groups, for example, have found that they are excellent at managing their automotive fleet at competitive prices and service levels and seek clients outside their organization. For most organizations full-scale commercialization is discouraged and shared services groups are held at providing external services only if surplus capacity exists without the need for additional capital or labor to meet the external service requirements. Once organizations move to full-scale commercialization, the internal services function becomes another business unit of the company.

In the advanced marketplace model, the goal is to provide internal clients with choice of the most effective supplier for the cost. Line managers have considerable choice and a say as to what services they intend to purchase, especially in the professional and senior technical services. This still may not mean that it is "no holds barred" choice. It might be that the internal corporate groups negotiate to supply a certain level and standard of services with the senior vice president, general manager or vice president of an operating group or company which their own middle managers will have to live with. Frequently the move from a marketplace to an advanced marketplace model takes at least two years. The shared services group needs a chance to get its quality and costs under control, to weed out unprofitable and unsatisfactory products and to earn the reputation of being in the service business. This takes time, especially where a lack of trust has built up over the years with the corporate groups wearing two hats: service and compliance. For some mature shared services organizations, the final plateau is to move shared services into a full enterprise model by operating it as an independent business.

The advanced marketplace model needs to evolve over time

SHARED SERVICES AS AN INDEPENDENT BUSINESS

Regardless of the legal structure, the idea in the independent business model for shared services is to operate as a separate business entity that provides products and services to a range of organizations beyond the original one where the need for shared services started. Shell Services International started as the internal shared service provider to the five key businesses of the Royal Dutch/Shell Group. It is now a separate company that is expected to be profitable as a separate business entity with clients both inside and outside the Shell group of companies. It has offices worldwide and employs 4,700 people.

As shared services evolve, these shared services businesses will eventually be competing with the major consulting and third party outsourcers. They will have a distinct competitive advantage in their own

---

SHELL SERVICES INTERNATIONAL

"Offering worldwide shared services to all enterprises both inside and outside the Royal Dutch/Shell group of companies."

◆ consultancy and business solutions

◆ HR services

◆ systems integration

◆ infrastructure technology

◆ business services.

---

sector since they have specific knowledge and expertise related to that industry. For example, Shell Services International will be able to market its distribution services to other oil and gas companies since it knows distribution and it knows the oil and gas business. It is a compelling market strategy to have core competencies in both the corporate function and in the sector itself. If a shared services financial center has managed to get its costs down and its service up, then it may be poised to operate as a separate business.

Mature shared services centers which have been operating for a few years, have driven their costs down and the customer culture upwards, might try to become the new competitors on the horizon. This is going to add to the competition where there are not only con-

FIGURE 2.6   A continuum of shared services models: the independent business model

BASIC	MARKETPLACE	ADVANCED MARKETPLACE	INDEPENDENT BUSINESS
• Consolidation of transactional/ administrative work • Focus on economies of scale • Services charged out to recover fully loaded costs • Objective to reduce costs and standardize processes	• Includes professional and advisory services • Separation of governance and service functions • Services charged out to recover fully loaded costs • Objective to reduce costs and improve service quality	• Client choice of supplier • Market based pricing • Possible external sales if surplus capacity • Objective to provide clients choice of most cost effective supplier	• Separate business entity • Profit is retained • Multiple organizations as clients • Objective is to generate revenue and profits for service company
Mandated services	Voluntary services	Voluntary services	Voluntary services

sulting companies and third party outsourcers but also shared services groups which not only know financial processing but know it in pharmaceuticals, in telecommunications or in the oil, gas and energy business. The lame excuse of the past that challenged the idea of outsourcing payroll or benefits administration or billing systems because third parties could not possibly understand the complexities of the business is going to be harder to defend. Some shared services groups are aggressive in their drive to operate a fully commercial operation and are going to be after your business for transactional processing if you are not careful or prepared.

Conclusion

In the evolution of models, there are choices for organizations which dare to cross the threshold from corporate bureaucracy to a service-minded organization. Despite the innate logic of shared services, debate and considerable discussion is required before any organization should consider the move. The range of reactions is often extremely emotional and quite dogmatic. It is not an easy strategy to enact well because it takes corporate discipline. Even though the gold exists and it is irrefutable, some organizations will not have the tenacity and willpower to force business units and operating companies into thinking like an integrated enterprise. Advocates of shared services feel like James Marshall and want to go around yelling "gold, gold!" The strategy is so obvious yet corporate politics are sometimes so strong that they can bury many a great idea. For those organizations which want to consider shared services, there is a logical process for implementation that is tried and true based on others which have successfully made the journey.

Chapter 3

THE ROUTE TOWARDS THE

IMPLEMENTATION OF

SHARED SERVICES

Gold prospectors always start their journey with a map. Since there is no "X" that marks the spot, the ground must be covered inch by inch

It is fine to talk about what shared services is, what it will do for organizations and what should be included, but how do you really go about putting it in place? For many people embarking down the road towards shared services and especially for those who are charged with putting it in place, the questions need to go deeper about how to get started, what to do first, what to do next and how long it should take.

The implementation of shared services is somewhat of a linear process that has been tested and fine tuned by many of those who have already traveled down the road. The steps are outlined in a logical sequence in figure 3.1. Although linear and sequential, there is often a need to loop back and revisit previous steps to make corrections and to revisit decisions when more information is presented. Some steps, like obtaining buy-in for shared services and building a service culture, are ongoing requirements that will never end.

Most organizations estimate that it takes anywhere from 12–18 months to implement shared services. If staff services are already centralized in one location, the shift is not as dramatic and will not take as long as when the services are decentralized across a number of business units scattered across countries. In other words, creating a service center for the Americas or a pan-European center will take more time to design and implement.

FIGURE 3.1   The roadmap to shared services

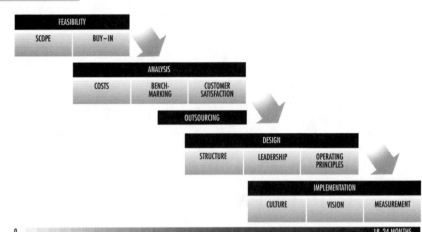

Implementation may be led either by the senior functional executive, such as the chief finance officer (CFO) or vice president of human resources, or it may be done through the appointment of a project manager or champion. Either way, it is important that there be one focal person who is identified and charged with the responsibility for the design of shared services.

The implementation process should typically take anywhere from 18–24 months from start to finish. This does not mean that the shared services design is 100% complete. Considerable reengineering and streamlining of processes are usually required once the centers are in place. If the implementation process is drawn out over too long a time frame, usually 24 months or greater, there is the danger of losing momentum and clients starting to lose interest. No one gets everything perfect the first time they take a step on the path to shared services. The best advice is for organizations to do the best they can and then move on. Once shared services is up and running, things can be fine tuned and modified. This is a much easier task than trying to rebuild momentum or client interest once it is lost. The following is an outline of the key implementation steps in shared services.

THE FEASIBILITY OF SHARED SERVICES FOR THE ORGANIZATION

Before embarking on the implementation journey it must be determined whether this is really the right strategy for your organization. Shared services must be looked at from the highest level to ensure there is congruence between the goals, objectives and principles of shared services and those of the organization. This is the beginning of the business case that will ultimately be presented to the executives to enlist their support and commitment for the move to shared services.

At this early stage it would be prudent to talk to other organizations or specialists who have had some depth of experience in shared services. Find out what their experience has been with shared services in general. It would be useful to get the answers to questions such as:

✦ What was your initial rationale for pursuing shared services?

✦ What were your goals and objectives for shared services?

✦ What did your executives like about the idea?

✦ What concerns did they express about moving to shared services?

✦ How did you get executive approval to proceed?

✦ What were the conditions set out by those who were resisting the move?

✦ What advice would you have for someone who is just starting the journey?

Scope

One of the key initial questions to be answered is what services are to be initially included in shared services. "Initially" because once shared services is up and operating effectively, additional services can always be added. In the start up of shared services it is advisable to begin with services where there is close to unanimous agreement regarding their inclusion. Where there is resistance or disagreement related to service inclusion, it's advisable to leave them out. It is better to get the center operating effectively with full endorsement. Once it is successful and clients see the benefits they will offer up the services that they did not want included at the outset.

Another scope issue is whether or not to include professional and advisory services. The goal of cost saving through consolidation relates mainly to transactional processing functions whereas professional advisory services is usually shared to improve performance and service. Cost saving is secondary for these services. If the primary driver for shared services is cost, then the best place to start is with the transactional processes. Most organizations start with transactional processing services and later offer professional and advisory services.

During the scoping exercise, the issue of outsourcing typically gets raised with questions about why the service is being consolidated internally when there are external providers who could do it better at less cost. This is a legitimate time to have this conversation; however, care must be taken to ensure the desire to outsource isn't based on anecdotal dissatisfaction with the present service or any incorrect assumptions about the availability and costs of outsource suppliers.

Buy-in

Shared services has to be driven from the top of the organization. Senior level buy-in is essential. The first step is to obtain executive endorsement to proceed with a more formalized feasibility study that will result in the development of a business case. The business case then needs to be reviewed and a "thumbs up" given for proceeding with shared services implementation. Some executive groups skip the business case altogether and provide a general agreement in principle to proceed based on the goals and principles. This usually happens where they have had previous experience or knowledge about successful shared services initiatives or when the CEO is in favour. Be cautious however, as it is important the executives have a full understanding of the issues and impacts as well as their responsibilities before proceeding. Otherwise when problems arise there may not be the support and commitment you anticipated.

Ultimately everyone in the organization needs to buy-in to shared services. One way or another if people are not shared services providers, they are clients of the shared services. The more clients know about what shared services can do for them, the more they will work to enhance its effectiveness. Buy-in therefore is not a one shot deal, it is a continuous process requiring multiple ambassadors who take the message formally and informally to the organization.

AN ANALYSIS OF THE CURRENT STATE

Once approval has been given to proceed with a detailed business plan, the first step is to obtain an understanding of the current state of the processes, the costs and how satisfied customers are with the services. This information provides the baseline upon which changes and improvements will be made. The first step in analysis is to identify and list the specific services that will be included in the initial shared services function.

Costs

Cost reduction is a key goal of shared services and the costs inherent in the current processes and services will be the basis for looking at future cost savings. The move to shared services is likely to require a different look at costs than past measurements. Previously the overall department budget for the payroll group, for example, provided a cost picture for the function. When moving to shared services it is essential to separate out specific cost items that will enable the calculation of the cost of processing a single payroll check, a travel and expense claim or an accounts payable invoice. The cost analysis must include all of the factors involved in a transaction including those associated with administration or overheads. These total costs will enable the calculation of fully loaded costs that are the basis of service pricing in shared services.

Benchmarking

Benchmarking involves the comparison of internal service costs with those of external service providers and those that are considered "best in class." Benchmarking at this stage in the process has two goals. Firstly, the data helps to assess whether it is viable to continue providing the service internally or whether the service should be outsourced. This information is a powerful tool for beginning to shift the culture since many staff groups do not really know how the costs of their services add up against external providers. The other goal of benchmarking is to create a baseline for measuring future improvements in cost savings. By getting information from other companies or suppliers who are best in class, the shared service group knows where to aim its sights. Benchmarking also needs to occur on an ongoing basis following the implementation of shared services. The shared services organization needs to compare its costs and practices continually with those of external suppliers and with in-house services of other organizations. It has to seek ways of reducing costs, increasing service quality and effectiveness.

If the benchmarking data shows the costs are significantly higher than best practices, the decision may still be to retain the service as a shared service with the provision that a plan for improved costs be put in place. The data is part of the solid foundation required to help the service group think like a business.

Customer satisfaction

Another component of the initial size-up and analysis is to develop a clear picture of the current level of client satisfaction with the services being provided. This picture will give an indication of the extent of change to the services and service delivery that will be required if shared services is to be successful. For organizations that would include more voluntary services this will provide an early indication of what clients are likely to commit themselves to

The move to shared services is about a significant mindset shift; where the client is in charge of evaluating service quality

purchasing. For many service providers this may be the first time that customer satisfaction information has been collected. Client satisfaction data at this time signals two things. First it signals to clients that things will be different and that their views on service quality are important and secondly it signals to employees in the services group that they must start to think and act differently.

At this point the business case is usually developed and presented to the executive. If the executive initially gave their agreement for a feasibility study of shared services then it is at this time that their endorsement for implementation is sought.

OUTSOURCING

Outsourcing suppliers are tapping on the windows of most organizations looking for an invitation to come in. These suppliers are springing up everywhere and are providing cost effective alternatives for the delivery of many internal services. For some executives, outsourcing may appear to be a better option than setting up a shared services organization. For employees in service functions, shared services may appear as an interim strategy before their function is outsourced. At this point in the process there may be functions that are likely candidates for outsourcing and they should be pursued, if for no other reason than to understand truly whether this is a viable alternative.

Care needs to be taken to ensure that the promises being made by the outsourced suppliers about cost saving and improved service quality are in fact an achievable reality. Some suppliers offer state-of-the-art systems and services at reasonable costs. Others do not and there would be very little gained by going to a mediocre supplier.

DESIGNING THE APPROACH TO SHARED SERVICES

Once the business plan and new direction is approved, one of the first tasks is to determine the structure and location of the shared services center or centers. It is also time to define specifically how shared services will operate within the organization through clearly defined operating principles. Even if a temporary project manager or acting leader has been assigned to implement shared services, someone needs to be more permanently identified as responsible for leading the new shared services organization.

Structure

There is no one best model for structuring a shared services organization. The optimum structure needs to be decided for the short term. One of the fundamental structural issues to be decided is whether the shared services organization is to be a stand alone entity or whether it will be connected to a functional group. Other decisions need to be made about the reporting level of the shared services organization. Options include whether it will report as a separate entity to the CEO, the senior finance executive, senior functional executive, such as human resources or information technology, or to a line business unit.

If the initial scope of services is to include professional and advisory services in addition to transactional processing, it is advisable to separate these into two organizational units: a center of scale for transactional processing activities, and a center of expertise for professional and advisory services. It is important, as well, to decide how governance-related activities will be separated from the delivery of services.

There are many issues and options when it comes to structures. Structures however are never permanent fixtures and there will no doubt be future reorganizations. Design the optimal structure to meet the immediate needs of establishing shared services and fine tune and modify as required.

Location

The location of shared services centers needs to be defined early on in the process. If it is to be at an existing location the change implications are not as dramatic as those following the decision to establish a new green field site. Both one time set-up costs and ongoing operational costs need to be identified at this time and considered in the decision. Non-cost factors such as the availability of the appropriate skills base and the desirability of proposed options can be major considerations in the long-term viability of any site.

An additional issue for consideration at this time is the number of centers to be established. Some organizations opt for one multi-function center, others establish multiple sites providing different services.

For organizations establishing shared services centers in Europe, the decisions become more complex as different countries with their unique languages, traditions and laws come into play. There is a broad range of European locations for consideration and careful analysis is required to identify those most appropriate for your organization.

Leadership

Leading a shared services organization requires a unique set of skills in

The skills required to manage staff involved in transactional processing differ from those for managing professional and advisory service providers

addition to those capabilities we normally attribute to excellent leaders of any business function. Careful consideration must be given to whether the new leader comes from within the organization or is hired externally to bring in a fresh perspective. In some cases a keen understanding of organizational processes and politics would be a great asset for the manager of the new shared services organization. Other organizations opt to bring in someone from outside the organization who has experience with shared services start-up and operation.

The focus of the leader of a center of scale needs to be on continual process improvement and cost reduction. They require the special capability required to motivate people whose job is to process data. Leaders of professional and advisory services need the orientation of managing a consulting firm.

Whatever the specific orientation of leadership for the new shared services organization, it is important that the leaders are appointed early on in the implementation process. There needs to be someone to take charge who has the overall accountability for success.

A best practice identified by Janet Faas, CEO of the Ontario Government Shared Services Bureau, which has consolidated services from across eighteen government ministries, is not to appoint the permanent leader too early. She believes there is a significant benefit for the new leader to come into the organization after some of the major battles have been fought. The decision to consolidate, the scope of services, and the operating principles are the most politically sensitive issues to resolve, and it is best if the new leader does not have to be associated with or wear the implications of these decisions.

Operating principles

The operation of any enterprise requires rules and procedures. For shared services many of these rules and procedures are new to the organization and a departure from traditional operations. It is important to define and obtain executive endorsement of operating principles before proceeding with formal implementation.

Operating principles include the rules related to outsourcing and freedom of supplier choice for business units. They also include how services will be priced and billed. Service level agreements need to be structured to provide clear definition of what services will be provided, at what price and within what quality standards. Service level agreements need to define both supplier and client expectations and obligations. Agreement and endorsement of these rules of operating are essential for the implementation step of shared services.

IMPLEMENTATION AND ONGOING OPERATIONS

The implementation stage is about throwing the switch. Services are now consolidated into the shared services center and are being provided to clients on a fee-for-service basis. Staff have moved to the new location or new staff have been hired to process transactions at the new green field location. Clients are anxious about service delivery and quality and are watching closely to ensure their needs are being met. The successful implementation of shared services requires a shift away from the traditional culture of most organizations. It also requires the definition of a compelling vision that captures the imagination of both shared services staff and clients. Ultimately the value of shared services must be quanttatively and qualitatively measured and reported.

Based on extensive experience and research Larry Giammo, managing director of the prestigious Corporate Leadership Council, identifies four essential factors related to shared services success.

1 **Managing costs must be a key focus**

   Business plans for shared services identify cost and non-cost impacts. Upon implementation and operation, service costs must be visibly reduced. While service quality in the eyes of the clients must be improved, there is a threshold level, beyond which clients are not willing to pay. It must be remembered that cost reduction is a primary goal of shared services. Many organizations, which significantly reduced administrative human resources work through consolidation and the implementation of integrated software systems, found after several years that the administrative headcount did not decrease. There must be a careful watch to ensure that staff numbers and costs are reduced following the reduction of work.

2 **Client feedback mechanisms are essential**

   With the consolidation of services there is an increased distance between service providers and clients. This "distance" may be physical as when staff and work are transferred to a remote center, or it may be more subtle with changes in reporting relationships and allegiance. The shared services must ensure that this space does not become a chasm of poor communication, unmet expectations and frustration. It is up to the service provider to build in effective and frequent mechanisms for ensuring client expectations are clearly understood and met.

3   Service flexibility is essential for client satisfaction

One of the goals frequently defined for shared services is process standardization. Shared services organizations, however, must ensure they do not compromise on meeting the flexibility requirements of their business unit clients. Software programs must be designed to enable the production of non-standard processes and one-off service requirements.

4   Transactional processing work requires a unique skill set

Traditional administrative work includes aspects of transactional processing as well as a broad diversity of other functions and tasks. In a transaction-focused shared services center the work is repetitive transactional processing. It requires a unique set of capabilities and skills and an orientation for this type of work. Organizations must not assume that those who perform administrative functions are the same people who should be transferred to shared services.

Culture change

The move to shared services will create anxiety within the organization. For many people there will be a great deal of fear about job loss. People will be concerned that in a full cost recovery environment they will never be able to compete with external suppliers and that the services they provide will ultimately be outsourced. On the other side of the coin there is a great deal of excitement about creating something new. People want to be successful and they want to be recognized as being valuable to the organization. People who gravitate to the excitement side will provide momentum and leadership to the new direction. They will be counterbalanced by those who will be in the way, who will want it to fail and will do their best to make this happen. Most people will sit on the fence, being pulled by both ends of the continuum. It is the job of the leader and those who fully endorse the move to bring others along. This will not happen without concrete actions and initiatives geared towards visibly rewarding desired behaviors and results.

The focus of the new shared services organization needs to be on service quality and client satisfaction

Vision

Shared services needs a rallying cry and a picture of the future that will capture the attention and imagination of the organization. The focus of the new organization needs to be on service quality and client satisfaction. Key client relationship roles must be defined within shared services. For some organizations the relationships become distinct management roles separate from the delivery of services. For others, the relationship function is built into the service delivery role of each and every person in shared services.

Measurement

The contribution that shared services makes to the organization must be evaluated and reported. Promises were made and expectations established in the business case about reduced costs and improved service quality in addition to numerous other performance-related results. Sooner or later the executive will want to know if these promises have been kept.

The cornerstone of shared services success is the level of client satisfaction with the services being provided and with the relationship that has been developed between service provider and client. While the evaluation of shared services performance and client satisfaction cannot occur until the centers have been operating effectively for some time, it is important in the implementation stage to define the parameters of how performance and success will be measured.

Summary

There is a lot to be done to put shared services in place and make it operate effectively. Each step must be carefully planned and executed. This will require a dedicated team of managers and team leaders who can drive the process throughout the organization. This cannot be done off the corner of someone's desk, this is a full-time senior management job.

Chapter 4

SCOPING SHARED SERVICES:
DEFINING THE BORDERS

Gold can be stretched or drawn more than any other metal. A single ounce of gold can be drawn into a wire over forty miles long, and that's without breaking

THE SCOPE OF POTENTIAL FUNCTIONS

A spectacular map of the Roman Empire hangs gracefully in one of the great rooms of the Vatican, the size of the vast territories under Rome's grip so startling at first glance. It is as though someone took a map of the world, laid it out flat, picked up a pen and began steadily at the farthest edges of the paper to draw lines here and there. Pen pressed deliberately as if to say, this will be part of the empire, this will not. Artificial divisions in retrospect, considering the modern map of Europe today. Just the same, there is something comforting and organized about lines and borders. There is a certain stability knowing what is yours and what is mine. So too in the business of shared services where there is a decision to be made as to how big and how wide the group should be designed.

Some organizations will take a wide sweep across the territory starting with a blank piece of paper and putting almost everything up to the light for consideration. These people will challenge conventional notions about what is core and what is not, what can be shared and what cannot. They will find common threads across diverse territories. Local geography and customs will be challenged for their authenticity in demanding unique services. Diverse services will be taken in the sweep:

51

purchasing, logistics, training, accounting, marketing, and sales support will be placed deliberately within the boundaries.

Others will choose a small and controlled boundary, such as financial processing, and implement it in text-book fashion, planned, orderly and down to the last detail. Tiny scope offers the possibility of learning outside the spotlight, narrowing the energy, taking the time to make things work properly. Executives who already have centralized functions may choose to start with services that are already in their boundary and in their control. No permission required to take centralized services and move them into a business model. Starting small and building success can often be the best way to demonstrate how a strategy works.

Choosing the boundaries and borders for shared services is one of the critical activities early on. Not that borders and scope cannot be revisited, they can and they will. It is a matter of making sure the opportunities have at least been considered before rejection.

DOW CHEMICAL

William S. Stavropoulos, CEO

Dow's Executive Committee has been directing a major move to reduce structural costs. We chose what we call the 80:20 program: 80% of the company's people work directly with the operation of the business units while the remaining 20% are in shared services or our leveraged and geographic resource groups.

Shared services

controllers
environment, health and safety
finance
human resources
information systems
legal
public affairs
purchasing
strategic department

Leveraged activities

manufacturing and engineering
integrated supply chain
research and development
marketing and sales
leveraged geographic activities

Deciding what to include and what not to include will depend on the image and reputation of the staff groups, the degree of centralization that already exists and the culture and orientation of the company. Is shared services a major break with tradition or a logical extension of current practice? Can the culture handle change of this nature? Is the company disciplined enough to stick to the rules of shared services? Finally, it will come down to the attitude of the person who is leading the strategic charge. Some people debate persuasively for nothing short of revolutionary change while others quietly argue the merits of incremental or evolutionary change: the broad sweep versus the narrow one.

On the evolution side, the premise is to take it slow, pilot one area and, like the author W.P. Kinsella said, "Build it and they will come." This stance would mean that finance converts one particular area such as billing or accounts payable and migrates business units that are willing. The long-term objective is to convince skeptics in the corporation that shared services does and can work. There is considerable merit in this idea provided that the organization has the time to wait for the evolution to gel and to get the cost savings out of the system. If a pilot is too small, if the scope is too little, organizations run the risk that no one even notices the great experiment. The savings and major culture shift to customer service is hard to see when the shared services unit is tiny in comparison to the overall size of the company. Forcing people and their functions to be included in shared services may be a bad idea since organizational men and women can find ways to scuttle the best of ideas if they are not committed to the outcome and success.

Steven Kerr is the chief learning officer and vice president of corporate development for General Electric, one of the oldest and most respected of the shared services alumni group. "Some shared services groups have already been disbanded, some are incredibly successful, some are doing pretty well." When asked to consider his working theory for the diversity of success even inside the same company, he pragmatically replies that he is not entirely sure.

GENERAL ELECTRIC

Steven Kerr, Chief Learning Officer

"Shared services, like outsourcing, is not a panacea for all functions. Sometimes it works and sometimes it is not the right strategy – especially if it has been forced upon reluctant business units. It is not a hammer!"

Give a little boy a hammer and he will soon find that everything he encounters is in need of hammering. Shared services is a good strategy, but it shouldn't be used as a hammer because it is not appropriate for all functions.

Leaders advocating the revolutionary orientation to change will argue that you should go for a whole function or functions since the effort of generating buy-in and managing the change will be about as much for two or three functions as for one. They will argue that you might as well ask for a wider scope up front and minimize the agony of picking off one function at a time. Reliant Energy is one company that began its design with a fairly wide scope of services (see Figure 4.1).

FIGURE 4.1   Reliant Energy's shared services

There are significant economies of scale in implementation costs for shared services when the scope is wider. One business case is developed rather than several. One transition plan is defined rather than one for each function. Just as in shared services, the cost to implement shared services is greatly enhanced when there is sufficient economy of scale.

Using terms like revolutionary change conjures up a bloody battle but in some companies, it may be better to go for the one big bang rather than an endless continuum of little skirmishes. If it is known at the outset that a wider scope for shared services is necessary, then it may be worthwhile to hold out for the bigger group of services. Drawing borders and boundaries is essentially an act of politics. Cynics who sneer and turn their nose up at the idea that politics is something to be managed should think again. The scope of shared services is an extremely political issue.

Even though a company or government might be in dire need of cost containment, line managers and heads of businesses will still often be reluctant to give up their own staff groups. It is a matter of turf and control. Edward De Pasquale, the executive director of Conemaugh Health Systems experienced a disappointing launch of shared services when he initially underestimated the complexity and politics of trying to consolidate financial shared services in a voluntary hospital association. Hospitals saw this as centralization plain and simple and had strong ideas on finance as a key lever. Having now

TABLE 4.1 Scope of potential functions for shared services in one company

	Transactional and administrative	Professional and technical
Finance	Accounts payable/receivable Payroll Credit and collections Customer billing Travel and expenses Tax filing and reporting General accounting External reporting	Financial analysis Business case support Capital planning Business analysis
Human resources	Benefits administration Pension administration Salary administration Employee records Claims Employee inquiries Job evaluation	Labor relations Organizational development Training and development Compensation and rewards Advisory services Health and safety
Information technology	Data center operations Network services Maintenance Help desk Data support	Application development Application architecture Software/hardware installation Strategy and training Telecommunications
Supply or support	Administrative support (includes: reception, clerical, secretarial) Travel arrangements Mail services Microfilming Fleet	Purchasing and warehousing Real estate Materials management Logistics and distribution Facilities management Public affairs Communications Graphic services Legal services Security services

SOURCE: Barbara E. Quinn and Robert S. Cooke

backed away from financial shared services, materials management, human resources and dietary services are new candidates for sharing and are predicted to be more easily adopted. It is unwise to ignore the politics of turf and control when considering the borders of shared services. Logic does not always win the day, but then whoever said organizations were necessarily logical?

Table 4.1 illustrates the potential range of functions that could be included in a shared services model for an organization.

You can see from the list of potential shared services functions that there is considerable scope and this list is growing. Marketing is now regularly defined as a potential shared service. In health care, there is a growing trend to share dietary and laundry services between facilities. In the financial sector, competing banks are creating shared processing centers. This is a dramatic turnaround, to imagine that

FIGURE 4.2 Shared services "snapshots"

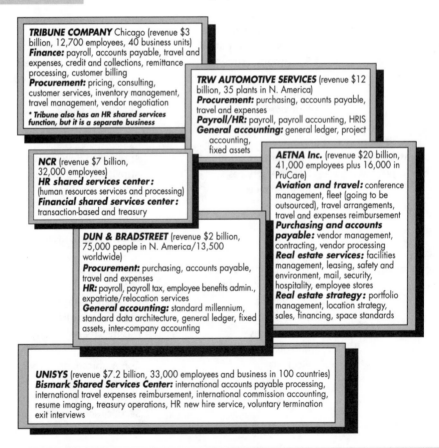

former enemies and competitors are forming joint ventures to reduce the cost of back room office operations.

Functions such as manufacturing, engineering and research, considered as core functions for most organizations, are now becoming candidates for shared services. Almost any function can be placed on the potential drawing board.

DEFINING THE BORDERS

There are three key areas to consider when defining the scope of shared services:

FIGURE 4.3   Three key areas

... *3 key areas*

image and profile   *degree of centralization*   *capability of managing change*

Where corporate functions occupy a dreaded position in that they have a poor image and reputation for service, there will be a great temptation to put more functions within the scope of shared services. After all, the compelling notion of an internal market economy finds line management quite willing to expand the scope if they see benefits to themselves. If human resources is seen by clients as ineffective or information technology as ridiculously expensive, the thought of making these groups client-focused and self-funding is an appealing proposition.

In this new millennium, there are still an amazing number of corporate functions which do not have a realistic grasp of their own image and reputation within the company. There are still corporate functions that have no formal client satisfaction feedback. According to customer service expert and author Chip Bell, only 10% of dissatisfied customers actually take the time to complain. If we transfer this idea to internal clients, we can be assured that there is likely to be some kind of reasonable correlation. It is not enough to sit back and wait passively for people either to complain or praise the group.

Many corporate staff groups have no idea how their clients perceive them. Are they seen as useful? Are they seen as competent? Are they seen as reliable? Are they seen as inadequate? It is essential to know this

FIGURE 4.4   What shared services can do for tomorrow's quality and costs

TODAY   **TOMORROW**

• ineffective	more effective •
• expensive	less costly •
• unresponsive	more responsive •
• bureaucratic	less bureaucratic •

Image and reputation are concerned with two principal elements: quality of service and the costs of the service

before defining the scope for shared services, since the selling of the strategy has to be based on fixing what is perceived to be wrong with the staff groups. Staff groups need a handle on how they are perceived and they need to know how their costs stack up against outside practices and how clients view the cost of their operation.

Cost is key but, in our view, cost is never the fundamental root cause of dissatisfaction with corporate and internal staff groups. When costs are perceived as too high, this is often symbolic of a deeper rooted cause related to dissatisfaction with quality. When executives complain of high corporate costs, they do not tend

The real issue is reputation

to say things like, "Golly, we have the best human resources function in the world even though it is really expensive". In corporate circles it is easier to complain about internal corporate functions by citing cost as the predominant cause for dissatisfaction. Cost is safe and neutral. It is easier saying you cost too much than saying we think your service is really bad.

It is easier to define the scope of shared services and to sell the strategy when the actual image and reputation is known. Shared services is a compelling strategy for staff groups that find themselves with a bad reputation for service and high costs to boot. Telling clients that shared services will mean providing products and services that they are willing to pay for is an appealing proposition. Who is going to turn down lower costs and better service?

Outsourcing

When scope and boundaries are being considered, the subject of outsourcing is likely to emerge. It will be a known fact that some services are already poor quality, overpriced, and non-core to the business. The question on people's minds will be, "Why go through an agonizing transition to shared services only to have to outsource two years later?" Although outsourcing may indeed be the right answer, the functions for now should be considered part of the scope and boundaries. Even if a function is outsourced, it can still be considered a shared service. The fact that someone else does the work doesn't take away the need to manage the service as a shared service.

Typical candidates that come up during scoping include:

+ printing
+ graphics and advertising
+ payroll
+ pensions and benefits administration
+ travel and expenses claims
+ vehicles: leasing and maintenance.

The reasons for these kinds of functions coming up during scoping are fairly obvious. In the printing game, very few companies want to make the kind of capital investment to stay up to date. Let printing companies invest in the high priced technology. In graphics and advertising, it is a question of getting access to the best talent available and not being restricted to internal groups that may or may not be state of the art. For payroll, pension and benefits, travel expense administration, and vehicle management it is simply a matter of scale and volume.

At the end of the scoping exercise, you should have a clear list of potential candidates for shared services to take upstairs for approval. If this initiative is being driven from the CFO's office, the CFO has a responsibility to raise the wider scope and potential for consideration even if out of their direct organizational control. The CEO and executives need to be made aware of the potential and they need to make the decision as to where to start or how much to include. Typically a business case is put together so it is essential to nail down the scope prior to getting executive agreement to explore shared services as a strategy.

Where the image and reputation of the corporate staff groups is poor, shared services is an excellent strategy for change and accountability. Although it may be tempting to simply outsource the function, it is not advisable to take something that is a disaster in the client's eyes and simply hurl it over the wall to an eager third party supplier. Shared services makes sense as an interim strategy even if the path to outsourcing seems paved in stone.

The degree of decentralization

The question of what scope to envisage also relates to whether the functions are already housed in a centralized function or whether there is a huge degree of decentralization. Where there is a high degree of disbursed functions across countries or geographic areas, it may be difficult to get business units and operating companies to offer up all of their localized services such as finance and human resources, whereas they may be willing to pilot one specific operation such as billing. Where the functions are already centralized to some degree, it is definitely recommended to go with the wider scope. If the CFO has information technology and human resources in addition to finance, it would be worthwhile to define a wider scope at the outset.

In fact, the clear direction would be to turn any centralized services into shared services and to make the strategy successful before going to the executive team for a wider scope. It is obviously going to be easier to get approval to turn central services into shared services than taking functions away and out of the business units.

The history and culture of decentralization has to be looked at within the company. Greater decentralization often occurs when organizations have been either in a monopoly or a cost plus environment which means there has been little accountability for improving the bottom line, so functions have sprung up as needed. Alternatively where individual operating companies have been very successful or suddenly become very core or strategic to the enterprise as a whole, they become good bargainers for getting what they want, even if it costs more. If they want their own human resources function or information systems group, they will tend to get it. The request usually comes at budget and sales projections time, when tempting targets are accompanied by a few additional full-time employees. So over time, the function grows from one or two people to entire departments with infrastructure and overheads.

If the cash flow warrants the costs, then companies will create what they think they need to be successful. In some cases, the complaints are completely valid. It just takes the loss of one big deal or one major sale due to the center bureaucracy for an operating executive to demand the creation of their own service groups. If they have the track record and the clout, decentralization will be permitted even though it is an irrefutable fact that decentralized corporate services cost the company more money. It is true that one cannot guarantee better service in a centralized environment, but you can guarantee lower costs overall to the enterprise as a whole.

In some cases operating companies have created their own units out of years of frustration with corporate or central groups which are perceived to be unresponsive

THE CULTURE AND STRATEGIC ORIENTATION

Finally, the overall culture and strategic orientation of the company is a determining factor in whether shared services should be considered and if it is, what the scope should include. If the organization has demonstrated success in managing major change or implementation of major new systems or projects then this is a competency that will be useful in the implementation of shared services. Moving to a marketplace economy is a significant culture shift for both the buyers of the services and the sellers. If the organization has a poor reputation for implementing major change and making it stick, then shared services will have a hard time getting off the ground. The nature of this strategy means it is top down driven and if the culture has a history of executives nodding in principle and then proceeding to do whatever they want, shared services and the scope of it is irrelevant. If this is the case, then the executive will pick a very tiny scope or pick a function that is largely perceived as not having much use and let them try to put shared services in place.

If the company has a dismal history of change started and then stopped before ever getting fully implemented, then it is likely that shared services will share the same fate. The discipline required to make shared services work suggests that there has to be a high degree of capability for managing difficult transitions. People in corporate functions are not all begging to move to an internal business enterprise model. There has to be considerable investment in changing the culture and helping people to make the transition from corporate bureaucrats to zealous service providers. Heads of business units will have to trust that the new shared services organization will provide at least the same quality as they are getting today. The CEO and executive team will have to be relentless in enforcing rules that do not permit duplication of functions once they have been designated as shared services. This means you cannot create a phantom local accounts payable or human resources group once the decision is made to go to shared services.

KRAFT FOODS

Bernie Kocanda, Director of Shared Services Center

"It is hard to demonstrate the value of moving to shared service unless there is real dissatisfaction with the service."

To be successful, a lot of change management has to happen; recognize the need for this. We are a very centralized company and even then, we had to position shared services as not just about costs but about improving the service.

Where there is a financial impetus to drive down costs, the scope may widen considerably. If business is rich, the cash cows of the enterprise may resist the scope when it impacts their own decentralized groups. So if one of the companies is very profitable, it is hard to argue for change unless the company operates in an integrated fashion or has a strategic vision to be a fully integrated enterprise. The issue of control is really at the heart of the matter. Some business units want control of functions that aren't even core to their central business. They will fight to keep a local accounts payable or billing operation even if it is costing the company more money overall. Unless someone tells them to think enterprise-wide or unless they see a compelling need to reduce operating costs, they will always err on the side of control.

The benefits for volume processing are easily evaluated with ready and available benchmarks to show the cost per transaction before and after shared services implementation. In the center of excellence or expertise approach, the benefits come from pooling expertise and leveraging the intellectual capital throughout the organization. For example, it is too cost prohibitive to have technical experts throughout a decentralized operation whereas a center approach can have a range of technical expertise readily available as needed. In human resources for example, operating companies will be unlikely to have the capacity to house senior experts in performance coaching, pension design, or organizational development to the same degree that you could have in a central approach. By concentrating technical expertise in one center, the enterprise as a whole has an opportunity to avail itself of deeper, more comprehensive knowledge on an as needed basis. The scale usually does not permit such a wide range of technical expertise at the local level.

In most cases, organizations are choosing the concept but not the language since it may be audacious to refer to a newly consolidated group as "the center of expertise," implying that expertise does not reside out in the field or in the operating businesses. Frequently, organizations choose more generic language such as Business Services when referring to a center of expertise.

The benefits of a center approach for scale include the ability to attempt removal of the natural hierarchy that exists in any corporate and internal function. In the world of corporate functions, it is clear that there is a distinct hierarchy between administrative and professional level functions, especially in finance and human resources. The administrative and processing people are definitely seen at the bottom of the power structure. When they are consolidated into one center, it can be motivating since there is more career latitude to move upwards within the center. With the right kind of leadership, clerical and administrative people can feel that what they do has meaning, that their services are important and that quality service counts. Most corporate groups are trying to shift their attention away from transactional and processing to concentrate efforts at the more strategic value-added level. Finance wants to be spending more time doing business decision support and controlling. Human resources wants to be doing strategic succession planning and deployment. Information technology wants to be working on long-term IT strategic investment, while supply wants to work on supply chain management.

At a conceptual level this is understandable. At a practical level however, it is important to recognize how valuable and important the transactional and administrative functions are to an organization. An accurate dental claim or pay-check will not make or break the company, but if not done properly will erode employees' perceptions of their employer. In functions such as billing, accounts receivable, and pension administration, it is absolutely critical to achieve high levels of quality for accuracy and responsiveness.

Dangerous hierarchies are being created where those in professional services are presumably strategic and value-added while those in administrative functions are low value-added and non-strategic. How would you like to come and work for the non-strategic, low-value-added department of our company?

One of the more disturbing trends floating around conferences and professional journals is using the term non-value-added to describe transactional and administrative work

So shared services offers the scale center the possibility to engage in a new world where transaction processing is the core business, where it is valued and cared about. In the expertise center, the new world offers a much greater leveraging of expertise with groups dedicated to becoming world class in their area of expertise. In actual terms, the center may be one actual physical location offering different levels of services.

Joseph W. Rahaim, a senior manager with Ernst and Young LLP, uses slides to describe scope that also breaks down traditional lines within staff functions and looks at life through a process lens. He warns that companies which have not addressed shared services must get on board quickly or remain at a competitive disadvantage.

FIGURE 4.5   Order to cash as defined by Ernst and Young LLP

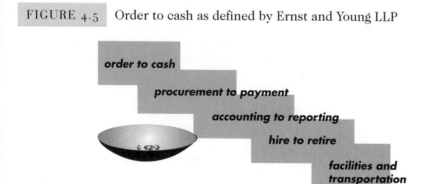

CONCLUSION

Leaders of corporate functions can benefit from the rigor in doing a business case for shared services. They should at least look at what results could be achieved even if there is a reluctance to go with shared services. The forward-looking leaders will put their own corporate and internal function to the test since sooner or later someone will tap them on the shoulder and ask why they have not considered shared services. A good answer can only be provided when the facts are there to back up the response. Even if shared services is not seen as viable, it is wiser for the corporate functions themselves to raise the idea for approval rather than have it dropped on their heads. The CFO, the vice president of finance, human resources, or supply should be banging on the executive door and presenting the idea to the executive. It is a question of leadership. Confident leaders are willing to explore ideas and test assumptions. Competent leaders are willing to imagine different and better ways of doing things. As Socrates said, "The unexamined life is not worth living." Corporate functions need to examine themselves and determine what and how they can improve. This does not mean that shared services is the only answer and it does not mean it is the right answer. The fundamental principle of integration and consolidation is worth exploring. The profound idea of tearing apart the governance role from the services role is worthwhile thinking about. Before examining shared services in too much depth, it is wise to go to the executive and get their agreement that the idea is worth pursuing. Get their endorsement for investment to investigate the strategy in further detail.

The idea that line management needs to be accountable for owning corporate policy is a worthwhile conversation at the executive table

The blank piece of paper needs to be laid out flat and the pen lines drawn around potential borders and boundaries for shared services. The definition of borders is a good decision for the executive to make. They too can lift their pens and make deft strokes as to what is in and what is out.

Chapter 5

SHARED SERVICES CANNOT BE
SOLD, IT CAN ONLY BE BOUGHT

Patience is possibly the single most important trait necessary for good prospecting. Recovering gold is a methodical process. It's hard work and cannot be rushed

EXECUTIVE TEAM DYNAMICS AND ITS IMPACT ON SHARED SERVICES

People firmly committed to the principles of shared services believe the inherent logic should make organizational acceptance a breeze. Like any brilliant idea, the assumption is that the act of understanding will cause people to come running. All that has to be done is to sell them the benefits and they will sign on the bottom line. Unfortunately, what may appear compelling and logical to some is not necessarily so for others. People will accept ideas only when they themselves come to the same conclusions in their own way and in their own time.

The executive of the organization must buy into the philosophy of shared services and come to its own conclusion that shared services is an idea worth pursuing. It must come to accept that in the long run shared services will win, that the executive will be the beneficiary of more effective and efficient services that will contribute to the organization's performance. It must personally accept that some short-term loss of control over resources it previously owned will provide longer term personal rewards.

In most cases, shared services is a strategy that is bought from the top down. This is not a grassroots idea, nor can it be implemented half

Shared services cannot operate as a "skunkworks" project

way. Tom Peters and Robert H. Waterman in their best selling book, *In Search of Excellence,* coined the phrase "skunkworks" to refer to a department where creative ideas could spawn and germinate outside the corporate bureaucracy. Shared services requires disciplined buy-in and commitment by all the members in the shared services operating environment: the stakeholders, the clients and users, and the management and staff of the organization.

There is a story from the training and development community that was frequently used in leadership programs. A pig and a chicken are walking down the street. The chicken turns to the pig and says, "How about getting some breakfast? Bacon and eggs would be great." The pig says, "Oh sure, bacon and eggs – for you this represents involvement but for me it is a total commitment!" Shared services is the bacon and the executive team must decide whether they have the commitment to put it on the corporate menu or not.

The term buy-in has become synonymous with the word commitment. Although involvement is also critical for success, ultimately it is commitment that will ensure the success and longevity of this initiative. Almost everybody in corporate life today talks about needing to get buy-in from somebody because commitment is the glue that will make some strategies stick while others will fade before they have even been properly implemented.

For the executive of the organization, there is a requirement to grasp the intellectual properties of shared services and the practical realities of moving to consolidation. For corporate groups that are contemplating a shared services model, and which will be the ones driving to get executive endorsement, there is a need for careful preparation. Depending on the dynamics of the executive team, obtaining buy-in and commitment can be more or less of a challenge. It is essential then to analyze the executive team dynamics ahead of time to determine how best to position shared services.

In corporate practice, terms such as Corporate Management Committee, Lead Officer Group and Executive Committee are frequently used. These are nice, neutral terms to describe the fact that, for the most part, the word "team" simply doesn't apply to the people at the top of the house. The problem is not that executives aren't natural team players or aren't oriented to being part of a team. It has more to do with corporate tradition and the selection criteria for executives. We select senior managers who are decisive, who will define a direction and focus the organization's resources on its achievement. Most organizations do not promote people to executive positions because they are conciliatory and excel at achieving consensus with their peers. It is not surprising that the

We often say the term "executive team" is in fact an oxymoron – "executive group" is a more apt description

concept of an executive "team" with the characteristics of shared account-ability and a cross-functional orientation is a bit of an oxymoron.

Either way, the structure and orientation of the executive team is a determining factor in the acceptance of any model of shared services. In an organization with a traditional executive group, individual operating companies or business units may be so strong and autonomous that they do not have to adopt enterprise-wide thinking or worry about cost savings to the overall company. In the traditional executive suite, each occupant is rewarded for delivering their own organization's results with few rewards or accolades for contributing to the performance of a paral-lel business unit or to the organization as a whole. In this model why would any individual executive agree to adopt shared services for the overall good unless they had to?

Many contemporary organizations are moving to a more integrated approach to executive operations. Typically driven by the vision and operating style of a CEO who sees the need for more cross corporate integration, the integrated team shares accountability for organizational performance beyond the realm of its own individual organizational enti-ties. In this model the decision to adopt shared services or not is based on the group's assessment of the overall good that would be derived by the organization.

Understanding the group dynamics of your organizational executive team is time well spent. In this context, we will explore the model as it relates to shared services. It will be more difficult to obtain agreement and to institute shared services where the company and executive are what we call traditional. If the executive team is integrated and the vision is towards an integrated organization, shared services will be easier to position and probably more acceptable.

TRADITIONAL MODEL: VERTICAL BUSINESS UNITS

Historically, executive groups have operated under what we call the tra-ditional model of executive teams where the CEO is the primary integrator, while the heads of the business units focus on running their individual business operations (see Figure 5.1). The primary objective of executive meetings is information sharing and might even be informally referred to as status reports or weekly updates. A fly on the wall at one of these meetings would see the CEO clearly chairing it, with individual executives making presentations or providing updates on issues from their respective business units. Although it looks like a group interac-tion, in fact the activity is one-way communication, with the main audience being the CEO. The other members are there to listen and absorb information that may or may not be pertinent to them.

FIGURE 5.1   A traditional model for executives

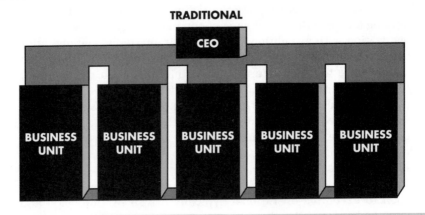

A senior vice president might update the group on a new initiative, the results of a study or on the last quarter's performance. Other executives, finishing off their morning scones and coffee, might be very interested, might even have been involved to some degree, but they are not there to question, challenge or make any decisions related to other people's business.

The motivation for operating as a traditional executive group mostly centers on the belief that there is no real interdependence between the various units, thus no basis for working together to make decisions or explore mutual issues. For organizations operating on the traditional model, this is essentially correct. The result of this mindset of autonomy is organizational units that operate very independently. In this independence mindset there is a great deal of resistance and sometimes outright indignation at any suggestion of increased centralization. Even though they might eventually accept that shared services would make their life easier and contribute to their organization's performance, the hurdle to jump over is their desire to retain control and ownership of their own resources and services.

The essence of the traditional group is that the individual executives have no real shared accountability for overall enterprise-wide performance. They may all have a similar bonus plan if the corporation hits its key performance targets on customer satisfaction, profitability and employee satisfaction, but individual vice presidents are held accountable only for their own piece of the business. The implementation of shared services is a corporate initiative that will contribute to overall corporate performance and cost savings. This is a tough sell to an executive who may not see this goal as congruent with his or her own.

In the traditional model it is the CEO who is the integrator and the arbitrator and the one who effectively acts as the ultimate judge and decision-maker. In this context, bringing shared services up to the executive table will mean that the CEO is basically the one who must buy the concept of shared services. Getting the CEO on board needs to be the initial step in getting approval to proceed. This will require one-on-one meetings with the CEO to ensure that he or she has a clear understanding of the organizational benefits that will accrue with shared services. It is the CEO who will ensure the operating principles required for success are put in place and followed.

INTEGRATED EXECUTIVE TEAMS

In an integrated executive team, there is a dual set of shared executive accountabilities that include both corporate and operating unit level objectives. This creates an environment where individual business unit heads hold each other accountable for the same set of corporate goals and targets, even though they don't have direct control over what goes on outside their own business unit. In this model, illustrated in Figure 5.2, each vice president has an accountability for corporate-wide decisions and an accountability to run their own business as they see fit.

With an integrated executive team, executive meeting becomes a group interaction. The primary reason for meeting is to make joint decisions on issues of a strategic nature, while information sharing becomes a secondary motive. A bird's eye view would reveal considerably more

FIGURE 5.2   An integrated executive team model

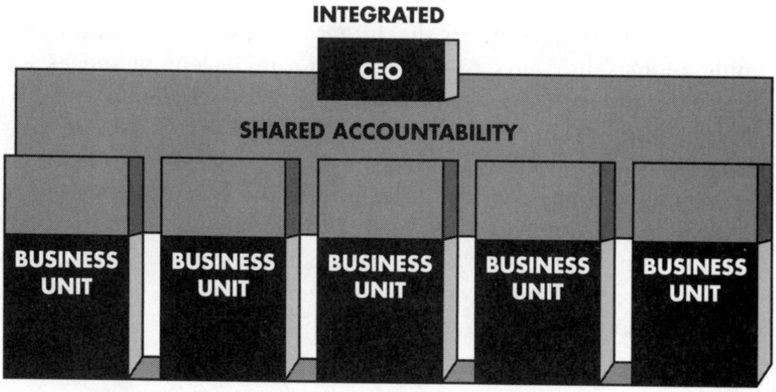

animated debate and discussion among executives and less one-way communication than would be seen in the traditional model.

The CEO in this model has a role to ensure that integration takes place but not to act as the actual integrator. Discussions and decisions are taken collectively, although not in all areas. This is not one gigantic "group experience" with the executives all roped together like a six pack of beer, running around deciding on everything, everywhere that goes on in the company. Rather this executive team has defined areas of shared accountability for very specific functions of the company's operation.

There is little one-on-one deal-making between the vice presidents and the CEO in an integrated group. In fact, when this model is successful and fully operational, it is considered poor form to make deals off to the side without coming to the executive table beforehand. It does not mean that all vice presidents are running all of the business units. Instead, one portion of the executive performance contract deals with shared accountability, while another portion deals with making decisions and running the individual's business unit.

In the integrated model, executives think as a corporate entity and meetings focus on addressing cross-corporate issues and answering key corporate questions. For example:

+ What are the key strategic issues facing the enterprise that we need to address?

+ What is our strategic response?

+ What is the best use of our capital for this year and the next few years if we are to ensure sustainability of the enterprise as a whole?

+ Where are we going to get our next leaders from so that the enterprise is sustainable in the long term?

+ What is the most appropriate allocation of capital across the enterprise to ensure the achievement of our overall performance targets?

Decisions that come to the integrated executive table have broad implications. They have to do with senior management succession planning, with compensation practices, with IT investments and corporate planning processes. They have to do with corporate functions and hence shared services. In the integrated model the decision to pursue shared services will be made by the team and in the best interests of the organization. Each member will weigh the benefits against the downsides but individual desire for power and control will be secondary to the evaluation of enterprise-wide value. Shared services is an easier sell to an integrated team.

THE EXECUTIVE PRESENTATION

Regardless of the model of how the executive team operates, getting its buy-in to shared services is essential. There are a number of factors that can contribute to increasing the probability of success. Executives need to see the big picture and not the details. They need to see the broad picture of what they can expect and what it will do for them. This means laying out the potential scope at the outset rather than have them discover later that shared services is wider than any one corporate function. It is better to position shared services as a business strategy directed at improving the overall cost and effectiveness of corporate and internal functions than it is to define cost savings narrowly in one process such as benefits processing or payroll.

At some point it will be necessary to appear before the executive team to present the concept of shared services and to obtain their commitment to pursue, at the minimum, an assessment of its viability for the corporation. These types of presentation typically last from thirty minutes to two hours depending on the executives' desire to probe into the details of the rationale. The presentation will have to be cleverly planned, requiring the need for advanced mental gymnastics to boil down reams of details into a few highly focused slides. Presenters at the executive table are always competing with a broad range of what we like to think are highly strategic items. Shared services is typically not high on most executives' list of issues requiring their attention or focus. The task can be daunting but careful planning will pay off.

The agenda items need to include a conceptual overview of shared services as well as a concrete discussion on its viability for the organization. There needs to be the opportunity to deal with some of the more controversial and high impact implications.

Who has recently had a discussion in their executive teams about whether it is worthwhile to check expense accounts or not and whose job it is? Who has talked recently about the concept of choice for buying internal services or not? Who has recently tried to explain that budget allocations have nothing to do with the real costs of services? Who has had a discussion recently about whether it makes sense to have duplicated functions across a range of companies in a range of countries? All this in thirty minutes!

> *The issue of governance, inherent in any shared services discussion, is fundamental and requires intelligent discourse*

There is a need to recognize that each member of the executive team will come with different levels of understanding of shared services. For some of them this will be the first time they have heard of the concept. Other members will be quite knowledgeable from their experiences in other organizations or from colleagues in other organizations who have already implemented shared services and are anxious to share their success stories.

Expect that at least one of those executives will have heard of it and may know more than you think. In one example, a controller who was introducing shared services to the executive wanted to make sure a full and wide picture of scope was presented since their CEO was currently an active board member of a well-known company that had successfully implemented multi-functional shared services. Some insiders were reluctant for the finance department to be so bold as to suggest that shared services could also apply to human resources, supply and information technology. The decision in this case was to present a broad scope that illustrated the potential for shared services even though the presenter from finance was going out on a limb and presenting far-reaching and politically sensitive options.

Many shared services initiatives have started in the finance function which naturally places a high degree of emphasis on the rigor of business case thinking: a requirement to spell out the benefits and potential savings along with the risks and costs for implementation. In some organizational cultures, it is unthinkable to proceed on any strategy without strong facts and figures while other cultures work more on an intuitive level. In these cultures if the executives like the sound of the shared services concept they will just give their blessing to put it in place. Knowing your culture is important for how much analysis needs to be done prior to going to the executive for buy-in.

BC HYDRO AND POWER AUTHORITY

David Harrison, Senior VP and CFO of Corporate and Financial Affairs

Although we did not do a formal business case, we were clear on what we were asking the corporate management committee to agree to in the presentation.

We went to the corporate management committee several times to make sure that there was a corporate executive endorsement. The concept of shared services is not hard to understand, but it is important that the rules are made clear in advance and that we as a corporate management committee know what to expect.

There are several options for making the presentation to the executive committee – the content may differ slightly for each company but the core principles remain the same. Before making any type of presentation to the executive, it would be prudent to try to meet each executive on an individual basis. This can accomplish several things. You can determine whether the executives have heard of shared services and what they think about it. Are they for or against the idea? The meeting ahead of time will also provide a heads up to the executives on the potential scope. A vice president of human resources, for example, would want to know ahead of time that his or her function was being potentially offered as a candidate for shared services. If the executive team is traditional, it is the CEO who must be influenced ahead of time since the CEO will in essence make the decision to agree in principle.

The following is a typical presentation made to executive committees on shared services for initial buy-in.

FIGURE 5.3   Slide one: objectives of the executive presentation

The initial presentation to an executive team on shared services is to ensure they clearly understand what shared services is about and the impact on the organization. It may be customized to reflect that the presentation is either informational or simply aimed to get a decision to proceed. Basically, the point of the first slide is to explain that you are going to provide a definition of what shared services is and is not. At this stage it is usually worthwhile to point out that shared services is not centralization. You also want to position the fact that you will be defining the impacts of moving to shared services, the key fundamentals and what executive decisions need to be made. As well, you want to provide an overview of the conditions for success. Finally, you would want to provide some advice for the executive on next steps.

The concept of dynamic internal marketplace is the cornerstone of shared services. Everything else about shared services is derived from this basic qualifier. It is important up front in the presentation to ensure

FIGURE 5.4   Slide two: what is shared services?

**WHAT IS
SHARED SERVICES?**

- Shared services creates a dynamic internal marketplace for services
- Shared services is like any business – customers determine its fate
- Shared services requires an understanding that the role is to provide a service at *cost, quality and timeliness* that is competitive with alternatives, to a clearly defined group of clients
- Shared services is *not* the same as "centralized functions" – the difference is the principle of the marketplace

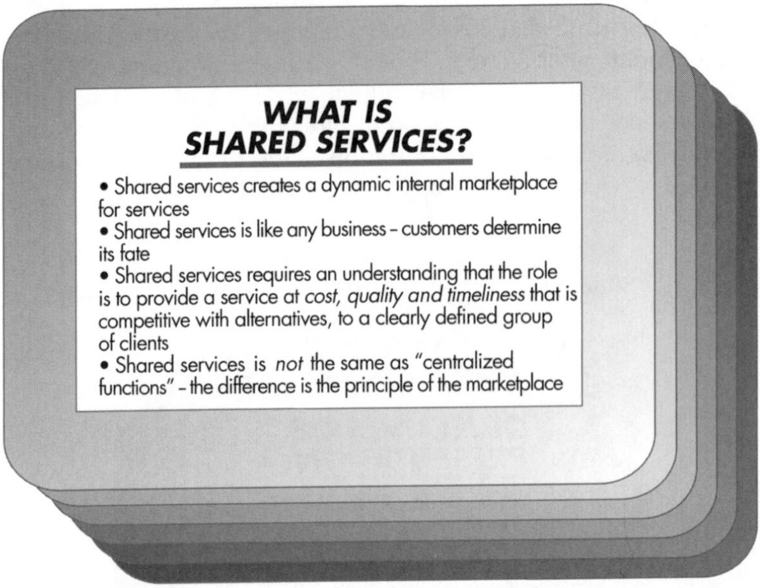

the executives have a clear picture of what this statement really means (see Figure 5.4). It is critical to get the element of choice and of meeting client needs for cost, quality and timeliness. It is usually helpful to provide a concrete example. If human resources goes to shared services, it means that clients will determine which products and services they want to purchase, at what level and what quality. While it is not recommended that the details of how customers determine the fate of the shared service function should be revealed, this is one of the key areas of interest for all customer group executives.

It is critical to point out how shared services differs from centralization, that under centralized functions the levels of acceptable quality and timeliness are typically defined by the centralized group for its own purpose or "the corporation's good." In a centralized accounts payable function they may, for example, produce check every two weeks because they have determined that this is the corporate standard. In a shared services function the frequency of check production would be that which meets the needs of the internal customers. In this opening to the presentation it would also be worthwhile to do your homework and point out organizations which are either corporately admired or are seen as competitors and have adopted shared services. Depending on the geographic scope of the organization it may also be useful to point out that shared services has been adopted by organizations in many countries.

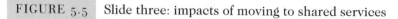

FIGURE 5.5   Slide three: impacts of moving to shared services

If shared services is to be bought into by the executive it will be based on the value it places on the impacts and the extent to which it accepts them. The executive will need some kind of proof, however, that this will occur. Examples will need to be presented that illustrate how things will be different (see Figure 5.5). The theory is that if corporate service functions are consolidated and focus on meeting the needs of internal clients, then the business unit clients will be able to focus more on doing what they do best and are rewarded for: running the business.

For most business unit executives the notion of having greater control over the services they receive is an easy sell

There will be a lot of skepticism about this issue. All that can be said at this point is that this is one of the benefits identified by others who have implemented shared services. A few comments or quotes from these organizations might get the skeptics to nod or at least mumble, "We'll see."

It must be stated unequivocally that consolidation will reduce the overall operating costs to the enterprise as a whole. Pointing out that there will be reduced costs due to the discontinuation of services that the client business units don't want is also useful in reinforcing that they are the drivers. It is wise to agree with operating companies which decry any form of consolidation as being less effective. In other words, in their eyes, it is more effective to have their local human resources, information technology, and accounting operations at their fingertips. This may be true but it is irrefutable that this strategy is costing the company as a whole more money. The issue is then affordability. Is this a luxury worth paying for? If it is, then shared services may not be appropriate for the organization.

Successful shared services depends on the ability to separate effectively the governance and control functions from the delivery of services. The concept is hard to explain and difficult to grasp. In this initial presentation to the executive it must be introduced and explained. At this point it should be sufficient to introduce the notion of the shift in accountability and control for policy compliance. Examples of what this really means will come later.

This slide builds on the concepts that were introduced in the previous slide. These are the fundamentals that will enable the benefits to be derived (see Figure 5.6). The ownership of services is meant to illustrate who calls the shots, who decides what services will be delivered, and at what cost. For many executives, who are still yawning at the idea of shared services as just another flaky initiative introduced by corporate groups, the notion of having choice over who supplies the services

FIGURE 5.6   Slide four: key fundamentals of shared services

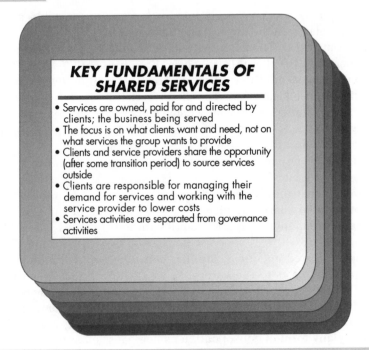

KEY FUNDAMENTALS OF SHARED SERVICES

- Services are owned, paid for and directed by clients; the business being served
- The focus is on what clients want and need, not on what services the group wants to provide
- Clients and service providers share the opportunity (after some transition period) to source services outside
- Clients are responsible for managing their demand for services and working with the service provider to lower costs
- Services activities are separated from governance activities

causes them to snap to attention. After years of poor service they see this as their chance to be able finally to buy high quality services from whoever they want. It is important that they don't get too excited. There is also an implied shared responsibility for making shared services successful. This means that both supplier and customers need to work together to reduce costs and ensure the successful operation of the service function. Clients need to predict demand volumes and communicate these to the shared services supplier. If there are

They need to appreciate that the decision to source external suppliers is a corporate decision that will never be made unilaterally by an individual executive

significant shifts in demand over the year then the two parties need to work together to mitigate the impact on the shared services business.

One of the ways to make this shift from corporate services to shared services is to revert the budget to the operating groups. In this way, they now own the money and in effect purchase the services from shared services. This is the only real concrete way to let line managers know this is not centralization in disguise.

The separation of governance functions from service delivery is a core point to shared services and is what shifts the accountability for policy compliance to line management. This point requires further clarification and to make the point the slides shown in Figure 5.7 are used. These slides are intended to begin the education process with the executive about the difference between the delivery of services and governance functions. This is a core and central issue for corporate functions within an organization. It is one agenda item that will get the attention of the executive. It is not very often that executive teams really talk about governance issues as they relate to their own corporate functions.

Accounts payable – expenses claims

Concrete examples must be presented to illustrate specifically what is meant by the separation of governance and service and the shift in accountability. Traditionally it is corporate functions which wear the control hat and enact policy through their own processes and transactions. In this scenario, clerks circle "unauthorized expenses" and either send the claim back to the originator, or call and cause the unsuspecting victim to squirm. This even occurs when there is a signature by the victim's boss. This is the policy enforcer role in full steam. In shared services, the opportunity exists to stop the payables function from being policy enforcer. In this new scenario, claims are processed if there is the right signature. Line management is accountable for ensuring compliance to policy.

Accounts payable clerks can wield control over vice presidents through the expenses claim process, especially if finance has typically been the enforcer

FIGURE 5.7   Slides five and six: defining governance and services

Facilities – office space

In the facilities area, there are frequently rigorous controls over how much cubicle space one is allowed, what kind of furniture is acceptable – veneer or solid wood, coffee table entitlement or not – depending on the level in the hierarchy. In the traditional model the facilities people are the corporate cops who decide who gets what. They become the enemy because they end up preventing people from getting what they want. Under shared services, facilities people are in the service business. This means that they don't say no to requests outside policy, but rather they suggest that the requester gets approval from his or her boss to go outside standards.

IT – hardware purchases

In information technology, hardware purchases are usually controlled by the information technology department. Under shared services, the CIO office would likely set policy for hardware standards and then the IT function would be able to offer its services without the encumbrance of being tied down by policy. In this case, like facilities, line managers who wish to deviate must get their line approval for doing so.

HR – labor relations

Finally, in human resources, the labor relations group is often the corporate gateway for allowing line managers to do or not to do certain things. Over time, it becomes clear that the labor relations department is actually the one which is accountable for labor relations as line managers must ask its permission for every transaction. In this model, line managers learn quickly that they should not trust their own judgement since someone else will make the decision and take the accountability. In shared services, the labor relations is truly advice only – the department does not have the power to say yes or no.

Ultimately senior executives will need to make decisions about how shared service will operate (see Figure 5.8). This presentation is not the time for these decisions; however, it is the time for executives to understand what will need to be decided before implementation. They will have to decide whether they want shared services to recover costs or whether they want to move to market-based pricing at the outset. It will be useful to indicate that most organizations opt for a phased-in move to market-based pricing if at all. It is an opportunity to get some feedback as to whether they want bundled or unbundled pricing. It is better for shared services organizations to have more bundling of services since there

The most important decisions will relate to how long the executive team will grant shared services exclusive supplier status and what mechanism will be used to consider outsourcing

FIGURE 5.8   Slide seven: executive decisions

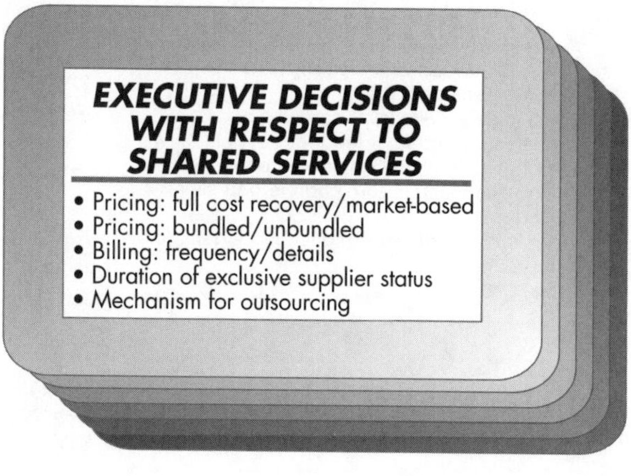

EXECUTIVE DECISIONS WITH RESPECT TO SHARED SERVICES

- Pricing: full cost recovery/market-based
- Pricing: bundled/unbundled
- Billing: frequency/details
- Duration of exclusive supplier status
- Mechanism for outsourcing

will be less infrastructure in the billing processes. Most customers, however, will opt for more unbundling since it will provide them with more options. In practice, a minimum time is generally eighteen months which is seen as the right amount of time for shared services to get up and running. The most favored method for outsourcing is to insist on a business case. For example, if one business unit or operation wants to purchase services and bypass the shared services group, it will have to make a cogent business case for approval by the executive team.

The business case is not designed to be an insurmountable barrier but rather to reflect the serious decision that is being taken to replicate services that are already a burden on the corporation. It is a decision not to be taken lightly and must have real cost benefits to be of value.

There will be many times during implementation, as functions are consolidated and people's lives are impacted, that employees and managers will question the direction

There is no point starting from scratch to experiment with shared services. Others have gone before and many lessons have been learned. This initial presentation is an ideal opportunity to share with the executives what has enabled others to be successful (see Figure 5.9). Because shared services is a top down and cross-organizational initiative each and every member of the executive must talk openly about their support and commitment. It is at these times that wavering executive support can kill the initiative. Unions or other employee representative bodies must be involved in mitigating adverse

FIGURE 5.9   Slide eight: what will make it successful?

WHAT WILL MAKE IT SUCCESSFUL?

- Visible executive endorsement for the move
- Involvement of the union
- Simple service level agreements
- Effective customer feedback system
- Shared Services Advisory Committee
- Investment in culture change and client education
- Alignment of performance management systems

employee impacts during the transition. At a minimum it must be ensured that the right protocols are in place. The rules and regulations for shared services need to be as simple as possible and service level agreements are no exception. It is imperative to ensure that the executives understand this from the outset.

Since it is defined that clients own, pay for and direct the services they receive it is essential that the shared services providers have effective feedback systems in place. Defining this up front as a criterion for success will increase the executives' confidence that they will be listened to. An option to raise at this point is the establishment of a shared services advisory committee or board that would consist of business unit executives and would provide overall direction to the functions.

The move to a shared strategy cannot be taken lightly. It requires new ways of operating for both suppliers and customers (see Figure 5.10). It will be important early in the process for executives to understand that investments must be made in culture change and in educating clients in how shared services will change their lives. The alignment of performance management systems is to ensure that people are rewarded for acquiring the new competencies required, and for achieving newly defined results.

Finally, it is critical that executives understand that a number of decisions are required before proceeding. Shared services is not for every organization. Can the organization handle a shift in accountability

FIGURE 5.10　Slide nine: advice for moving forward

to line management? Can the corporate functions make the shift that it will take to operate as a business within a business? The answers to these will determine the extent to which the organization should proceed with shared services. Once the fundamental direction is endorsed, the executive team will need to come together to make decisions on a number of more detailed operational issues. Most importantly the team needs to stick with the decision, to be supportive when things blow up and to be available to provide further direction and support as required.

SmithKline Beecham

Milan F. Kunz, VP, Director of Marketing Sciences and Services

One of the keys to our success with shared services was the degree of top management commitment and direct involvement. They monitored our progress bi-weekly and approved every blueprint and management structure along the way. This was effective in signaling the strategic importance of shared services.

Once the executive team has made a decision for conceptual buy-in, the analysis and planning has to begin. The depth and breadth of analysis will depend on the culture and orientation of the company and probably from where the strategy is being led. Patience and a methodical process are the prospector's tools for finding gold. So too in the analysis of shared services! Rushing to design and implement is likely to cause shared services to be a quick and unsuccessful flash in the pan.

Chapter 6

THE INITIAL SIZE-UP:
UNDERSTANDING WHERE YOU ARE

*It doesn't matter how good your gold detector is. If you aren't in a gold
producing area then you have no chance of finding gold*

A sailing school instructor was helping a group of students learn the old-
fashioned method of navigation using a compass and a chart. The task
was to get from point A to point B. Excited, the students pored over the
chart, so beautiful, it could be framed as a painting, tiny shapes of islands
and numbers dwarfed by a single delicate compass rose. The instructor
told the students one simple but complicated fact of navigation; and that is
that you cannot get to anywhere unless you know where you are. It suddenly dawned on the students that the compass and chart were rendered
meaningless without the precise understanding of where that moving boat
was in terms of speed, distance and time. Getting to the destination of
shared services cannot be accomplished without this same clear precision.

Once executive approval to proceed with the implementation of a
shared services strategy has been obtained the internal service functions
must develop a clear picture of the current "as is" state of their business.
This includes listing and categorizing all functions and major activities
being performed, determining the costs associated with these activities,
comparing costs to external benchmarks and investigating the extent of
customer satisfaction with current products and services. This understanding of the current state of the business is the foundation upon which future
decisions will be made by the shared services function. The listing and categorizing of functions and activities is also the basis for initial discussions
with clients regarding their product and service requirements. The costing
and benchmarking information will provide an initial insight into what specific services will cost clients and whether the costs are competitive with

external providers of similar services. In some cases the costing and comparison to external suppliers results in the identification of functions that could be outsourced immediately in order to save money.

The "as is" picture is made up of the following:

+ a current list of the products and services presently being offered;
+ the costs to produce and deliver the products and services;
+ comparison of costs to external benchmarks;
+ the degree of customer satisfaction with current products and services.

THE "AS IS" PICTURE — CURRENT PRODUCTS AND SERVICES

The process of actually defining products and services is often perceived as an extremely useful exercise on its own. For example, finance groups may say they provide financial advice. But what do they actually mean? What is the product here? What is the service? Financial advice needs to be broken down further. Financial advice products and services could be business case analysis and preparation, capital planning or financial modeling for acquisitions. Most importantly, who are the services intended for? In shared services, there is a definite requirement to specify and delineate the range of products and services and to clarify to whom they are delivered.

Figure 6.1 is a model of the shared services operating environment. Stakeholders of shared services, represented by the CEO and board in most organizations, are accountable for defining the overall mandate and direction of the shared services organization. External suppliers provide services to the shared services group as required. Clients and users reside in the business units and are the customers of shared services. Clients are senior managers who typically engage or contract for services while users are individuals and groups who actually utilize the services. External customers are the ultimate customers of the enterprise as a whole. This system model is designed to illustrate the dynamic inter-relationship between all the elements the shared services environment.

The list of current functions and activities needs to be identified as either services provided to clients or to stakeholders. This is where a high degree of discussion and strong leadership needs to occur.

People find it both difficult and useful to think about the provision of corporate and internal functions as businesses. Some groups have never really thought about their work in terms of a menu of products and services. As well, it is new thinking to begin to try to separate those

FIGURE 6.1   The shared services operating environment

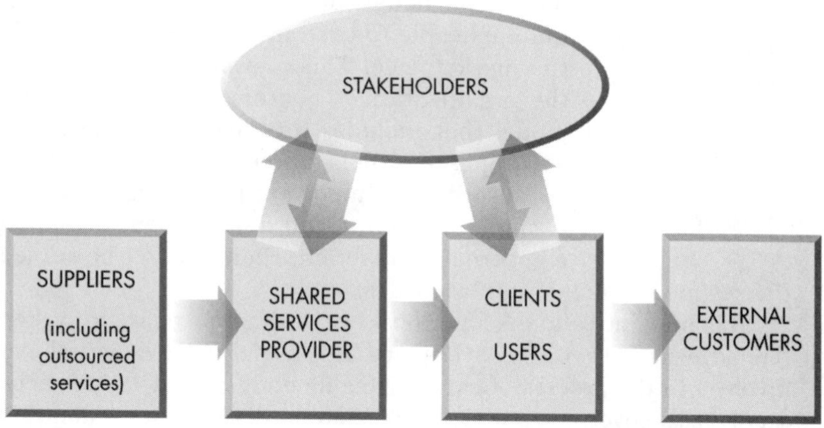

SOURCE: Barbara E. Quinn and Robert S. Cooke

functions that are directed for governance purposes and those that are pure services directed at internal clients or operating companies.

The three categories of functions and activities are defined as follows:

✦   those that are provided to internal business units, the clients and users and are therefore "*services*";

✦   those that are provided upwards to the stakeholders, the executive and board, or are policy/standards oriented and are "*governance*";

✦   those that are internally driven: "*internal overheads and administration of the shared services provider*".

As functions are allocated between services, governance and administration it becomes clear what functions are being performed and for whom. Frequently this task is done with a small design team. Experienced managers of shared services claim that this beginning definition of products and services and internal clients is one of the most powerful elements in beginning to shape the new business culture. Many corporate functions have never thought about what they do in terms of products and services for internal clients or for the executive. The product and service language essentially is marketing-oriented and starts to establish the new mindset of shared services.

The service and governance debate

There is always a great deal of debate around the definitions of service and governance and subsequently what functions or activities

Separating activities into services and governance can be daunting, with people arguing for their services being governance and above marketplace rules

fall into each category. For many people there is comfort in knowing that what they do is governance: on behalf of the executive and therefore not applicable to customer choice and the rules of the marketplace. This is especially an issue when the organization is contemplating a marketplace model that includes professional services. People will argue that their function is governance-related because it is so important to the organization. For example if training and development is defined as a governance function, then it won't be subject to the regime of the marketplace rules.

It is imperative to take a critical eye during this phase to make sure that governance is really governance. It is useful to have neutral experts involved in the process of categorizing functions and activities between service and governance who can mediate in disagreements and provide expert opinions as required.

The allocation of functions and activities between governance and service is not a scientific exercise but is more of an intuitive process, unique to each organization. Organizations have developed customized definitions that reflect their environment, politics and orientation to corporate functions.

Table 6.1 gives some product and service listings to illustrate how the various products and services can fall into the categories. This list of products and services is offered as an example of the format and content that needs to be defined to explore shared services. Sometimes the lists are quite revealing. This is the beginning of thinking like a business. This is where the services are identified and this is where the conversation points to the fact that governance, although critical, is not the majority of the function.

We find that some groups have more trouble than others defining products and services. Providing concrete models and templates such as this are helpful since it provides a starting point for moving forward. There is no requirement to start from a blank page.

When corporate and internal groups develop their first cut at the product and service listing, it is sometimes surprising for them to discover that providing services makes up the majority of their activities. In other words, those activities that are governance in nature are few although they are critical. This process of defining products and services is the first step to operating a business within the business.

The thinking framework for products and services is to define what is done and more importantly for whom the products and services are intended. This is where some groups discover that they are not always entirely sure where certain services are directed. One of the fundamental ground rules of operating a shared services function is ensuring that

TABLE 6.1	Analysis of human resources	
Services	**Governance functions**	**Administration and overheads**
Professional/advisory ✦ HR generalist consulting services ✦ Recruitment and selection services ✦ Compensation services ✦ Labor relations advice and guidance ✦ Grievance assistance ✦ Training and development Transactional processing ✦ Payroll ✦ Benefits administration ✦ Pension services ✦ Claims management	✦ Corporate HR information and records ✦ Corporate HR policy development ✦ Compensation ✦ Benefits ✦ Equity/diversity ✦ Labor relations ✦ Corporate succession planning ✦ Top level executive development	✦ General administration ✦ Planning and scheduling ✦ Time sheets ✦ Wordprocessing, telephone answering ✦ General filing, mail processing, reporting ✦ Budgets and business planning ✦ Internal meetings ✦ Staff development ✦ Committee participation ✦ Business development and marketing ✦ Staff development

only products and services where there is an identified paying client are produced or delivered. Many corporate professional services functions, like human resources, develop products and services that they believe the organization needs. In isolation of any client or organizational demand, change management models and training programs emerge from cubicles whose occupants have no contact with real line managers and have little sense of their expectations and what they want. In shared services only products and services whose need has been defined by a paying client should be produced.

THE "AS IS" PICTURE – CURRENT PRODUCT AND SERVICE COSTS

Once the product and service listing is done, the next step is to begin to define what the costs are in producing and delivering them. One of the cornerstone principles of shared services is the recovery of fully loaded costs from clients for the services being provided. Once there is a calculation and understanding of fully loaded costs, which include direct and indirect costs, then the price of services to clients can be determined.

Human resources groups have to understand what it actually costs them to recruit a person. Information technology departments must unwind what they do so that they can actually cost out how much it takes to write a customized application for a business unit. Finance groups have to understand the cost of one transaction in payroll or payables. Supply has to understand how much one package costs to ship.

This process of understanding costs is one of the most significant and powerful elements in beginning to change the culture and mindset. Often, this is brand new information. It has never occurred to functional corporate people to examine how much certain activities cost or how much it costs to produce their products and services. More importantly, corporate people begin to develop a clearer picture of who these products and services are aimed at.

Product and service costing can be done either in a very detailed fashion or in a broader way using the best available data. One of the preferred methods for determining costs is a form of ABC or activity based costing. ABC is a systematic process for defining the costs in any given process. This is the core part of understanding where any function stands today. Activity based costing will provide management with a thorough identification of the actual costs that will stand the test of rigor. In shared services it is critical to know all the costs associated with the production of products and services.

In a traditional allocation model, service costs usually do not include overhead items such as phones, computer hardware and software, office space, and management overhead. Moving to a full cost recovery model means that there has to be a provision for these types of costs as well as depreciation, finance charges, and taxes related to shared services. This loading in of all costs is essential as a base for what will eventually become prices.

New integrated business information systems enable the capture of detailed costs and can make the task of determining product and service costs easier. It is important, however, to ensure that the new system is not driving how the shared services business operates but that the system is designed or modified to capture the scope and nature of cost information that the shared services group requires.

For the shared services groups which will be contemplating a marketplace model and beyond into eventual commercialization where services are sold externally, it is essential to have a clear and accurate cost picture with all costs loaded in so that comparisons with external suppliers can be easily made.

Where service organizations have dependencies on assets or are in asset intensive businesses such as property management, theoretically the cost of capital and depreciation should be built into the financial structure. However, it is believed that certain well-known best practice data and benchmarking data does not load in the depreciation costs which artificially lower costs. For example, here is a typical chart of benchmarked data:

TABLE 6.2	Transactional costs in a finance function		
	Accts Rec.	**Accts Payable**	**Payroll**
Fortune 100 mean	$16.00	$8.00	$6.00
Shared services mean	$7.80	$4.44	$2.77
Best practice company	$5.60	$0.80	$0.70
Best practice productivity	16,000	55,000	3,000

It is critical to know what costs are loaded into these numbers. If system depreciation costs, for example, are not built into IT service costs or the costs for transactional processing then the rates will be artificially low. While this may look good to the client it is not realistic since these costs must be recovered somewhere. Moving these costs somewhere else is not the point nor is burying the costs of depreciation. Fundamental to shared services is the recovery of fully loaded costs from clients. If the costs are not fully loaded or are kept artificially low then it is impossible for clients or shared services functions to make effective decisions related to product offerings. If the real fully loaded costs, for example, are significantly higher than those of external suppliers then clients and shared services suppliers need to be able to make effective decisions on outsourcing.

The process of identifying all costs included in the production of products and services can be considerably time consuming and may not be the strong point of the people involved, finance excepted. It is worthwhile getting the finance department involved in taking the lead even if shared services is being implemented in human resources or information technology.

While some organizations may believe they have a pretty good handle on their internal costs, in practice this is rare. In many cases allocated budget dollars have little to do with the actual cost data required for shared services implementation. Although certain specific charges may be known, this is not enough detail to enable a move to pricing.

The traditional allocation system leads to complacency over the years

Some organizations do not have the internal expertise to determine activity cost and do not have an integrated business information system to provide them with the information. For these organizations it would be wise to seek external help from someone qualified in these types of costing methods.

Activity based costing is a tool for strategic and operational decision making and attributes costs to products and services based on an analysis of the causes of these costs. The methodology basically traces and allocates costs by examining in detail the various activities performed to produce the products and services. This results in a clear cause and effect relationship between activities performed, their associated costs, and their resulting output.

HUSKY OIL

Reg K. Milley, VP of Corporate Administration

I felt that the discipline of ABC costing was a worthwhile skill for the staff in corporate services to learn. It is a concrete way to understand what their own services actually cost to produce.

Rather than bring in outside experts, we chose to train our own people in activity based costing. This learning is important to shift corporate staff groups to thinking more like a business.

Activity based costing generally involves a series of sequential and logical steps that enable the final assembly of relevant costs for carrying out the services. Once the specific services for which costing will be done are identified, all the activities performed to produce, market, and deliver the services (activity analysis) are identified and listed. For each activity a cost must be allocated as either labor or some other resource that is consumed in carrying out the activity. For each activity or series of activities other direct or indirect costs are also added. Once all activity costs are defined the activities and their associated costs are linked together so the costs of the service can be tabulated. While other elements of formalized ABC involve the management and control of the process activities, for the purpose of determining service costs this is as far as you need to go at this time.

While the process of activity based costing can sound daunting it is the level of rigor required for ensuring that charges to clients are based on true fully loaded costs. So it is for shared services. The identification of what it really costs to deliver a service can be an *The understanding* enlightening and disheartening exercise. It is *of costs is essential* enlightening as this is often the first time staff will *to running a* have an appreciation of what it really costs them to *successful enterprise* perform certain services. It can be disheartening at the same time because the costs are usually much higher than anyone would have guessed. Couple that with an intuitive sense of what customers really think of the products and services and you have some interesting and dynamic management information.

Once fully loaded costs are calculated, many internal service groups are shocked by what look like astronomical overhead burdens. For many, there is a sinking feeling that they will be rendered noncompetitive with external suppliers simply based on the burdens they must carry. Real estate and facilities charges, for example, elicit radical responses such as, "Let's move out of the corporate head office into a new site, maybe in the manager's basement," so their costs can become more competitive. For most internal functions, however, they have little choice over where they are located. While in the

One of the key trends in the consulting industry has been the move to shared office spaces to reduce overhead and premises costs

short term there may also be little ability to impact facilities costs, concrete measures can be taken towards reduced costs. This move is consistent with the practices of telecommuting – more people working out of their homes – and the emphasis on consultants spending more time in the consulting industry, for example, having three offices for every two people in contrast to the old standard of everyone having an office. Traditional office space averaged about 86 ft² per consultant and the move to workstations reduced this to 56 ft². The move to "hoteling" or shared office space reduces space to 5.5 ft² per consultant. The objective is to reduce occupancy costs by increasing densities.

It is possible, over time, to reduce the overhead burdens carried by the internal service groups. For many, the calculation of fully loaded costs for their services is the first time there is true realization of the cost of being part of an organization. These groups need to work on strategies for getting these costs down if they are to become competitive with the costs of external suppliers of similar services. In other cases the reality must hit home: there is no way to compete with the lower costs of external suppliers and the organization needs to work at moving away from the strategy of having internal suppliers for that service.

THE "AS IS" PICTURE – COMPARISON TO EXTERNAL BENCHMARKS

A benchmark is a measured "best-in-class" achievement where the performance level is recognized as the standard of excellence. Benchmarking is the process of comparing and measuring ourselves against both qualitative and quantitative practices and performance in other organizations. We all know that somewhere else in the world someone else is most likely doing something that we do in a more effective and efficient manner. It makes logical sense that we should do our best to learn from the best.

Qualitative benchmarking is the process of comparing ourselves against the excellent practices of others. In the initial stages of the implementation of shared services qualitative benchmarking will enable us to learn about the best practices in setting up shared services. Shared services is a relatively new strategy; however, there have been many successful implementations. Rather than experiment through trial and error, it makes sense to learn from those who have successfully gone before.

During the initial stages of shared services implementation the focus is typically on quantitative benchmarking to determine if service costs are in line with local suppliers of similar services. The rationale for obtaining cost benchmarks at this time is to consider the possibility of outsourcing specific functions in the initial stages of moving to shared services. For example, if you have an internal service where the costs are very high compared to external benchmarked suppliers, the right decision may be to outsource the services rather than move them into a shared services organization. Typical examples include internal travel services and print shops where local external suppliers can provide comparable or better levels of service at significantly reduced costs.

Benchmark data like any source of numerical comparative data is highly subject to interpretation and a great deal of care must be taken to ensure that the services being compared are similar and that the costs comparisons are relevant and reliable. It is important that internal service costs are fully loaded in that all costs associated with the delivery of the service, including asset depreciation, are included. It is only valid to compare fully loaded internal service costs to the prices charged by external suppliers.

Subsequent benchmarking with other internal suppliers of similar services can provide valuable input into the development of perfor-

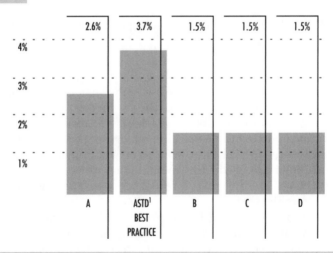

FIGURE 6.2   Percentage of payroll spent on training

mance targets for the new shared services organization. It is useful for defining targets for the new organization not only in service costs but also in areas such as staffing levels and customer satisfaction levels. When direct cost-to-cost comparisons cannot be made, sometimes a comparison of ratios is useful. For example, human resources benchmarks will point to a ratio of one HR person to every 125–150 employees. This can be useful in comparing the overall staff numbers in HR prior to shared services. In finance, the cost of processing one transaction is usually used as the benchmark. This means understanding the costs to process one paycheck or one invoice and comparing internal costs to the benchmark. This type of comparison is useful in determining the need for consolidating transactional processing in order to reduce costs to the level of comparative benchmark organizations.

In a recent benchmarking exercise a financial institution wanted to know if its training costs were in line with other comparable financial institutions. While on the surface this looks simple it was discovered that none of the institutions involved captured the same information in the same manner or included the same factors in the numbers.

While benchmarking is sound in principle there is a need for deep probing to ensure that what is being compared is relevant and valid

Two of the key comparisons in this exercise were the total number of dollars spent on training per employee and the percentage of payroll spent on training (see Figure 6.2). Sounds straightforward! All you do is divide the total amount of money spent on training by the number of employees and then use the same total training dollars over the total payroll dollars as a percentage. The easiest number to determine should be the number of employees in each organization, except that some organizations use full-time equivalents (FTEs) and others use headcount. Headcount is the number of people on the payroll including part-timers and job-sharers and this number is larger than the number of FTE which is the number of employees occupying a full-time position. There could be three part-time people, for example, occupying one full-time position.

The determination of total training dollars turned out to be a very complex exercise and to this day after considerable effort it is doubtful that the numbers from the different financial institutions are direct comparisons. The make-up of total training expenditure can include a number of components. The most typical include internal training department and trainer salaries and external training expenditure. External training expenditure includes the cost of courses paid to educational institutions and private suppliers plus any associated cost of travel, accommodation and materials. While the cost of the training department and trainer salaries should be straightforward, in many organizations people who deliver courses do this as a part of another job not related to training. How are these costs captured?

Other areas of training costs are less consistently tracked and include the salaries associated with trainees while they are in attendance at training courses. In some organizations this can represent over 25% of total training expenditure. Many published benchmark studies of training expenditure do not specify whether trainee salaries are included. The authors of these studies can have no way of confirming what was included in total training expenditure submitted by study participants.

The costs of training premises is another associated training cost that is inconsistently tracked. In some organizations the costs of owned training facilities can reach 10–15% of total training expenditure. Sometimes these costs are buried in the real estate group or allocated to operating units and never appear on the training balance sheet. In other organizations major training facilities are owned by the training group and appear on their statement.

Bank of Canada

Richard Julien, Director of Client and Employee Services
Shared services continues to evolve. One of our major clients told us he sees light at the end of the tunnel. We know we still have to keep working at being competitive and cost efficient.

It sounds like a simple exercise. Benchmark the dollars spent per employee on training with other similar financial institutions. It is not only difficult to understand exactly what is included in other organizations' numbers, it is usually just as difficult to understand what is included in your own cost numbers.

It is also important to step back and take a good look at the fundamental rationale for doing the benchmarking. What will the results tell us about our business? For a benchmark of training expenditure per employee, is a high number or a low number best? If we are higher than other organizations, does that mean we are more committed to training or does it mean we are inefficient? Other typical training benchmarks are related to the number or percentage of employees who receive training and the number of training days per employee. If a high number or percentage of employees are receiving training, is this a good thing? A high number may mean there is no strategic allocation of training to where it will have the most impact; it is a sweeping strategy and potentially meaningless. The number of training days per employee is another questionable area for benchmarking. The trend in training is towards workplace-based, just-in-time training delivered with the assistance of technology. Does a benchmark indicating a high number of training days show a greater commitment to training? Does a low number indicate less commitment or even less training? Not necessarily. A low number of training days per employee may indicate the organization is in the fore-front of providing more efficient and effective workplace-based learning.

Proceed with benchmarking, but do it cautiously and with a great deal of skepticism. Only valid comparisons are of value and most of the time determining validity is the most difficult exercise of all.

The "as is" picture – client satisfaction

Although many corporate functions believe they have an intuitive sense of how they are being evaluated, there can be a real wake up call when clients are asked to pay. The real determination of satisfaction is when they are willing to pay for the services they use. It is therefore very important at this stage to get a true picture of internal client satisfaction with current products and services. They often cannot produce any kind of tangible evidence on the degree of satisfaction or dissatisfaction with their products and services. In the absence of any real data, there is a requirement to get some sort of evaluative data before the full implementation of shared

Surprisingly many corporate and internal service groups do not have any formal data on how they are evaluated or viewed by their clients

services. The data can be collected in a formal or informal matter, qualitatively or quantitatively. Some efficient strategies for collecting customer satisfaction data include:

+ face-to-face interviews with selected senior clients and middle managers of client groups;
+ telephone surveys of a few selected clients;
+ quick electronic or paper surveys with a few selected clients.

The real issue of obtaining client satisfaction information at this point is to get an initial perspective on what products and services clients are likely to agree to buy from the shared services group. Low levels of client satisfaction are a red flag that the products must be changed or services improved. Sometimes products and services that have formed the traditional offering of the service groups are simply not wanted. In other instances clients are so dissatisfied with the quality of the services that they will push for alternative suppliers once shared services is implemented. This is important information to have early on in the process of moving to shared services.

It is often very disheartening for people in the services function to hear negative feedback regarding their favorite products and services

Once shared services is implemented and operating, there is a need to carry out regular assessments of customer satisfaction

and it is especially devastating to see them removed from the repertoire. That biannual report that your staff dedicate hours of overtime to producing on time can be given the thumbs down once customers are asked to cough up the $1,000 cost. No one ever read it and no one knew this until they went out and asked clients if they were willing to pay for it. This information will help the function fine tune its product offerings and the quality of its service delivery. The only candidates qualified to assess and evaluate services are the clients of the service. The requirement for ongoing client satisfaction data is now etched in stone. No turning back.

BUILDING THE BUSINESS CASE TO PROCEED

This completes the initial size up or the "as is" picture. Further approvals to proceed with the implementation of shared services will be based on the business case that is developed from this initial assessment. The business case will need to identify cost savings and targets for enhanced product and service quality and customer satisfaction. Depending on the culture of the organization, this will have to be either very detailed or very conceptual. Either way, the building of the foundation of data that includes actual costs and client satisfaction is important for the future.

TRW's EXPERIENCE WITH ITS BUSINESS CASE

✦ The business case should be viewed as a strategic investment and should insist on a minimum return of investment and not be justified by headcount reductions alone.

✦ Our business case was sponsored by the CFO and corporate controller and was based primarily on hard savings; we did not attempt to qualify soft savings including the shift of finance to higher value-added tasks.

✦ Our case is a constantly referenced document; conditions change but the recommendations and results remain the baseline.

✦ The business case is not a project plan.

✦ The business case should be communicated to all levels of the organization.

TRW Automotive found its business case to be an excellent tool for implementation. TRW held many workshops to collect information on current processes and to motivate involvement in developing process visions. The process of developing the business case was an excellent tool for building user and client buy-in to the vision of shared services.

Tribune Company also used a business case as part of its implementation process.

TRIBUNE COMPANY

✦ Our business case focused on cost savings and showed a potential of $1.1 million.

✦ We also defined qualitative benefits and they included the following:

　– allows managers more time for decision support services

　– enables company-wide sharing of expertise

　– helps to standardize company financial policy

　– facilitates favorable pricing

　– centralizes billing and collections for national advertisers.

You can see that two different approaches were taken: one that emphasized hard savings and one that included soft savings in addition to pure dollars. Knowing what style of business case will work is entirely dependent on corporate and organizational culture.

During the process of size-up, one of the issues that will rear its head is the option of outsourcing. If a service is out of line with outside benchmarks for cost and is seen as very poorly performing, there may be a requirement to pursue the possibility of taking the service outside. As the sailing instructor said, "To get anywhere you have to know where you are." This critical analysis helps organizations decide where to go next.

NOTES

1   American Society for Training and Development

Chapter 7

STRATEGIC OUTSOURCING

King Midas, granted the privilege of a wish, asked the god Dionysus that whatever he touched become gold. When he came to his palace, he discovered that indeed, whatever he touched became gold. In this way, he was prevented from eating and now was being tortured with hunger. So he begged the god to take away the superb gift

POSSIBLE MOTIVES FOR OUTSOURCING

The strategy of outsourcing is a bit like the Midas touch: sometimes it is a superb gift and sometimes it is not what organizations are expecting and so they want it taken back. Glittering promises apparently do not always live up to their claims. The term backsourcing has already emerged to describe the practice of companies taking back previously outsourced functions. According to a recent article in *Business Europe* a study of outsourcing that was done in the US showed 70% of companies were satisfied with the results while 30% were not satisfied.[1] Clearly we know that sometimes outsourcing works and sometimes it does not. This is the question to answer: why this divergence in opinion? To know this, we need to understand what criteria organizations used to evaluate success. What were these companies really trying to accomplish in the first place?

As Peter Drucker said, "The leader of the past was a person who knew how to tell. The leader of the future will be a person who knows how to ask."[2] Leaders must question how staff work has traditionally been done and ask whether there isn't a better way of doing it. The ability to challenge and debate strategies such as outsourcing and shared services is an essential executive skill. All too often though, leaders do not spend the time to delve into complex questions, preferring to latch on to the strategy of the year and proclaim it as the new white knight. Judging from the burgeoning growth in outsourcing, which is predicted to be over the $200 billion mark by the year 2000, organizations are going in droves for the ride.

The availability of new third party suppliers and complementary information technology makes outsourcing more attractive than in the past (see Table 7.1). Just the fact of having options means that companies will increasingly look around before making the assumption that the service will have to be performed internally. If you didn't like your travel and expenses reporting or technology development departments in the 1960s, 70s or even 80s, there weren't a lot of options around. Everybody pretty well had their own services back then. Staff groups were not questioned all that much about alternatives to having the services inside or whether they had recently compared themselves to the latest outsourcer. Then, albeit slowly, certain services began to move outside the corporation.

Mature entrants have been outsourced for some time. It was not all that long ago that companies had their own cafeterias, people taking care of plants and fixtures, full print shops, internal travel departments and telephone operations departments. Companies had their own architects and civil engineers to not only design and construct their buildings but to maintain them from cradle to grave. Over time, many organizations realized that these activities were not core to the business, even though they were very important, and that outsiders could do it more effectively. Today, most organizations are even shedding their own properties, never mind building them from scratch.

TABLE 7.1   Trends in outsourcing

Mature entrants	Middle age entrants	New wave entrants
✓ payroll	✓ information systems	✓ logistics
✓ facilities	and technology	✓ materials management
✓ food services	✓ disbursement accounting	✓ sales and marketing
✓ management services,	✓ human resources	✓ human resources
i.e. construction	✓ travel and expenses	✓ accounting
✓ document processing	reporting	✓ engineering
✓ pension and benefits	✓ mailroom services	✓ manufacturing
administration	✓ property management	✓ legal services
✓ travel services		✓ research
✓ telecommunications		

The middle entrants are experiencing the highest growth right now. Just ask companies like Gelco in travel and expenses reporting, Fidelity in human resources administration, IBM and Compaq for technology services to name a few. For example, IBM Global Services was worth $25.7 billion revenue in 1997, the largest information technology services provider in the world with more than 465 strategic outsourcing contracts. How fast are companies shedding technology services? Outsourcing is IBM's fastest growing segment of all its businesses.

In looking at the new wave entrants to the outsource market, it is obvious that companies are widening their assumptions about what is strategic and what is not. Imagine manufacturing companies outsourcing manufacturing. It would have been heresy not very long ago to consider taking sales and marketing out to a third party. Some companies are challenging boundaries for what is essentially core by putting almost everything up on the table as a candidate for outsourcing. Many traditional insiders, however, cling to the same old myth – "outsiders won't know the business and the culture the way we do." External suppliers can offer more than knowing the business, they can offer knowledge on what other companies or even competitors are doing. Granted, there is something of a bandwagon effect taking place in outsourcing before the final results have been posted. Executives can feel pressured to leap if everyone else is doing it too.

Ashridge Strategic Management Center

Hertfordshire, England

In the United Kingdom, financial functions, except taxation, seem to have the lowest level of outsourcing activity in our research.

The highest proportion of outsourcing seems to be in pension administration, training and education, legal, property services, and insurance.

Another growth area for outsourcing comes with the entrance of firms offering to take over what has been traditionally considered a key internal function: marketing. An example of a growing player in this arena is Mosaic Group Inc. which provides outsourced marketing services to over 100 clients. The company has doubled its revenue over the past year and the demand for its services is growing dramatically. Services include:

+ product launches
+ sampling programs
+ direct marketing
+ conferences and trade shows

+ database management
+ point of sale activities.

Clients say Mosaic can execute a marketing program at 60–70% of the cost of companies doing it themselves in-house.

RICHARD HAYS

Author of *Internal Service Excellence*

An outsourcer says to a frustrated company, I have an aspirin and I can relieve your pain.

Outsourcers are selling. They are doing very well at it but in some cases are overselling. A company has to be very careful. They should get their staff functions in good shape before going outside.

Rather than jump on the bandwagon, leaders really need to practice inquiry and challenge fundamental assumptions prior to adopting a radical strategy such as outsourcing. Once the services are taken out, along with the intellectual capital and resources, it is not all that easy to reverse the decision. Real job losses are a consequence, although in some cases, the third party may volunteer to take over the people. Just the same, it is equally traumatic for people to in effect leave one employer and go to another one. Outsourcing is not a decision to be taken lightly even though it might conceivably be the right one.

The stress and emotional impact of outsourcing causes deep and unmistakable rifts. Real job losses are a consequence

The idea is to be very clear on the "why" of the decision. What are the essential motives for taking services out and placing them with a third party?

+ out of sheer frustration?
+ for cost savings?
+ to take advantage of world-class practices?
+ to avoid investment in future technologies?
+ out of a dogmatic philosophy to get out of non-core business?

There are many legitimate reasons, but sheer frustration is not one of them. One chief executive officer who outsourced the entire information technology function of a pulp and paper company admitted that more work should have been done internally to figure out what was wrong before turning over their problems to someone else. The executive was simply fed up with the cost overruns, the complaints of underperformance, and saw outsourcing as an easy answer to the problems. This frustration had been building up for years and yet it came as a complete surprise to the unsuspecting and naïve information technology group which obviously had no idea of how it was really perceived. The company's subsequent experience with a third party supplier has caused the organization to learn a hard lesson: that they did not think carefully about what they were trying to accomplish other than to rid themselves of a problem. The results have been less than stellar to date. Frustration in and of itself is clearly not the best rationale even though it might be completely understandable. It's too bad the information technology group did not see it coming but it was the one at fault in this scenario. Costs were not the only reason for its demise, although they were part of the problem.

Outsourcing for cost savings

One of the biggest myths is the assumption that outsourcing automatically saves money. Maybe and maybe not according to the Corporate Leadership Council which found that sometimes the strategy resulted in cost savings and sometimes it ended up costing more.[3]

Companies which enter into a contracting proposition with a third party supplier sometimes do not even know their own costs yet they are presumably making some kind of comparison. This is why it is a good idea to consider the discipline of shared services analysis prior to a leap to outsourcing. How else can a good comparison be made between internal services and a third party? This kind of analysis is a baseline against which to measure and evaluate outsource suppliers. Without this data, internal staff groups or unsuspecting companies may be unconsciously negotiating a contract with a third party in bad faith or asking for unreasonable performance standards.

Having this information means reasonable trade-offs can be made along with reasonable performance expectations. If costs are going to increase post outsourcing, then it is important to know what gains are being made either with respect to improved service levels or being in a better position to meet rising client expectations. For example, if payroll costs will increase but there is access to a help desk twenty-four hours a day, this may be a reasonable trade-off.

TABLE 7.2   The shared services "as is" picture

the costs to produce staff services	benchmarked costs for same services	degree of satisfaction with the services

Big dollar differences

When outsource suppliers offer incredible savings, it is wise to examine where they are finding the leverage or what is accounting for such a difference. If outsource suppliers are offering substantially lower prices without substantially different processes or technology, this should be a warning flag for organizations which are going to be surprised later on when they are charged for every single additional function requested. The supplier will be bidding low to get the initial work but it will turn out to be mutually unattractive over the long term since no one wants to lose money and no company wants to spend more money than it planned. Many organizations will report after the honeymoon of a new third party has worn off, that they are being charged line by line for each additional request or service. Fair enough since the outsource suppliers are in business for profit and cannot afford to simply give away services for free. This now poses an enormous political problem for the staff executive which will have to go back a year into the third party arrangement and inform the surprised executive team that costs have in effect gone up compared to internal services. This is not insurmountable since cost containment can be a new expectation of the supplier, it is just better to know this in advance and build in contingencies ahead of time. Outsourcing still may be the right answer in the long term.

In theory you should be able to outsource to the best in the world, up the value and lower the cost.[4] Selected vendors should have the ability to demonstrate world-class processes at the lowest costs. This is not always the case and many suppliers fall into the lower left of the following figure.

FIGURE 7.1   Cost and value

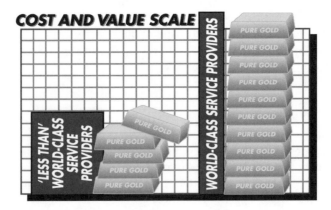

Sometimes organizations may receive somewhat better value for marginally higher costs. This is obviously a win compared to the status quo. In this scenario companies and third parties need to work together to reduce costs and improve performance. Contracts should clearly indicate promises to improve over a specified period of time. Dwight H. Mills, leader of rewards and resources at Owens Corning, says companies should not expect to move sideways, that outsourcing has got to yield benefits from the effort of making it work.

Most problematic is where organizations are outsourcing services and attaining comparable or lower value for comparable or higher costs of doing it internally. These organizations should rethink their outsourcing strategy or seek alternative suppliers as soon as possible.

Organizations should be looking for world-class suppliers at world-class costs whenever possible.

GUNN PARTNERS

Bob Gunn

Organizations which outsource their own less than world-class services to less than world-class providers are in for serious trouble down the line.

Staff groups have to become far more relevant, valuable and effective by changing and improving the actual way work gets done. If outsourcers are using old processes to crank out work, what has been gained in the long run?

Access to world-class practices

In the transactional processing business, the numbers are increasingly compelling to argue in favor of outsourcing. A financial institution might have an excellent payment center that on average completes 200 million transactions a year while a third party supplier might offer the possibility that comes from completing 1.8 billion transactions a year. This is the magnitude of scale companies are seizing. No matter how good and how smart the people and management are in the 200 million transaction center, they will never be able to compete on a unit price basis the way the 1.8 billion processor can. Total System Services Inc. of Columbus, Georgia is one of these suppliers that compete on a world scale by offering low cost, high value financial services processing.

TOTAL SYSTEM SERVICES INC.®

Richard W. Ussery, Chairman of the Board and CEO

We continue to set our sights on one goal, one destiny: to become the world's best information technology processing company. We know where we are going. We know how to get there.

The advantage of capturing economics of scale is really not about unit cost but more about saving organizations from making their own capital investment in business areas that are not their core business.

In financial processing, best practices in shared services can mean reducing the cost of processing an invoice from $16 to $7.80.[5] Big savings to the bottom line. Administrative functions and high paper processing areas are obvious choices for what to outsource as companies pounce on squeezing savings from what are being called "back office operations." James Bryan Quinn (1992) sums it up rather nicely by saying, "When a company internally produces a service, whether in the value chain or in a staff function, that others can produce more effectively externally, it sacrifices competitive advantage." Back room operations can drag down a company's advantage. The public sector's shrinking budget problem may already have caused too much cutting to the bone for essential services and so they can expect big gains from considering reduced overhead costs.

World-class capability

Companies wanting access to world-class practices or world-class capability may find outsourcing an attractive alternative. Retention is rearing its ugly head as companies scramble to attract and retain highly skilled technology people. Growth opportunities are richer for information technology people when they are working in a larger technology environment. For example, firms such as Andersen Consulting, CGI in Canada, and Cap Gemini find it easier to attract technology staff due to the opportunities for growth and learning in new technologies. Companies are once again chasing information technology staff, wooing them with retention bonuses, perks and prizes, so they don't leave. It may be easier in the long run to access the world-class talent from technology suppliers which will do a better job of ensuring a steady supply. At least that is the claim.

Outsourcing to improve service

Since it is clear that costs on some occasions increase when services are outsourced, a working hypothesis may be that companies find it easier to position outsourcing as cost related rather than service related. There is an overwhelming culture in most large organizations of excessive politeness, of saying one thing and meaning another. It is quite possible that many organizations choose to position the often unpopular decision to outsource as a cost savings initiative. This is corporately more palatable than saying, we think the service is so lousy that we would rather pay more because at least we will get some value. It is easier to blame a decision on impersonal facts and figures than point finger at organizational colleagues and tell them they are not up to scratch.

On the other hand, some functions may have to be outsourced simply because they cannot be salvaged. If a human resources or information technology function has no credibility with senior executives and has an impossibly poor reputation for delivering service, there may be no choice other than going outside to a third party supplier. If it's going to take too much of an investment or it's going to take too long to raise the bar of performance and profile, then it might be more expedient to work immediately on moving the services to a professional external supplier. Shared services would be an alternative strategy if the company wanted to give the staff group the opportunity to reinvent itself.

Outsourcing to avoid future investments

Companies with legacy systems in technology may choose outsourcing as a preventive measure against major capital investments. Some companies may outsource to get access to new technologies without their own capital investment.

XEROX CANADA

Sheila Reid, Chief Information Officer

It is far better to capture the benefits of new technologies with a third party. We don't have to invest our own capital.

We decided to outsource all of our information technology services except new development. We had a lot of old legacy systems and did not see it as a smart move to reinvest our own capital to get up to speed. Far better to find a supplier who has already made the investment.

Companies rightly question the need to invest this capital when they can take advantage of the technology using someone else's capital. This is the rationale for going to third party outsourcers which can spread their capital investment across many companies.

The dogma of non-core

Some companies truly believe that only core competencies should be retained in-house and everything else should be taken outside. Organizations are even moving away from retaining their own manufacturing and marketing departments. The great athletic shoemaker Nike does not even make its own shoes! It decided it was better at everything else which included research and development, design, distribution and sales and marketing. In essence, a manufacturer which doesn't manufacture! Automakers are not manufacturing the whole car, they have outsourced the production of parts and components, choosing to buy rather than make. They have become designers, assemblers and marketers of vehicles. This practice is rooted in the assumption and belief that a company must work to define and retain its core competencies and then shed the rest. Sony's core competency is miniaturization, Toys R Us has world-class information and distribution systems, Black and Decker's core competency is small electric motor technology.

The definition of core competencies provides companies with a good foundation for deciding whether they should exploit their core competency across other fields and what core functions should be retained or outsourced. For example, one of Walmart's core competencies is in logistics skills, which would allow the company to diversify into other markets provided that logistics was a key success factor. Financial institutions are outsourcing their credit card processing, while some utilities and telecommunications companies are outsourcing customer call centers. This represents new thinking and new ideas about what is core and what can be done better, cheaper and faster by outside suppliers. Credit cards to banks and call centers to telephone companies seem like inseparable peas in a pod yet analysts are busy sharpening their pencils, firing up their electronic spreadsheets and looking to all processes in the chain for ways to maximize company value.

There are a few sacred cows, however, that we believe organizations should never sacrifice no matter how compelling the argument.

GOVERNANCE NOT FOR SALE

One area that should not be outsourced is the governance piece of any staff function.

Governance functions are services directed upwards to stakeholders which include the board and the top executive team (see Figure 7.2). Additional stakeholders may be regulators and other pro-

FIGURE 7.2 The direction of governance functions

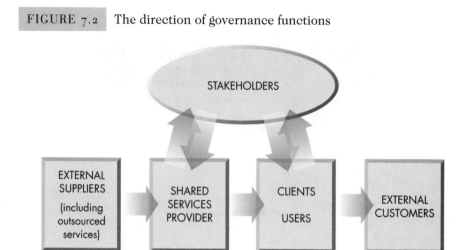

fessional governing bodies. Stakeholders are those parties that place constraints on how the shared services group operates. For example, in finance, there are codes of professional conduct that dictate how work is performed.

Staff departments have a governance role, which is directed at protecting the overall assets of the company and not at meeting individual client needs. The requirement to have compensation policies is aimed at protecting the company in the long term from chaotic or exorbitant pay practices. Individual business units may not like the compensation policy, preferring, in fact, to do what they please but the board and the executives must insist on corporate policies to minimize their liability. In other words, governance is not voluntary, it is mandated service on behalf of the board or executive. Governance functions are identified in figure 7.3.

In practice then, a company may choose to take all general accounting transactions to an outside supplier, it may even choose to take all accounting services outside, but it should never take away the controller function. In information technology, people mistakenly believe that they can simply outsource everything, thus doing away with the chief information officer role. Wrong thinking! The governance role for information technology is designed to protect the assets for the shareholder. A third party supplier does not have the same shareholder and in fact their interests may be diametrically opposite. Therefore it would be unwise to relinquish internal controls to an outsider and maybe even irresponsible. "Penny wise, pound foolish," as the British say.

Eliminating the salary of the chief information officer is not a good investment decision. You may think you are saving money now but you

FIGURE 7.3   Governance functions

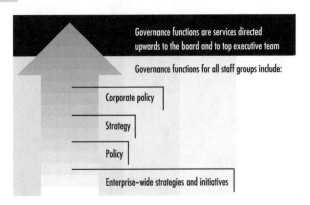

Governance functions are services directed upwards to the board and to top executive team

Governance functions for all staff groups include:

Corporate policy

Strategy

Policy

Enterprise-wide strategies and initiatives

will be paying heartily later when you realize that no one person is really looking after the whole picture of information for your shareholders.

Although outsourcing may look like a handy solution that will instantly wash away all the troubles, it is wiser to figure out if the function is in the right shape to turn over and to select a date that takes into account the housekeeping required to package up the function. There is a popular myth that you simply toss a basket of work over the wall and the supplier catches it in mid air and hits the ground running. If the function is a mess, is poorly run and disorganized, this is not the time to simply bundle it up and toss it over the wall. No third party supplier can possibly take over a completely ineffective operation and just magically turn it around. Although they might say they will try!

DILEMMAS IN OUTSOURCING

At a recent conference aptly titled "Strategic Outsourcing," one of the presenters, who just happened to be an executive in an insurance company selling its relocation services, proudly presented an overhead slide that outrageously claimed without any substantiation that "companies which outsource are more financially stable." Says who? Half truths are bandied about with great flourish. "Ninety-eight percent of some form of human resources is outsourced." No kidding, since for decades most companies have used outside insurance companies for benefits and actuaries for pension administration.

Cynics have plenty to crow about when it comes to the outsourcing crush. Here are the top three reasons for companies to be cynical about outsourcing:

1 Consulting companies' net profit: "A hand that feeds itself."

2 Loss of control and risk in third party arrangements.

3 Fulcrum pendulum – the tendency for business to swing in wide arcs from one strategy to the direct opposite.

Consulting companies' net profit: a hand that feeds itself

Consulting companies and suppliers can make a lot of money by taking over your company's staff departments. The lucrative business of delivering services is estimated at over $282 billion with a growth rate predicted at 20%.[6]

Cynics may find it intriguing that the same consulting groups that help executives make decisions on outsourcing just happen to have their own outsourcing businesses. When one consulting company was pressed to answer the question as to whether it wasn't a conflict of interest to be out advising companies on the one hand to outsource and on the other to offer up their very own outsourcing services, the partner replied, "Not really." He calmly justified the rationale by drawing two boxes on a piece of paper and stating that there were two separate divisions: one that tells companies to go for outsourcing and the other a potential supplier for the company to consider. There is something fundamentally disagreeable about this arrangement. Not a legal or strictly ethical issue but surely a potential moral dilemma. No doubt consulting companies have what are known as "Chinese walls" between the various divisions – the term used to describe legal barriers of non-disclosure. Not flagrant conflict of interest but hard to imagine how a consulting company could be that neutral when so much is at stake. Consulting companies which have been involved in strategy work with clients would definitely have an advantage at "Request for proposal" time given their inside knowledge of the drivers for outsourcing and what needs to be accomplished. Smart executives should ideally insist that consultants who advise them on outsourcing will not be able to gain directly from the decision.

Consulting companies are very good at selling and right now outsourcing is for sale. It is no secret that consultants and third party suppliers are much better at selling and presentation skills than the majority of internal staff groups. Presentations and pitches are rehearsed and timed. A lot of preparation goes into selling and building relationships, a lesson that needs learning by internal groups incidentally, and it may seem seductively simple to outsource functions with inadequate analysis of the consequences.

Loss of control and risk in the third party arrangement

Cynics may also fear the loss of control and potential risks from putting your business in someone else's hands, someone who does not necessarily have your best interests at heart. Business is in business for profit. As Lee Kercher, state chief network officer for the California State Department of Information Technology, put it at a recent conference, "Consultants' goals are not necessarily your goals." The issue here is for the outsourcer to return a profit pure and clear. While your success is important to them as an ongoing source of revenue, they are not really looking out for you the way you look out for yourself. Terms like "strategic partnerships" are inviting. What a strategic partnership means is debatable. Understandably, it is a noble and worthwhile aim to work with vendors who operate in a partnership spirit, but the idea of suppliers being true partners is not very practical unless there is a legal strategic partnership in place with mutual financial stakes and mutual interests on the table. This is a strategy of co-sourcing or joint ventures such as when Royal Bank Financial Group formed an alliance with S1 technologies to develop Internet banking.

Many companies may question outsourcing strategies on the grounds of loss of control. However, as Howard Spode of PricewaterhouseCoopers argued in a recent article, "Actually, outsourcing can gain you control, because you can deliver better service visibility and discipline with better cost control."[7] This may be a bit of a stretch since the issues of control are more to do with future risk and the ability of third parties to sustain performance over the long term.

Most outsourcing stories point to the rosy picture of success, the potential upside. The failures and problems with third party outsourcers are still not out in broad daylight.[8] There are not many reports of failure since companies do not want a feature story on how they spent more money taking information technology services outside the company. Alternately there is no desire for publicity by outsourcers as to how they were unable to live up to the claims made at sales pitch time. Anyone interested in hearing the dark side to consulting pitches has only to read *Dangerous Company*.[9] the scathing and juicy "tell all" book about inside the powerful consulting world. Lawsuits, previously either unheard of or well-hidden, are beginning to emerge as frustrated companies choose to sue consulting groups that have failed to live up to their promises.

Cynics might talk about the vulnerability for a company which has relinquished control into the hands of an outside party. Who is to say that these suppliers will not change their processes and philosophy and in essence begin to dictate to companies what they are going to get. For example, imagine that your company is one of twenty companies using the same outside supplier and imagine that you are one of the smaller ones. The majority of companies decide to go in a new direction for processing that does not meet your expectations. No problem, the contract is clear. You can get out of the contract legally. The only problem is now you have disbanded your own group and it is not so easy to start up a new organization, staff it and go back to doing functions that you recently outsourced.

In accounts payable, it may be possible to get the service done cheaper outside but this is the key link to suppliers and can be the first indicator of supplier issues or problems. In accounts receivable, cheaper, yes, but it is the key direct link to customers and where many customer issues may become evident. Telephone companies which outsource their call centers may not find this to be a good strategy in the long run. Some companies are already moving away from call centers and going for highly personalized service.

They may be customer oriented but their loyalties lie elsewhere. These third party suppliers are developing into enormous companies and who is to say that they will be able to hold the enterprise together. Consulting companies which start up outsourcing divisions will come to realize over time just what kind of challenges there are in running a company that is not based on purely intellectual capital and professional services. Consulting companies which advise other companies on how to build a strong culture and motivate staff had better listen and practice their own advice since they will now be charged with motivation and retention issues themselves.

> *There is a certain lack of control in working with people who are not your own staff, who have an allegiance to their home company and not to yours*

Traditionally, large consulting companies are quite hierarchical. Partners do relationship management, partners are the ones who define and change proprietary models and processes. It will be interesting to see how they fare at running major companies with a workforce that expects real involvement. Not all consulting firms are structured the same way. The recent skirmish within KPMG where the Canada group wanted to merge with Andersen and break away from KPMG International seemed, from the press coverage, to be an issue of how they were treated. Organizations are putting their staff groups out into consulting companies and third party suppliers with the clear assumption that they will be there in the morning. The size of consulting companies and third party suppliers is growing considerably. Growth is difficult to manage.

Whoever said "the devil is in the details" couldn't be more insightful when it comes to reading the fine print in a third party contract for services. Many organizations have leapt on the train waving the illusion of lower costs only to discover that costs are increasing steadily. Being in the business for profit, third parties are excessively rigorous about charging clients for every single thing asked for or performed. Always accommodating and exceedingly service minded, suppliers are only too happy to generate a few extra reports, do some extra human resource interviewing, or work last minute on the preparation of a presentation to the board. These services might just be over and above the terms of the existing contract. The shock of additional charges may take awhile to be noticed but when it sinks in, there may be a lot of disappointment and a bitter feeling of having been oversold the benefits of outsourcing. As David Garrison, Chief Procurement Officer for Aetna Insurance, said at a recent conference, "One of the biggest pitfalls in working with a third party supplier is underestimating the talent of a supplier to write themselves a good contract." His advice is to ensure that you have a proper commercial negotiator on your side who can account for economic changes, and who understands the dizzying world of costs.

THE FUTURE OF OUTSOURCING

FIGURE 7.4   The Fulcrum Pendulum

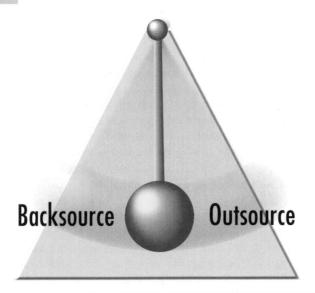

Fulcrum pendulum: the tendency for business to swing in wide arcs from one strategy to the direct opposite

Pure cynicism aside, there is always the fulcrum pendulum to consider, whereby the strategy of tomorrow is diametrically opposed to that of today. It is just the way the world works and outsourcing is still in the honeymoon phase. Conceivably outsourcing is just at the beginning of the growth curve, and it will continue to double and triple in expansion. It is hard to predict the future but we do know that whatever goes up, usually goes down. No doubt, at the end of the day, the transactional processing and true back office operations will continue to be out-sourced to large-scale mega processing operators. Hopefully, these operators like other organizations will learn how to build strong and inviting cultures and in essence become famous household names. There will probably be some retrenchment in the professional services area with a trend to backsourcing.

The visionary habits of the top outsourcers

We want to know all about the visionary suppliers and consultants. We want books written about them so we can contrast and compare what they stand for. For example, Hewlett-Packard is widely known for a collaborative and participative culture, 3M for innovation, Citicorp for expansionism due to size and services, and Ford for people being the source of its strength. Who will emerge from among the outsourced suppliers as the General Electric or Johnson and Johnson of tomorrow?[10] If Motorola claims to exist for superior prod-ucts at fair prices and Sony for experiencing the sheer joy that comes from technology, what will the new outsourcers be known for and how will we find out?

It is in the professional side of staff functions that the pendulum has the greatest possibility to swing backwards. In the 1970s and early 1980s in Canada, a lot of large public accounting firms grew their human resources organizational development practice only to have it disintegrate largely by the mid-80s with a return to basics. This caused a rebirth in internal consulting units due to the supply drying up. Accounting and consulting firms also moved away from audit as a core practice, causing most companies to reinstate an internal audit function. This trend is reversing as public accounting and consulting companies want to reclaim audit as one of their core service offerings. Human resources, information technology, finance and supply are under siege as companies look to the new knight on the horizon called "outsourcing." Should we or shouldn't we? For anyone who has been around long enough in corporate life, it is not inconceivable to imagine companies arguing for growing their own staff groups in-house, because outside suppliers are just not meeting expectations. Outsourcing still has another five to seven years of growth before any swing back.

The principal point is that outsourcing is a legitimate and sound strategy provided that it is seen as just that. It needs to be selective and seen as one of many options. It is not a Midas touch. Shared services is the first step. Staff groups either within shared services or contemplating shared services should be the ones to make the decision on outsourcing. After all, they should be in the best position to read the fine print and to know whether it is a good deal or not. It does take courage and leadership to be the one to tap yourself on the shoulder and decide to take services to the outside market. Far better for marketing or finance to make the call than to have the executive look down their long noses and point to the door. So given that shared services is the first step, it will take someone to lead the expedition and a structure put in place to make it happen.

NOTES

1 'Farming out shared services', (April, 1999), *Business Europe,* (The Economist Intelligence Unit).

2 The Drucker Foundation, Leader of the Future

3 Corporate Leadership Council. Companies pay an annual fee of $50,000 to join the council, in return for their research into human resources best practices

4 James Bryan Quinn, 1992

5 Bob Gunn at Reengineering Conference

6 Maurice Greaver II 1999

7 KPMG study as quoted by Maurice Greaver II, 1999

8 "Farming out shared service", (April, 1999), *Business Europe,* (The Economist Intelligence Unit)

9 James O'Shea and Charles Madigan, 1997

10 James Collins and Jerry Porras, 1994

Chapter 8

ORGANIZING AND LEADING
SHARED SERVICES

*The Internet is a goldmine for organizing the business of prospecting.
Everything from binoculars, hammers, gloves, sample bags, eye pro-
tection, a red jacket, dust masks and bear bangers to ward off the
lumbering animals! Hobby or not, this is an organized sport*

At some point during implementation, there is a need to figure out
the structure, location and leadership of the shared services operation. What is the right shape of the organization, who should it report to
and who should be in charge? Organizational structure is usually a topic
that generates great interest and enthusiasm since everyone typically
has an opinion on what the best design looks like. There is probably no
better corporate pastime than drawing and doodling boxes on white
boards, flipcharts, and pieces of paper whenever the chance arises.
Academic pundits and earnest consultants will tell you that form follows
structure, but in practice there is always a lot of energy when executives
are given the task of drawing possible options for structure. There is
something artistic and powerful about etching the boxes this way and
that way. In reality, most seasoned executives know that structure in
and of itself does not produce anything. The theory of organizational
design is that a bad design can impede performance but it is never the
cause for success either. No one has yet come up with a paper on effective shared services that lays claim to the superb organizational design
as the critical driver.

The question of who should lead shared services is perhaps the
more intriguing proposition. Should the person be from inside the staff
organization, or should the organization take a bold leap and either go
outside to the business units or even more dramatically, go right out-

side the corporation to find a seasoned shared service implementor? There is only one real way to approach the structure and leadership issue and that is to plan for success. Imagine that the scope might expand later, that new clients and customers may be added and need to be integrated into shared services. This will provide a design that is flexible enough to prevent a reorganization every time new functions are added to shared services.

The structuring, location and leadership issues will arise at different times in different organizations. In some cases, the structure is scoped out when going to the executive team for buy-in and commitment. In others, it is following the business case and the decision to implement. The timing will differ based on how shared services was introduced to the organization. Although structure is not a solution unto itself, it can obviously help the effort to transform corporate functions into operating businesses.

SHARED SERVICES AS A SEPARATE ENTITY

We believe that shared services must be set up as a separate and distinct entity with its own executive as illustrated in figure 8.1. A separate organization allows shared services to be seen clearly as new and improved while also enabling a distinct separation of governance from services. It sends a clear message to the rest of the organization that something is dramatically different from what existed before.

Most large-scale shared services organizations have established separate entities at the start. Jim Bryant, who set up shared services

FIGURE 8.1   Shared services as a separate organization

for Baxter Healthcare, not only agrees with the need for a separate entity but is a huge proponent of the green field space. Advocates of this concept will point to the benefits of starting over, of creating a brand new culture that is capable of establishing excellent internal client service. Whether a new location or just a separate organization, it is a distinct advantage to be seen as different than the corporate head office functions.

Where the size of shared services is not sufficient to warrant a complete and separate operating structure the alternative is to set up shared services under the various existing functional units with no common reporting point. In this model human resources transactional processing related to employee data, benefits, and compensation administration would be set up under the HR function while processing related to disbursements, travel and expenses, and receivables would be under the finance group. While this model will have minimal disruption for the functional groups themselves, it will be difficult to convince the rest of the organization that anything is different. The establishment of a separate shared services organization with its own executive reporting structure sends a clear signal that something is new. This is not corporate as usual. A new entity helps to create a different culture, and can enable the shift to a more client-centered and service-focused organization.

SEPARATION OF SHARED SERVICES FROM GOVERNANCE FUNCTIONS

The other advantage of a distinct shared services group is the ability to separate clearly shared services from the corporate governance functions. This is necessary to provide clarity to the services role and to reduce the visible relationship to the corporate role of policy development and compliance. The corporate office functions include:

✦ development of corporate policy, guidelines and frameworks;

✦ auditing to ensure compliance with corporate policy;

✦ strategic direction including vision and goal setting;

✦ promoting and communicating use of best practices;

✦ performance monitoring;

✦ co-ordination and management of corporate wide initiatives on behalf of the executive.

When policies are created, the governance groups will have to tap into expertise in the shared services group. For example, if corporate human resources needs to revamp its compensation policies, it will want to consult compensation experts in shared services. It is better to keep the separation clean in the client's eyes.

SEPARATION OF TRANSACTIONAL PROCESSING FROM PROFESSIONAL AND ADVISORY SERVICES

For most organizations which have opted to include professional and advisory services in shared services there is a recognition that most of the synergy comes from separating the transactional processing functions from the professional and advisory functions. The functions are typically separated into what are commonly referred to as "centers of scale" for transactional processing and as "centers of expertise" for professional and advisory services, as illustrated in figure 8.2.

We believe that the structural separation of transactional processing from professional and advisory functions is key, since the management and operation of these two service groupings are very different. The orientation for running the transactional processing business is about economies of scale, process efficiencies and the effective use of technology. The orientation for the manager of a professional and advisory service business is more like running a consulting firm and it takes special skill and expertise to lead professional experts.

Figure 8.3 is a sample structural model that establishes a separate shared services organization distinct from corporate governance functions with the transactional processing services split from the professional and advisory services.

FIGURE 8.2   Centers of scale and centers of expertise

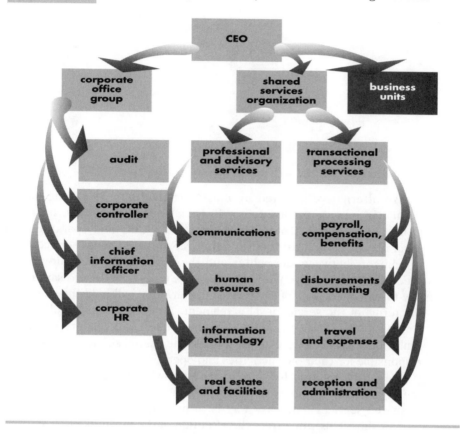

FIGURE 8.3   Sample of a separate entity shared services organization

SHARED SERVICES REPORTING

While the actual reporting structure for shared services organizations differs considerably, many report to a senior finance executive since this was the starting place for many shared services operations. Differences in reporting are typically due to size, scope and geography of the organization as well as cultural norms around reporting levels. In some organizations shared services reports through the operating business units. When Kaiser Permanente established its San Diego, California based shared services center, it reported to the vice presidents of the operating units as outlined in figure 8.4. In this structure, day-to-day service center decisions, as well as service levels, are directly influenced by the business units that may or may not be acting in unison.

FIGURE 8.4   Kaiser Permanente shared services organization, San Diego

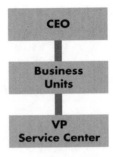

An alternative selected by most organizations, including Kaiser Permanente at its service center in Fort Worth, Texas, is to have the shared services organization reporting to the CEO and operating as a separate entity as illustrated in figure 8.5. In this model service level agreements between the center and the different business units governed the relationship. While the business units have less to say in the day-to-day operations of the service center, they will hold the center to the terms of the service level agreement. American Express followed a similar model; rather than having shared services leaders report to senior business unit executives, it made the shared services units solely responsible for their own activities and operations.

Reporting relationships are a sign of power in organizations and if the organization wants to send a strong message about the importance of shared services, one easy way is to provide a very senior reporting relationship. This will attract the attention of the business units and the organization, especially the staff within shared services.

FIGURE 8.5   Shared services center as a separate entity reporting to the CEO

INTERNAL STRUCTURES OF SHARED SERVICES ORGANIZATIONS

Once the macro reporting structure is in place and the reporting lines are clear, it is essential to decide what kind of internal management structure is required. In traditional bureaucracies, the number of management levels is often a convenience for the internal group. The fact that clients have to go up and down levels within the hierarchy for a decision typically doesn't bother old-fashioned corporate groups. Nor does the cost of management infrastructure. Now in full cost recovery mode, the number of levels of management is significant since the cost of that management infrastructure will have to be loaded into the rates and prices. So you have to ask if your clients would be willing to pay those additional fees for the extra management.

The best illustration of the difference between a traditional finance structure and a shared services structure can be found at American Express Europe. Ralph Andrette, vice president and general manager of American Express Services Europe Limited, uses a slide, illustrated in figure 8.6, to show the reduction from seven levels to four.

In thinking about new structures, the requirement is to start with the functionality necessary and then to determine the minimum number of layers possible. As Ralph Andrette points out, a flatter organization raises the level of customer contact and decision making at all levels. Any good structural design begins with the thinking of what needs to be accomplished and what functions are required. While structure in and of itself does not do anything, it can either facilitate or impede success. Shared ser-

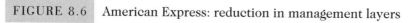

FIGURE 8.6   American Express: reduction in management layers

vices requires a structural design that will contribute to the business goals, as well as facilitate customer contact. Obviously the number of management layers is significant. Too many layers will impede empowerment and empowerment is what is needed for people to provide high quality service to their clients. People need the autonomy and authority to solve client issues without the hindrance of a multi-level bureaucracy. Waiting for the boss or the boss's boss is not always a winning client strategy. In general, the rule of thumb is to design in the minimum layers of management and supervision required for an effective operation.

The internal structures of the shared service centers themselves vary, depending on size and scope. Multi-functional shared services organizations require more complex structures than single focus groups. The Unisys Shared Services Center in Bismarck, North Dakota is a multi-functional organization supplying services to 33,000 employees in 100 companies. Its structure, illustrated in figure 8.7, is relatively flat with five managers and a staff to manager ratio of 20:1. There are no first line supervisors or team leaders.

Alternatively, other shared service organizations have opted to structure along process lines or have combined like functional services. The provincial Government of Ontario, Canada has structured its shared services organization with clusters of functions bundled to provide discrete service offerings. The structure for the province's Shared Services Bureau is illustrated in figure 8.8. The shared services, including an employee help desk, employee data transactions, financial transactions and general administrative services, report to the general manager of service operations. Also included in the structure of the bureau is a business

FIGURE 8.7   Unisys Shared Services Center

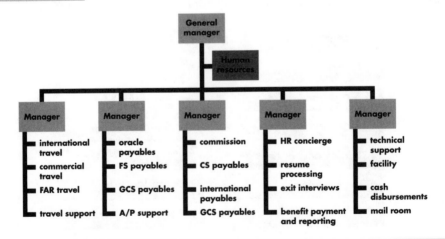

FIGURE 8.8   Ontario Government Shared Services Bureau, Canada

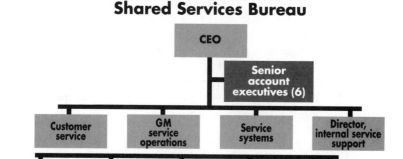

improvement function that provides ongoing support to improve process efficiency and effectiveness continuously as well as organizational development, change management, communications and marketing support. The bureau has a staff of almost 1,400 providing services to eighteen government ministries.

FIGURE 8.9   JD Edwards & Company financial services centers

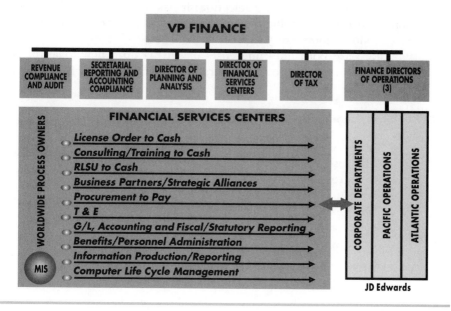

Some organizations have aligned their structures with internal processes. JD Edwards & Company has four shared services centers serving the Americas, Europe, Asia Pacific and Japan. The three directors of the service centers report to the director of financial services centers. The directors are accountable for ensuring the needs of the operational unit clients are being met. For each of the ten processes, as illustrated in figure 8.9, there is a worldwide process manager who is responsible for continuous improvements and changes to a process and for ensuring worldwide process consistency. For example, there is a process manager responsible for the worldwide license order to cash process.

Locating shared services centers

The search for the best location for the shared service organization ranges from a simple decision to locate in available space or within current facilities to the international search for the best new "green field" site. The key decisions in site selection are whether to locate close to current operations or at a more remote site, whether to have single or multiple sites, and whether to co-locate with clients or to stand alone.

The criteria for selecting a location are consistent across most organizations which are looking for a place to put their shared services center. Moran, Stahl & Boyer is an Atlanta, Georgia based consulting firm that specializes in site selection. It has defined a list of considerations, illustrated in table 8.1, which range from labor availability and costs, to local community support and image.

There are both one-time costs of setting up a new location, and ongoing cost and non-cost considerations. Moran, Stahl & Boyer defines

TABLE 8.1   Moran, Stahl & Boyer: criteria for site selection

✓ labor availability	✓ business taxes
✓ labor cost	✓ power reliability
✓ facility costs	✓ communications
✓ access to company facilities	✓ infrastructure
✓ labor quality	✓ incentives
✓ quality of life	✓ community image
✓ air access	✓ community support for business

the one-time costs of setting up a new center location as those related to employee relocation for workers moving to the new location and the separation costs for leaving the organization. There are also one-time costs for moving office furniture, fixtures and equipment, and for moving and setting up technology hardware.

Recurring costs for consideration are employee salaries and benefits, ongoing facilities costs, rent, operations and maintenance. Non-cost issues are those related to how far people have to travel on a daily basis to come to work and the quality of life that employees can enjoy in the new community. These recurring and longer term cost and non-cost considerations will have the greatest impact on the sustained success and performance of the shared services organization.

Whirlpool Europe defined its selection criteria for its shared services center location as those shown in Figure 8.10.

FIGURE 8.10   Selection criteria for Whirlpool Europe

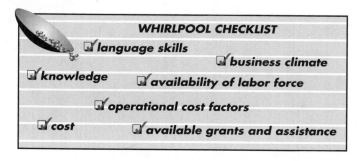

Following an analysis of sites against its criteria, Whirlpool Europe ended up selecting Dublin, Ireland as a green field site for its shared services center. It assessed that Dublin offered a flexible labor environment that also enabled the company to hire financial staff with the language skills it needed. The location also provided a reasonably low cost, but productive infrastructure and an adequate technology infrastructure.

Dun & Bradstreet grappled with how many sites to have and what to have in the sites. It looked at the option of having one site that contained all the shared services functions, multiple sites with one major function in each site and having two sites with all functions at each site. The three options were then compared against service, cost efficiency, information, and technology factors as outlined in figure 8.11. Following the analysis of the options it was clear to the company that a single multi-functional site was most effective in meeting its objectives.

FIGURE 8.11   Dun & Bradstreet: assessment of options

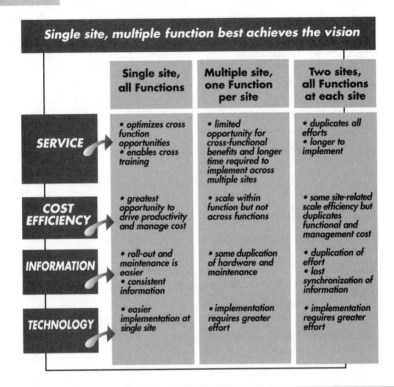

As organizations move to a marketplace or advanced marketplace model of shared services many of the professional and advisory services require face to face interaction with clients. As a result proximity to client is a key factor. Some organizations have found it most effective to have professional and advisory staff co-located with their clients on an ongoing or project basis. For those which co-locate their resources within a client's premises the location of the shared services office is less a factor. Other organizations have opted for establishing a professional and advisory service center to obtain the synergies of staff working together and sharing experience in a single location. In both models it is best to locate the center closer to the corporate center and in a major city since it is easier to attract and retain highly qualified staff for the professional and advisory role.

There is much debate about "green field" versus "brown field" sites. Green field sites typically consist of new physical facility and new employees who may have little experience with the organization. Proponents of this model point to the need to make a fresh start and to show the organization that something is different. There is a view that leaving behind redundant labor can be an incentive and acceler- ate the change to client-focused organization.

KAISER PERMANENTE

Nate Oubre, VP Shared Business

Ensure you understand the complexities of the work being consolidated into the green field site and make sure you retain some of the best employees who ran the legacy processes to help in the transition.

When we established our Houston based green field site, we started a fresh with brand new staff. We then told business units, "Give us all your files." After we had all the files sent to the center, we quickly real- ized we couldn't read or understand what they meant. We needed people who had worked with the legacy systems and had the practical knowledge. A lot was never written down. People just knew how to make things work.

LOCATING IN EUROPE

Issues around location in more complex regions such as Europe (and similar conditions apply to other multi-country regions) include more than just the typical questions of abandoning the mindset and culture of the old organization and building a new service-oriented culture with new people. When moves take place across a region as wide as Europe with major differences in company and labor law, taxation, culture and work habits, there is a greater diversity of factors to consider.

When Baxter International announced its move to create its European shared services center in Dublin, it was just one part of restructuring its European back office which included the finance and purchasing func- tions. In doing so it followed on the heels of Whirlpool Europe, Allergan, Informix and others, which have made Ireland one of the most popular locations in Europe for establishing shared services centers.

Helping to attract new shared services centers is a well-educated, youthful workforce, eager for employment in the new economy. So much so that Ireland, a long time exporter of labour, has seen the return in large numbers of qualified professionals eager to move to quality jobs in their home locations. This is all taking place on the back of progres- sive government policies, which, at least for the time being, continue to offer exceptional incentives in the form of low corporate taxes to attract incoming investment.

Legal operating company frameworks such as "commissionaire" structures, which have been created through Irish entities, enable companies with operations in several European countries to treat their subsidiaries as sales agents of their Irish center and benefit from low corporate taxation for their entire European operations. Though how long this will last remains to be seen given the pressure in Europe for tax harmonization amongst EU members.

In recent years, thanks to the influx of new shared services centers and the large number of international call centers that have preceded them for companies such as Dell, Gateway, American Airlines and many others, Dublin has taken on the appearance of a boom town. Not only is there visible growth in the support economy, with new hotels, restaurants and bars, but also the concomitant increase in real estate values raising prices to levels comparable with other Western European capitals.

Shared services centers are now likely to move to locations further from Dublin, as the labor pool begins to come under strain, and special skills such as foreign languages become more difficult to find.

KPMG, London

Rory Colfer, Principal EMU Consultant

One of the micro economic effects of the single currency EMU is that businesses can now locate in any part of the eurozone without being forced to consider hedging their investment in a particular national currency.

EMU (Economic and Monetary Union) will be a key catalyst in forcing businesses to reconsider their operational structures as we move into a new millennium with a Europe that wants to be treated as a single economic entity. We do not yet see a timeframe where a company headquartered in San Francisco runs its worldwide operations from there. We still have European headquarters for the time being.

Historically more expensive in terms of labor costs, the Netherlands and Belgium, especially Flanders, also stand out as popular locations in Europe for new shared services units. Geographically in reach of most major Western European markets and with a history of being outward-focused, due to relatively small internal markets, they have a high percentage of multi-lingual inhabitants and a flexibility and work ethic that results in high levels of productivity. The Netherlands, which according to Vanderwicken's *Financial Digest* claims to have attracted 400 US companies to establish centralized administrative operations in the last three years, emphasizes its multilingual labor pools, modern infrastructures and sometimes tax breaks too.

Assuming that the right skills were available and costs were kept low, logic would suggest that in these days of high speed communication and data lines and integrated systems, location of shared services centers would matter less. This would be missing the point. If you are unwinding years of corporate history and power bases, moving to a location which is independent and geographically central to your customers is an attractive proposition. No one unit appears to get preferential treatment simply because it's close to the SSCs, and the people in the function get to make a fresh start.

Politically it may be difficult to argue against locating the new shared services center at an existing location where there could be low-cost space available. However, if it means being based at the headquarters, or within a major operating unit, you run the risk of being seen either as a part of the corporate center and controlling activities, rather than providing services your clients need, or risk appearing to favor the large unit with which you are co-located.

Neutral locations, if affordable, are important. From the shared services perspective, they are close to all their clients. In the case of shared services centers, it is closeness, not absence, that makes the heart grow fonder!

THE CULTURE AND LANGUAGE OF LOCATION

Paris is Paris, it's not France! At least that's what you'll hear from most French people not actually born in Paris. And it's a fact that the use and sound of the French language varies infinitely from one part of France to another. A shared services center which does not communicate in the appropriate French regional dialect may be taking things too far, but if your clients are in South East Asia, you will certainly have to accommodate regional variations in the use of Chinese for example to ensure effective communication. Anything less and you will have a diplomatic incident and at worst you will end up with total resistance and no clients.

Complexities of language and culture are frequently used as reasons not to implement shared services. Genuine, well-intentioned arguments for service excellence frequently mask delaying tactics by would-be resistors. It is important to deal sensitively with issues of culture and language. Careful planning, selective hiring or transfer of the right skills is necessary. However, the scale provided by shared services centers makes these issues easier to deal with, and the cost reductions and general improvement in service quality more than compensate for any minor accommodations that have to be made.

The location of the shared services organization is a key strategic decision that dictates the path that the shared services organization will take. Emotionally most people are committed to a preferred place. It is important that a great deal of thought and critical analysis be placed on this decision since once the decision is made, most organizations are committed for a long period of time. It better be the right decision. Finally, it will come down to the leadership of shared services. Sometimes, finding the right leader or leaders is what will make this strategy work.

LEADING THE SHARED SERVICES ORGANIZATION

The recruitment and selection of all shared service staff, including executives, is probably one of the most critical tasks anyone can undertake. Leadership of shared services takes certain kinds of people who can both build strong relationships with clients and build a positive climate for achievement within the center and get the job done. Strong skills in working with people is essential.

Maverick organizations, those which regularly make bold moves and operate in a culture where people earn the right to positions, and nothing is taken for granted, may well choose to do what is maybe considered to be outrageous, and that is to go outside and hire somebody new to head up the shared services organization. Going outside the organization to hire a senior executive still causes cries and whispers on the inside. If the outsider comes from another kind of industry, the cries are even louder. There is always skepticism about the ability of traditional leaders of corporate functions to make the big leap to heading an internal enterprise called shared services. They do not see a traditional corporate finance, human resources, information technology, or supply person as having the right stuff to lead a business within a business. Going outside to fill the senior position signals a major change.

An outside search will enable an experienced shared services leader to be selected. In an organization where the scope of shared services is considerable, the risks may be higher if the choice becomes an internal one. Where corporate functions have a poor reputation and an image to improve, it may be wise to get new blood into the function. Since shared services has been around for a number of years, an external search can yield a candidate who has had experience in making the transition. An outsider may be able to bring credibility to the strategy. The advantage of no baggage can be a quick and early win for the new shared services organization.

Naturally, there is always a flip side to the external search process. On the negative side, an external search may send out the wrong signal. People from within may see shared services as an even bigger threat. If the culture of the organization is such that outsiders are in fact seen as odd and unnatural, it may be wiser to go with the devil you know than with the one you don't.

Most large and traditional organizations will tend to select leaders from within the ranks even if they don't necessarily exhibit the ideal degree of entrepreneurial and service-minded characteristics. In our experience, we have seen leaders rise to the challenge and exhibit enormous capacity for leading a significant change such as shared services. An internal selection sends a signal to the organization that the power to lead resides within. It typically provides more optimism that the leader of shared services will at least understand the business of the enterprise.

In many cases, the leader's job may be a case of default in that whoever has been leading the charge and making the presentations outlined in the previous chapters is likely to be the one to take the helm. The process of understanding shared services and trying to get executive commitment to the idea usually is a key step in beginning the transition from a corporate mindset to a business mindset.

Nonetheless, there is usually considerable debate over who should lead the shared services organization. Many of the managers and staff within the shared services organization will want someone new, someone from outside the corporate and internal ranks, someone from a sales and marketing background who can lead the organization forward. There will be others from within who would be highly suspicious of someone from outside, unsure of a foreigner from sales and marketing, coming into information technology or human resources. This contingent would be more comfortable with an insider. This translates to a finance person to lead a financial services operation, an HR type to lead HR shared services and so on.

Ultimately, it takes a leader who is successful at running a business. It takes someone who has credibility within the organization and who is seen as competent to run this new enterprise. This can mean someone who is quiet and competent. It does not take a textbook view of leadership to make shared services successful. It does take considerable tenacity however to make shared services work. The required capabilities of leaders for shared services are not dramatically different from the skill requirements of leaders in any business function. While emphasis may be required in specific areas related to service orientation and change leadership, generally the list of requirements is consistent. A typical example of leadership skills for shared services from Kaiser Permanente is outlined below:

+ decisive
+ empowered to make decisions
+ strategic/systems thinker
+ service orientation

+ cultural competence
+ strong communicator
+ ability to influence
+ team focused
+ understands change leadership
+ results oriented
+ confidence/initiative
+ develops others
+ personal development.

Whether the recruitment is external or internal, it is recommended that the criteria be very clear and that the CEO or senior executive spends time articulating what kind of profile the leader should possess. Let us look at the following page which is the actual profile of a leader done by an external search firm.

This description applies generally to running any shared services operation. It is not specifically aimed at running a financial transactional center or a professional and advisory center. There are specific leadership skills that are different, however, for leading these two different types of shared services organizations and this is one of the reasons we advocate the separation of transactional processing from professional and advisory services.

LEADING THE TRANSACTIONAL PROCESSING CENTER

For centers of scale providing transactional processing services, the kind of leader required is one who can and will take an inspired position to managing what is basically a production center. This job requires a leader who can make the center of scale into a highly prized and valued service center. This is a leader who takes pure joy in managing transactional and administrative work, who sees the value and loves the idea of reducing the transactional unit cost of one disbursement from $8 to $5. Leaders of transactional processing service centers are people who have a genuine interest in the idea of business process improvement since one of their principal roles is to improve process and lower operational costs. These kinds of managers are those people who really relish the thought of creating a motivating culture where people in clerical or technical ranks can blossom and find tremendous satisfaction in doing transactional work. Not a job for just anyone!

THE POSITION

The Director of Shared Services Europe is expected to provide leadership for the continuing smooth operation of the unit and to manage its continuing development.

As the Director is unlikely to possess the functional expertise required for every service, leadership skills and a profound understanding of what it takes to manage a service-oriented administrative organization are the keys to success.

The ability to establish a close working relationship with client units and with functional heads is essential to understand client needs and to put effective resources in place to meet them. Experience of operating in a large, complex, US based corporate environment is important.

The function of Director, Shared Services has three major dimensions: strategy and organizational development, active, hands-on involvement leading a shared services organization and development of future service offerings.

THE MAIN TASKS OF THE DIRECTOR OF SHARED SERVICES WILL BE:

+ To define and gain approval for the shared services strategy in Europe, its budgets and for its implementation
+ To lead and motivate an effective service organization
+ To rapidly establish personal credibility as the unit's leader
+ To take an active, hands-on role in key relationships with business leaders
+ To ensure the unit continues to provide effective, efficient services
+ To seek and ensure implementation of improvements in service delivery
+ To expand the range of services, to grow the business
+ To manage the operating budget from X million to X plus million
+ To lead the specification and implementation of IT systems that support business units and the center's activities.

THE IDEAL CANDIDATE

The ideal candidate is someone with a thorough understanding of corporate strategy, business needs and the European economic and political environment, as well as exceptional people management skills which drive these activities. The Director needs the ability to persuade business leaders that opportunities to reduce cost and raise effectiveness can be realized through sharing services with other business units and sites and through standardization and implementing common systems.

The ideal candidate has the maturity to work effectively in a multi-functional environment and the ability to handle ambiguity. The following personal characteristics are considered to be essential:

Leadership
Open, flexible, and with a down to earth manner that gains the respect of colleagues

Interpersonal
A team player whose energy and communication skills make this person a persuasive negotiator and relationship builder

Handles complexity
Able to handle ambiguity that arises in a service environment in a complex, diverse and geographically widespread organization

Thinker/doer
A clear thinker, able to translate knowledge and understanding of the business, economic and political environment into actionable strategies and willing to make decisions independently in pursuit of the strategy.

SOURCE: Andrew Kris, Amrop International

The core competencies and skills for such a manager and leader would likely include the following:

+ consistently demonstrates a client service attitude;
+ motivates and retains staff;
+ builds a climate for achievement;
+ understands how to implement business process improvement;
+ fiscally manages a business.

LEADING PROFESSIONAL AND ADVISORY SERVICES

If the model for shared services includes professional and advisory services, leaders are now in the business of running a professional services enterprise. Anyone who has ever participated in the executive search for the head of a professional consulting firm or a practice leader will attest to the fact that it is a very difficult search. The toughest management challenge has to be leading groups of knowledge workers. Professionals need guidance with their ideas and approaches while also needing to work independently and autonomously on projects from inception through to completion. It is a delicate balancing act to shape and guide without being overbearing.

Ask any high technology firm or management consulting profession how hard it is to balance controls with intellectual autonomy and you will find a similar response. These are competing demands within a professional services firm. On the one hand, there is the need to market and sell the business while on the other hand producing profitable products and services. Ratios of administration and the cost of sell-through to revenue are real issues. Monitoring progress against targets and careful attention to the bottom line is a given in the external professional service or consulting business. These are new behaviors for the shared services leader especially if the candidate has come from inside the company.

The leader's job is even more difficult when you layer it over a corporate entity that has traditionally been a monopoly with little accountability for profitability and a positive client service reputation. It is truly an art to manage strong-willed professionals who have grown up in a somewhat entitled culture and have now been cut loose to earn their way for profit. In the book *Managing the Professional Services Firm*, David Maister claims that, "people may adopt the wrong assumption that the typical professional firm is made up of intelligent, energetic individuals, who can be relied upon to be autonomous, self-starting professionals with no need to be managed. Professionals can be the toughest people to manage. They require involvement, nurturing, acknowledgement, feedback and assorted other care and feeding. Managing a professional and advisory service center is not for the faint of heart."

DAVID MAISTER

Leading author on professional service firms

Despite the scarcity of professional people, people management is still low on the priority list for most external and internal service groups.

The aspects of good people management is not a soft and easy issue but the basics of good supervision on work, thoughtful management of work assignments so people build skills, helping people to learn and grow. In most internal and external service firms, it is still a sink or swim environment.

The reality is that the best managers in professional services firms add a very special value. A manager's time in a professional services firm can be divided into five categories:

+ administrative and financial matters;
+ doing professional billable work;
+ personal marketing and selling;
+ general client relations;
+ dealing and talking with senior professionals and staff.

Maister claims that the biggest payoff areas are in dealing and talking with professionals and staff which should account for 30–60% of the week, and client relations which should account for 20–40% of the week. The emphasis on administration should be minimal and the issue of billable work and marketing will vary according to the structure of the firm.

In the case where there is an obvious leader for shared services it may be simplest to have the person just take over the position. For example, if the chief financial officer or vice president of administration already has functions such as human resources, information technology, and supply management under their wing, then it is often an obvious choice to simply anoint the leader. The advantage here is that this leader will know the business and culture really well and not make any obvious gaffes. Naturally, it is assumed that this leader has credibility with other line management executives. If not, problems will loom ahead. Remember, in shared services there is usually an evolution towards market-based pricing and client choices, so it is incumbent on the leader of the shared services organization to quickly get the business up to speed by earning a reputation for high quality delivery at the right price. Once the leader is in place for the shared services organization, the next step is to build the infrastructure necessary to make the strategy succeed.

Chapter 9

THE FOUNDATION FOR SUCCESS

Every time you touch a key on the computer, its gold connectors carry messages to the computer's brain. Gold is still the number one specification and foundation for virtually all military equipment from nuclear submarines to space stations due to its incredible property of being virtually indestructible

Building the business of shared services means starting with a solid foundation, one that is strong enough to withstand the pressures that come with implementing any new corporate strategy. Not so much making shared services indestructible but rather making sure that certain key elements are solidly in place for success. These elements are an important foundation in shaping the business within a business mentality.

These are the critical elements that need to be built into the foundation:

1 Operating principles that need to be agreed to by the CEO and executive.

2 Pricing models and structure.

3 Service level agreements.

4 Internal billing for services.

To get started, the leader must develop a clear set of operating principles that need to be endorsed by the corporate executive team. These principles are designed to enable the shared services organization to succeed by spelling out certain conditions for the operation. These are known informally as the rules. They govern what is in and what is out for the shared services organization. For example, there needs to be a rule about outsourcing. Secondly, once the rules are agreed to, there needs to be a planned and orderly approach to what prices will be charged and how they will be charged. Too many pricing models will mean a costly infrastructure that will be a burden on the costs. Once the prices are set, there is a need to define service level agreements with internal clients that lay out the level and standard of products and services at what price. For example, for $8 per transaction in finance, there will be a standard of 96% accuracy. Lastly, there is a need to design new internal systems for tracking and billing time. People now have to be accountable for where their time is spent.

KEY OPERATING PRINCIPLES FOR SHARED SERVICES SUCCESS

There are a number of principles that are essential for shared service success. The following are those for which we usually recommend the leader seeks endorsement at the beginning of implementation:

+ there will be no duplication of services in business units once the service is designated as a shared service;

+ services will be charged at a rate to cover fully loaded costs;

+ governance-related activities will be paid for by the executive;

+ during an initial grace period (18–24 months) shared service functions will have exclusive supplier status;

+ following the grace period, decisions to outsource services will be made in the best interest of the corporation and will be based on a business case analysis;

+ business units have a joint accountability with the shared services organization to reduce operating costs and ensure the success of shared services;

+ the shared services organization will benchmark its costs with external best practices and will gather internal client satisfaction feedback;

+ the shared services organization will report annually to the corporate executive committee on costs and satisfaction level;

+ a shift in line management accountability.

The shift to shared services requires increased corporate discipline and a shift to enterprise-wide thinking. To that end, it is critical to ensure the principles are endorsed so that the shared services group can have a legitimate go at success. These principles in essence provide for a fair playing field at the start. The principles are not mutually exclusive but are interwoven in many ways.

No duplication of services

For shared services to optimize the scale and benefits, it is necessary to have approval that there will be only one shared services supplier. If business units are able to opt out and leave the shared services group with sunk costs and stranded assets the expected efficiencies and cost savings will not be realized. There needs to be only one source for any specified service. This means that once it is decided that certain functions are to be consolidated into a shared services center the business units no longer have the option of performing these services themselves. There must be a clear definition of what specific services are being transferred to the shared services organization. If it is decided that human resources generalist services are to become a shared professional and advisory service the business units will no longer retain resources to carry out these functions.

The business units must agree to respect the entity and not create their own phantom organizations in direct competition with the shared services group. In cases where business units have had a high degree of autonomy and little consequence for failure to comply with corporate standards, it can be difficult to impose these kinds of principles for success. For this reason the principles must be agreed to at the highest level in the organization and line executives must be held accountable for living up to the intent of the agreement.

Charge out at fully loaded costs

The shared service organization must charge out its services to recover fully loaded costs. This means that the true cost of the service is visible to the business unit. The business units must understand how the rates and prices are built and that the rates are fully loaded. Figure 9.1 illustrates the components of what is included in a fully loaded charge out rate.

There are four key cost components that need to be looked at in any shared service operation:

1 Service labor costs are those, including benefits, incurred in carrying out services on behalf of the client. These include the labor costs for carrying out transactional processing as well as the labor costs of providing professional and advisory services.

2 Governance labor costs are those associated with the development of corporate policies, procedures, standards and guidelines carried out on behalf of the executive.

3 Administrative costs are the labor costs for carrying out internal administrative work such as contract administration, time tracking and other work that is non-client specific such as meeting atten-

dance, committee participation and marketing. These include the labor costs of administrative support staff as well as management and executives of the shared services organization.

4   Overhead costs are those incurred for the facilities that the group occupies and could include heat, rent, telephone, furnishings and equipment such as computers, photocopiers.

Charge out rates for shared services that are designed to recover fully loaded costs must therefore include service, administration and overhead costs. The total of these costs is what must be recovered by the organization in a defined time or budget period.

Administration and overhead costs are key areas for attention if the fully loaded rates are perceived to be too high or are out of line with externally benchmarked cost. A major impact on administrative costs is the number of levels of management in the shared services organization. These need to be minimized so that the costs for administration are not overly high. It is also paramount that the ratio of

| **service costs** | + | **administration costs** | + | **overhead costs** | = | **fully loaded costs** |

FIGURE 9.1   Components that go into building the charge out rate

Service costs	**Governance charges**
• Labor costs to carry out transactional, administrative or professional, advisory work for clients	• Labor costs to develop corporate policies, procedures, standards and guidelines
• Charged back to clients based on negotiated service level agreements	• Charged back to the executive office or as a corporate-wide allocation
• Charged at a rate to recover fully loaded costs or at prices comparable to external suppliers (market-based pricing)	

Administration	**Overheads**
• Labor costs, including benefits for doing administrative work (e.g. contract admin, time tracking) and work that is non-client specific (e.g. attending meetings, committee participation, marketing)	• Costs incurred for facilities (e.g. rent, heat, telephone, furnishings) and equipment (e.g. computers)

Administration and overhead costs are built into rates charged for client services and governance functions

billable to non-billable time be carefully monitored. If groups spend too much time on their own development or in meetings that are non-billable, it will soon be readily apparent that the target for recoveries will be hard to meet. Overhead costs can be dramatically impacted by the location chosen for the shared services center. Rent charges in large urban office spaces can significantly increase costs to clients.

Governance will be paid for by the executive

Most organizations will want to try to separate the governance function from the services function. This will also apply to the recovery of costs. In other words, if the executive and board require significant services that pull shared services away from being able to recover from internal clients, this will impede the ability for shared services to stand on its own two feet. The costs incurred in carrying out governance activities, including the associated administration and overhead costs, need to be visibly separated from the costs of delivering services to clients.

While there may be no desire to actually charge the executive for these services the costs need to be visible and separate. At Mutual Life of Canada, there was a very deliberate move to make these charges transparent. Marianne Elliot, the vice president of shared services at the time, wanted to send clear signals to the top of the house about what the purchasing patterns were. If the business units were going to have to pay for products and services, they reckoned that the executive should do likewise and experience life as a paying choosing client.

Grace period

Everyone needs a fighting chance to get their organization up and operating before clients pass judgement and go outside to purchase services externally. It is therefore advisable to give a window of the first eighteen months to two years during which clients have no choice but to use the internal service provider. This does not mean that the shared services group has a monopoly for all services. If the organization regularly used external consultants for a certain kind of work, for example, then this practice would continue. If the standard practice was to use internals for this work, then it would be expected that this would continue for a period of 18–24 months. This grace period is to help the shared services group organize itself and to "get its act together" without the threat of clients moving on to alternative suppliers. The group needs the opportunity to fine-tune and revise its products and services, lower costs, and improve client satisfaction.

The grace period is a required element for success. In the long term, a business case should be required before any services are sought from an outside provider. This is not intended as a bureau-

The move to shared services is not a recipe for anarchy

cratic exercise but rather imposes a rigor on any decision to outsource services. The decision to move to shared services is often greeted with glee by business unit clients who now feel they can buy the services they want from wherever they want. Decisions to outsource services are in many cases made by the shared services group when it realizes its costs or service quality are not competitive. Internal and external service costs must be carefully analyzed to ensure that they are truly comparable. Even when it is clear that external service costs are truly lower there are a number of factors that impact the viability of going outside. If the organization will end up with a number of stranded assets as a result of going outside, these costs would have to be built into the business case.

Joint accountability for reducing costs and shared services success

Unlike a typical client/supplier relationship there needs to be clear joint accountability for ensuring success of the shared services group. As "partners," business units must do their best to ensure that they do not act in a way that puts undue financial burdens or demands on the shared services function. This would mean dramatically reducing demand mid-way through the budget cycle. Business units must live up to commitments related to service volumes and if their needs change they need to work with the shared services group to mitigate the impact on the shared services business.

In many cases, it is obvious from the start that costs are higher in shared services compared to external suppliers. This is due to a number of reasons. It could be that the negotiated labor rates are high, it could mean that the office space is expensive. It could also mean too many steps in a process due to corporate practice and the bureaucracy of tradition. For example, it may cost $10 to process a financial transaction due to the inaccurate inputs from the business units or the fact that the corporate group must hound business units for their inputs. In these cases, the business unit executive could help shared services reduce its process by doing a better job of the front-end and should have an accountability to do so.

Once the shared services organization begins to explore the costs of providing products and services and making a concentrated effort to lower costs, it will be apparent that the business units need to participate in the cost reduction process. Many of the issues which could enable the shared services group to reduce costs are not in their direct control and it is only with the support and assistance of the business units that these cost savings can be realized.

A shift in line management accountability

Fundamentally, shared services offers the opportunity to make a dramatic shift in accountability, especially in the policy area. Most service centers are getting out of the business of checking checkers. In the travel and expense administration area, line managers need to take accountability for their signature. Why should shared service groups check for policy compliance when the boss has already signed the expense report? Who is in charge anyway? This kind of double checking is simply not affordable any longer and it is high time that line managers accepted their role in getting their people to abide by company policy.

One of the surprising dilemmas for shared service groups is what to do when demand exceeds supply. Although most new shared service groups in a marketplace model are afraid of having to reduce staff because of lower demand, many groups have found in fact that demand has gone up. On the one hand, a shared services group could decide it will incrementally staff up to meet this demand but on the other hand, this may not be in the best interests of the corporation. To deal effectively with this scenario, shared service groups need to escalate this dilemma to the senior executive level of the business unit. Executives need to make a collective decision or alternatively need to prioritize which services are the most important.

Benchmarking and customer feedback

It is wise to let the executive know that benchmarking will be a regular form of doing business so that the shared services group can provide realistic comparisons of costs on demand: apples for apples. The practice of benchmarking is commonplace although you can always find people bucking the trend and finding all kinds of ways and reasons for not doing so. In shared services, it is a necessary element to success. The leaders of shared services have a responsibility to ensure that their products and services are defensible on the price points, that the prices are reasonable *vis-à-vis* the external marketplace.

The companion to price is the need to engineer a defensible formalized client feedback about the level of satisfaction business units have with the shared services group. These two pieces of data should help to dissuade the negative ones from seeing this as just another centralization exercise.

This commitment to benchmarking and formalized client feedback sends a positive message that this is going to be a business model and not a corporate exercise in control. It shows a willingness to operate in a fact-based environment, in an atmosphere of candid comparison, in a place where shared services offers itself up to outside scrutiny. This commitment alone can often improve the reputation and profile of many corporate and internal functions. It is a sign of maturity and openness.

Report annually

There should be an annual reporting back to the CEO and executive group on the results and outcomes of the shared services' past operating year. This is a good business practice and one that is a reliable method for holding shared services accountable for progress. The reporting out needs to include the target and the actual rate of recovery of fully loaded costs. In addition to the financials, there should be an overview of the internal client feedback, pointing out the biggest areas of strength and the areas for improvement. There needs to be an accompanying action plan for addressing the areas requiring improvement.

At this time, it would be wise for shared services to make any recommendations on changes in the principles and to give any advice on services that should be outsourced. In other words, the outsourcing decision should ultimately be left up to the CEO and executive. This annual reporting time is a taking stock of the past year with a nod to the future. For example, if the past year has shown that in one area of service the costs are still too high compared to external vendors and the client satisfaction is low, this is an obvious choice for outsourcing. The executive may still choose to retain this service in-house even though the data is compelling, requiring the shared services group to work harder at either lowering costs or improving satisfaction. After all, this is not a simple mathematical formula.

You can see from looking at the set of principles that they do in fact lay important groundwork for the business of shared services to get off on the right foot. Once these principles have been understood and agreed to by the CEO and executive committee, the focus for the shared services organization is to take a turn inwards. The next major piece of work has to do with pricing, service level agreements and internal systems for billing and tracking.

PRICING MODELS

Pricing and charging business units or other clients for services is a fundamental tool for establishing the shared services function as a true business within the business. It is an essential vehicle for shifting the culture of the shared services group and for changing the attitude of clients. When the shared service organization is treated purely as a cost center, it is almost impossible to convince people that things are any different than they were under centralization of services.

IBM Canada's Customer Support Operations group, a shared services group, moved from an allocation approach to a direct charge or usage basis. The implications, illustrated in Figure 9.2, showed clearly that clients were in the driving seat of defining service options and volumes.

FIGURE 9.2   IBM Canada's Customer Support Operations group

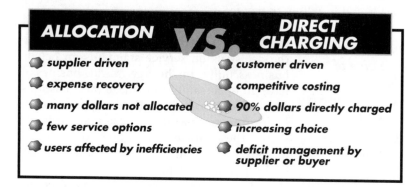

One of the most important impacts of direct charging for services is to shift people's attitudes away from a cost focus to one of pricing. When people think pricing, they automatically begin to think in terms of unbundling products and services, maximizing choice for internal clients. Although it may be tempting to create a number of different price models, the word simple still needs to apply.

The two most common ways for pricing are transaction-based and service- or project-based. For transactional processing services provided in the basic model of shared service, the predominant methodology for pricing is transaction-based where the price of the service is based on the unit volume of the service being provided. Pricing is based on a transaction cost such as $6 per accounts payable transaction or $5 for a dental claim processed. Pricing for transactional processes are usually an easier proposition since the transactions are finite and can be clearly bounded. For transactional processing services the other form of pricing is service-based where the price is based on an annual price for services being provided – a lump sum fee of say $350,000 for employee benefits processing.

For transactional processes using transaction-based pricing there can be unbundled optional pricing levels based on different service quality or service delivery requirements. For example:

✦ regular transactions @ $6 per transaction

✦ rush (within eight hours) @ $12

✦ rush (within one hour) @ $200.

This example shows the need to define pricing based on actual costs and that prices will differ depending on the standard expected. Likewise in network services in IT, the price will be higher if the standard is for 0–5% downtime versus 5%–10%. The business units in this case are accountable for deciding which standard their business needs and is willing to pay for.

This thinking and understanding of what different businesses may need is fundamental to defining a range of pricing models

In the old days of corporate centralization, it was the corporate and internal functions that made the decisions on service standards on behalf of the business units. In the new world, business leaders have an opportunity to manage their businesses and make decisions on standards required to run the operation successfully. These standards will vary across the companies and operating units. People directly involved in the work itself need to be a part of this pricing modeling.

Professional and advisory services are a much more complicated proposition when it comes to pricing. The basic pricing options for professional and advisory work, however, are not that different from transactional processing pricing. There is transaction-based pricing that is based on the unit volume of service delivered and there is service/project pricing. Transaction-based pricing for professional and advisory functions can be based on hourly or daily rates but relate to the amount of time and resources that are allocated to the client. Service/project-based pricing is based on a price for a specified package of work or a project or is based on an annual or budget period fee for services, similar to a retainer fee for a specified level of ongoing services.

The goal in pricing is to keep it as simple as possible. It is recommended that hourly rates be avoided since they are complex to manage and typically are offensive to clients. Hourly rate pricing requires a costly infrastructure to track time and hours. Generally, professional firms adopt a combination of daily rates and overall fixed project costs. There may be some pricing of products on a fixed basis. This is in mature organizations where the costs have been well established and consulting firms have confidence in publishing fixed rates for some of their products and services.

One of the key dilemmas is whether to differentiate daily rates according to the level of the resource. In other words, do you charge different rates for a more senior financial advisor than an intermediate or junior advisor? Although consulting firms and law practices do differentiate, it is our experience that a smoothed out rate for shared services advisory staff will make for better balance in the short term.

In the long term, it may be necessary to set differentiated rates but it is not recommended in the short term especially in what we will call traditional cultures and organizations. In large, formerly regulated industries such as telecommunications and the energy sector or in the public sector, it would be a complete shock to publicly show the different rates based on experience or hot skills and knowledge. Pricing would now make wages quite transparent in a way that has not been done before.

In maverick organizations with strong entrepreneurial cultures and those with survival of the fittest cultures, it may be quite appropriate to go for differentiation early on. In this kind of shared services model, there would need to be a recognition that rates may differ depending on demand. In external firms, if the demand for a consultant goes up, the rate typically follows. Imagine a bidding war internally for the same person from information technology.

Differentiation will add infrastructure costs since it is cheaper to manage with smoothed out rates. These are some of the decisions that need to be made early on in pricing. Reliant Energy established clear pricing objectives at the start of its shared services implementation as outlined in figure 9.3.

When you boil down the objective of pricing, it is to send the right price signals. The idea is to give enough information so that clients can make informed decisions. Generally, there is a basic level of service and an enhanced level of service: providing different prices enables clients to make their own decision as to what is best for them.

Market-based pricing

Up to this point we have discussed the concept of pricing to recover fully loaded costs. As organizations move to the advanced marketplace model, prices charged to clients shift to being tied to those of similar services available from the external marketplace. Market-based pricing, in contrast to full-cost recovery, is not based on the goal of recovering all the service costs but on being competitively priced with external suppliers of similar services. While some services are unique

FIGURE 9.3   Reliant Energy's pricing objectives

RELIANT ENERGY'S pricing objectives

- *to provide the appropriate price signals to help customers make better decisions;*

- *to provide proper charging mechanisms based on utilization from business units;*

- *to provide a set of cost management tools to help business units determine the relationship between cost and value of services in order to meet current and future requirements.*

to each organization it can be argued that a high percentage of the services could be purchased from external suppliers. Many business unit managers are aware of external suppliers and their prices and question paying higher prices for internal services. In this model all services are compared with any alternative service available to the customer and comparative prices are used to establish internal service market-based prices.

The key dilemma in moving to market-based pricing is making provision for costs that are under-recovered as a result of this approach to pricing. These provisions could include reducing overheads, increasing efficiency and, in some cases, eventually outsourcing the service if it cannot become competitive.

Shared services functions which have moved to market-based pricing are typically prevented from making a profit except on services sold commercially in the external marketplace. When internal "profits" are generated by the shared services group due to the relationship between its market-based prices and actual costs, some organizations return the profits to the clients in the form of dividends or for future pre-paid services. In other organizations, however, these profits are used for capital purchases to enable further cost reductions of the shared services. Once the pricing models are set, it is time to begin the process of service level agreements.

SERVICE LEVEL AGREEMENTS

A service level agreement (SLA) is the contract that defines the relationship between the shared services supplier and a client. These contracts need to be simple and clear and are not in place to define the resolution of every conceivable circumstance that could arise in the course of doing business. The advice that is provided consistently over time by shared services organizations is "make them simple." It is essential not to create bureaucratic infrastructure with complicated service level agreements that include pages of legalistic boilerplate and "what ifs." This simply won't work and will add enormous costs to the shared services organization. Therefore there has to be a principle for simplicity up front.

In organizations where there is low trust and low mutual respect, business units have been known to press for more complexity than need be. This is where business units will want endless standards spelled out like legal service contracts with external suppliers. In this case, it is critical to try to accommodate their needs. Ideally service level agreements are about one to two pages in length and spell out the description of services, the standards of service such as response time or quality. For example, do you commit to providing an accuracy rate of 100% or a response time on the help desk within half an hour?

Service level agreements need to answer, in a concise and simple manner, the following questions:

◆ What does the client expect?

◆ What will we supply or deliver?

◆ How frequently do we need to supply it?

◆ To what quality standard?

◆ At what price?

◆ What are the clients' obligations?

FIGURE 9.4   Sample service level agreement from Reliant Energy

Service Level Agreement

Supplier name (Shared services unit) _____

Contract Period: From_____ To _____

Business Unit name:_____

1. Description of products and/or services to be provided
   End products or services to be delivered
   Level of service to be provided

2. Service standards and performance measures
   Deadlines, response times
   Quality standards e.g. Accuracy or uptime

3. Pricing
   Charges for services being provided
   Method and frequency for charges

4. Operating principles
   Handling of excess demand, consequences for failure
   to meet standards
   Major contingencies

5. Improvement targets
   Specific improvement targets for selected cost and
   service standard indicators

_____   _____
Signed Shared Services Unit   Signed Business Unit Executive

✦ What happens if we don't meet these expectations?

✦ What happens if client doesn't meet their obligations?

✦ What recourse do we both have if there is failure on both sides?

Source: Service level agreement content from Kaiser Permanente

Kaiser Permanente describes four steps to the development of a service level agreement. The steps, illustrated in table 9.1, start with an initial identification of what services are being considered for which client and generally how the relationship will be defined between the players. The second step involves defining the responsibilities of both the shared services provider and the business unit client. This step also includes a description of how the services will flow to the client. Once these basics are defined and agreed to, the specifics of what services will be provided, at what cost and within what standards of performance, are negotiated. This step also includes agreement on what consequences, positive and negative, there will be for performance above or below the agreed upon performance standard. Finally they describe the review process necessary to ensure the required levels of performance and client satisfaction are achieved.

TABLE 9.1 Kaiser Permanente: four steps to service level agreement definition

1. Identify	2. Define	3. Negotiate	4. Review
Scope: What are the services provided by the shared services center?	**Responsibilities:** What is the delineation of responsibility between the shared services center and the business unit?	**Responsiveness:** What are the agreed upon service levels?	**Performance:** Did the shared service center meet its targets?
Participants: Which business units are involved?		**Costs:** What will client pay for the services provided?	**Compliance:** Did each party comply with the defined agreement?
Relationships: How are service centers related to each other? How is each service center related to each business unit?	**Requirements:** What capabilities are required by the business units?	**Measures:** How will the parties measure responsiveness, accuracy?	**Satisfaction:** Are both parties satisfied with the results?
	Interfaces: How will information and services flow between the service center and the business unit?	**Consequences:** What are each party's incentives, bonuses, and penalties?	**Scope:** Are there other products or services that must be included in the next agreement?

One key issue with service level agreements is the level at which they are signed. It is recommended that service level agreements be signed at the senior executive level of the business unit. Generally, this agreement should cover the core products and services. The rationale for one major service level agreement per business unit is that you do not want middle management wheeling and dealing, cherry picking services as they see fit. Rather you need to achieve overall agreement on the core suite of products and services as well as an estimate of how much discretionary service they plan on purchasing.

In the first year of shared services operation, it is essential to get a good handle on the expectations for service volumes and level. Service level agreements are a way of doing this. The other advantage of SLAs is that they provide a useful vehicle for educating the clients in informal ways about how and why rates are the way they are, and what is done on their behalf. This is frequently the first time that clients develop an understanding of what services are provided and what goes into the provision. They may find out, for example, that it costs them money when corporate and internal units double check inputs from the business units.

INTERNAL BILLING FOR SERVICES

Once the pricing models are developed and service level agreements signed and sealed, the last part of infrastructure has to do with establishing a billing strategy and methodology. Recent concerns from

FIGURE 9.5   Summary of pricing and billing strategies

BILLING STRATEGY	COMMENTS
No billing for services	- provides customer with no visible recognition of service value - can result in unrealistic service expectations with no recognition of impact
Allocation of service costs	- no relationship between services used and cost to customer - similar issues to no billing
Direct charging – full cost recovery	- visible relationship between service volumes used and cost to customer - pressures from customers to reduce costs
Direct charging – market-based pricing	- less pressure from customers to reduce service costs - service function must be financially viable or services should be outsourced

experienced shared services organizations demonstrate that building too much infrastructure for the purposes of internal billing can reverse the positive effects expected. Billing methods should not be cumbersome or expensive to implement. Figure 9.5 provides a summary of various pricing and billing approaches.

It is not recommended to invest large sums of capital to create an internal billing system. There is a story on the shared services conference circuit that reportedly has one shared services group making a case to the executive team for a $12 million internal billing system which needless to say was turned back post haste.

Most shared service organizations stop short of sending an invoice for work performed but rather send a summary statement of charges on a monthly basis. This ensures that both parties are conscious of the state of the nation at any given time.

TIME TRACKING

If you thought completing time sheets was a thing of the past, think again. It looks different, it is on a screen but it is the same concept. EAP systems such as SAP and Peoplesoft have reinvented the process of having people account, at a detailed level, where they spend their time and on what. In shared services, time tracking is essential. Shared services staff must take accountability for managing their time and take a disciplined approach to managing the costs of providing services. This is where the culture change begins. Most companies have some kind of tracking system for payment purposes but the one for shared services has to have real meat and real teeth. It is a priority for staff in consulting roles.

New shared services providers in professional advisory services often grossly underestimate their true costs when expressed on a daily or hourly basis. Some staff will be shocked when confronted with the reality of their costs expressed in terms of billable minutes. Asking the question, "What have you done in the last five minutes that a client would be willing to pay you $10.40 for?" is a powerful way to bring home the reality of what it means to be a provider of professional advisory services.

At a collective level, the shared service groups need to understand how they are doing on recovering costs. At an individual level, staff have to understand how they are personally doing against their time or project estimates. In the past, a professional might estimate it would take five or six days to prepare a report. Whether they were over or under the estimate this would not be a big problem. Now fast forward to shared services: imagine that the report was quoted to take five or six days and actually took ten to twelve. This is now a big issue and has to be reconciled. To know this fact however meant that the time was accurately tracked.

The first year will be a large adjustment period for the staff in shared services, especially for the professional advisory people who now have to take accountability for estimating correctly and for tracking their effort. If the estimate was just plain wrong, then the shared services organization is going to have a problem meeting recovery targets and will have to make adjustments. If time overruns were caused by changed requirements on the part of the client, then the advisor will have to go back and re-contract for a new price.

There are many questions and dilemmas of this nature that will arise in the billing and tracking process. If the technology and systems are easily available and adaptable to internal billing, automation can help. Software systems that track time are readily available. Simple manual systems can be just as effective. A paper stapled inside a project file folder can also do the trick for tracking time spent.

The very process of tracking and billing is what will start to change the culture for the shared services organization. It is an essential tool for change. It is difficult to isolate issues such as culture change in the implementation of shared services because at this point, the change is happening. For the leaders of shared services, these tasks in setting up shared services provide the right vehicle for conversations with staff and with clients.

Defining the principles of operating, designing the pricing options and service level agreements all contribute to the transformation of a corporate function into a business. They are important tools, they are the mechanics of shared services implementation. They are not the whole story though. The real key to implementing shared services successfully is the ability to shift the culture away from bureaucracy to a service mindset.

Chapter 10

CREATING A CULTURE
OF COMMITMENT

You can't damage gold by getting it wet or leaving it exposed to the elements. Unlike silver, copper and aluminium, gold is as bright and shiny as the day it was dug out of the ground. Gold is enduring

It was Jack Welch, chairman of General Electric, who once brilliantly captured the difficulties of turning strategy into action when he said, "The soft stuff is the hard stuff." The degree of culture change required to enact shared services successfully is enormous. To make shared services endure the inevitable storms, there will have to be a long process of culture change. Failure to pay attention to the soft side of change is a recipe for underperformance or worse, abandonment of the strategy before it even gets off the ground. The reality of corporate politics and strategy is that executives often fail at execution for two reasons. By the time big corporate strategies and initiatives achieve the endorsement and approval to go ahead, executives often unconsciously think the job is done and move on to the next major issue on their busy agendas. Secondly, executives often underestimate the amount of work that has to be done in helping people get through this kind of dramatic change. Culture change is core to success, it is what will make shared services endure.

The job is not done, just because the decision has been made! Executives who were involved in the decision process may feel they have crossed the finish line, whilst the rest of the organization is trying to figure out how to qualify for the race and what the course entails. Executives who have been successful at making shared services a reality will all tell you that they had to work hard at the culture piece. As Bertil Wrethag, president of ABB Support Services, said, "We worked hard on culture because we wanted a partnership with our clients but we also knew that unless our own people felt and behaved like partners with each other, we would never get there." Sound strategies that make things better always result in change to existing rules and practices and change means resistance. As Steven Kerr, the chief learning officer for GE, says, "People don't resist change, they resist being changed." Executives are often amazed when faced with less than enthusiastic staff. They are disappointed that staff don't share their enthusiasm even though it is perfectly normal. What has to be learned is that anything worth doing will be difficult to implement. It's not easy when there are the rules of the new market-place to learn. People endorse initiatives easily and early when they have little meaning or are seen as irrelevant. On the other hand, strategies that cause deep philosophical debate are the ones that have meaning. Shared services is a strategy that should cause vigorous discussion. It is a profoundly different direction for corporate staff groups which now have to think about surviving on the strength of their products and services, and on their ability to build strong client relationships. It can on occasion cause enormous upheaval with displacement of staff and be a tough transition.

All too often we hear shared service pundits going into enormous detail about the mechanics and the technical details of implementation. Everything from ERP systems and commissionaire structures, all the way to how to handle the Euro or design a new technology interface. These receive critical attention. Yet, when it comes to the most difficult and complex part of the transition, changing attitudes and behaviors to create a service culture, there is very little action to back it up. "We need to put a change management program in place," is sometimes as far as it gets. Even the term change management sounds like a mechanical process as if one simply inserts a disc into a machine and *voilà* it plays. Getting people ready to accept shared services takes considerable effort and investment. Just because management and executives think it is a great idea doesn't mean staff will flock to sign on board. The major lessons in this process from experienced implementers are the following:

+ expect anxiety and skepticism;
+ accept the reality that there will be attrition;
+ plan to communicate at least ten times more than you expected;
+ do not sugar-coat the truth at any time;
+ treat displaced people with dignity;
+ get managers to bring staff on board: don't do their job;
+ get people focused on improving service to clients.

STAFF INTRIGUES AND CONCERNS WITH SHARED SERVICES

During the process of getting employee commitment, we have found it useful to find out early on from staff what intrigues them and what concerns them about shared services. This helps to create a platform for communication and education throughout the process by building on the positives as well as managing the negative aspects. Here are the most frequent answers.

People do find the idea of shared services intriguing. There is energy for moving away from a corporate bureaucracy to being part of a service business that is accountable for delivering quality. People find it exciting to be at the start of something new, to begin from a blank page and try to get it right. Staff in corporate groups who are moving to a marketplace model are genuinely keen to separate out policy from services and try this new and fundamentally different model. There are many staff groups which want the chance to be part of a new operating model and although anxious about the future are still able to see the benefits.

FIGURE 10.1   What intrigues people about shared services

What concerns people

The first and foremost concern has to do with the potential for layoffs and feared job losses. This is a legitimate concern and may well become reality if the organization is considering a green field site or a geographic location different than where the critical mass of people are located. As well, corporate groups are naturally concerned about their ability to compete, to provide quality services at prices the clients will be willing to pay for. There is also an underlying concern about the ability to pull off the strategy, to bring people's skills up to speed, to get the whole team working in the same direction, and that is to be client-centered. There is usually a dawning recognition of the difficulty involved to amalgamate and consolidate dispersed geographic centers. At the very heart of the concerns, though, is the fundamental fear of job loss (see Figure 10.2).

Job loss can be a reality

The potential for job loss is a fact when organizations choose to create a new location or need to amalgamate and consolidate dispersed geographic centers. To expect that staff will be happy over the fact that

FIGURE 10.2   Concerns about implementing shared services

service will be increased and costs lowered even though they don't have a job is unrealistic to say the least. The hard reality is that employees are naturally going to be worried about themselves. And so they should be! For organizations in unionized environments, the protocols and rules are pretty clear about layoffs and redundancies when it comes to the terms of the settlement. But the fundamental issue is how do executives position the move to shared services and how can an organization minimize the damage from such a tough decision? There is no question that the strategy needs to be positioned. People need to paint the big picture for staff, outline the cost savings and benefits to the organization as a whole in order to try to provide reasons for the move. At the end of the day, if the answer is still job loss for individuals, the organization should have an answer as to what it is offering displaced people. Facts do not soften the blow, although it is essential to take the time to educate staff on the numbers and cost savings being achieved through consolidation.

The job losses are mainly centered around consolidation and standardization which impact people in the transactional processing area. Moving to global finance centers definitely displaces staff. Some organizations do a better job than others when it comes to managing downsizing. There may be some opportunity to absorb people into other jobs but at the end of the day, staff numbers will have to be reduced in order to realize the benefits outlined in the business case.

Where layoffs are almost impossible

For countries and companies that tend to offer more of a safety net to their employees due to cultural norms, or might even have stringent labor agreements that prohibit layoffs without penalty, there are still opportunities. The answer is to declare the employees surplus and not design the redundant staff into the center. Decisions such as layoffs are negative at best and it is better to deal with people impacted swiftly and with dignity. It is critical to get across messages to staff that this has nothing to do with their performance, that everyone has tried their best but that the only solution is a move to shared services.

> *The worst thing any shared service center can do is have too many staff, especially when some of the staff have no long-term future with the organization*

Given that implementation of shared services is anywhere from 12–18 months, there is time to try to minimize impacts through good human resource strategies such as early retirement, incentives to resign, and a careful hands-on managing of staff through this difficult process. Some organizations will use good position control to try to have as many displaced people as possible placed in other jobs. Ideally, organizations will involve the union executive early on in the process so that they too can help in the transition.

Some organizations will not have such severe people impacts due to the nature of their shared service designs and may be looking at a much smaller scale of operation than a worldwide financial processing center. No matter what the size, there has to be a concentrated effort at education and understanding so that managers and staff affected are part of the process. Although there will never be one perfect time or 100% commitment for the idea, the requirement is to get the consolidation in place and to start the change process. Darcy Volk, general manager of the Unisys Shared Services Center, captures this notion brilliantly when she says, "Even if you get it in ugly, get it in." This is why shared services has failed when organizations toy around with reengineering before consolidating the services or when corporate staff groups try to implement it without top executive support.

THE DYNAMICS OF EMPLOYEE BUY-IN AND COMMITMENT

When faced with the ideology of shared services, there is a tendency for people to be overly enthusiastic about the benefits. After all, the stories for cost savings are pretty amazing.

Here are a few unrealistic thoughts. It is working if:

+ everyone buys in and is totally committed;

+ people stay and don't leave;

+ I could get all new people; the old ones just won't work; staff just don't get it;

+ we could train our internal clients to deal with us, they would like us better.

Much has been written about organizational change and how to achieve the elusive buy-in and commitment. It is unrealistic to believe that you will get everyone to buy in and, in fact, you don't want everyone to buy in, especially at the beginning. It is far better to be realistic and consider the following. Think of the 30–30–30 rule and assume 10% are somewhere in between. There are about 30% of employees who will drive the change, 30 percent who will sit on the fence – these people are the swing factor and could go either way – and the bottom 30% who will not do much to help. In fact, they will block the change.

| TABLE 10.1 | The dynamics of buy-in and commitment | | |

Top 30%	Middle 30%	Lower 30%
Top 30% of employees and managers – these are the people who will embrace shared services, grab the bull by the horns, and say it is about time. These are the people who will make it happen. Watch out, some of these people are quiet, unassuming, and not the ones who necessarily look and act like stereotypical champions of change. People in this category are generally the top performers within staff groups and are confident in the role of the groups, in their own ability to make things happen despite the bureaucracy. For these kinds of people, this is an opportunity to separate the wheat from the chaff, to make staff people accountable for delivering what clients want. Entrepreneurs at heart, shared services provides an opportunity for these people to test out what it would be like to be in the business world where results are directly tied to effort. Shared services is a motivator and can often work to retain top performers who find it difficult to shine in a traditional corporate staff culture.	Middle 30% of employees and managers – they are ambivalent. They are like the swing factor in politics that can make or topple a political party in the polls. They could get on board but will wait and see what happens and who ends up in the top 30% category. People in this category might also be happy to see shared services fail. People in this category are torn. They see the innate logic of shared services and know that it could work. They also are afraid of losing control and fear that clients will not want their services. These are generally good performers and may even be top performers but they lack confidence in either themselves or their products and services. Solid corporate performers at heart, shared services offers too much ambiguity and too many unknowns. Work is not as predictable as it once was and there is a fear of how it will all turn out. These people need convincing and reassurance to help them move forward.	Lower 30% of employees and managers – they do not believe in making corporate staff functions operate like a business. They believe in the inherent right of corporate staff groups to control, to operate according to their own professional standards. They fundamentally resist moving to an open marketplace. They see themselves as corporate guardians, there to protect the organization from itself. People in this category can be strong resistors and in some cases, actually try to sabotage shared services. They will use the "we are all one company" line to defend the status quo and insist that it is not proper to introduce the concept of internal clients. They will suggest that the company should operate as one big team with external customers being the only real customers. Corporate staffers at heart, these people believe that they know what is best for clients and that they are the ones to determine what kind of products, services, and policies are good for the organization. They will be hard to convince but there are some that over time will be able to make a slight shift although they will likely never be champions.

Attrition wanted

It could be said that one measure of success for any major significant shift in business strategy is the number of people who leave the organization because of fundamental disagreement with corporate direction or an inability to act in a manner compatible with the new strategy. Although the idea of creating opportunities for attrition may seem contradictory, there are benefits to attrition during the implementation of shared services. There are staff who will not be able to or want to operate in a model of accountability and service. Attrition is not firing but rather creating the kind of environment where people are able to identify that they do not fit. To achieve this kind of attrition, the executive of shared services must actively support and endorse the idea that attrition is not a bad thing and that it will assist people who ask to move on, by helping them find alternative employment within or outside the company.

Acknowledging that attrition is normal can be a liberating experience and demonstrate an uncommon degree of honesty and respect for staff. The move to shared services can be insurmountable to corporate people who have spent twenty or even thirty years being the corporate cop, being in control, and setting their own internal standards for quality. The very thought of business units choosing what reports they want and evaluating corporate staff on the quality of their service is simply too much for some people. Far better to help them exit gracefully and with dignity.

A CLEAN SWEEP

The idea of starting with a clean slate appeals to some newly appointed shared services leaders who may fantasize about wiping everyone out and starting over with new people. This factor alone can be the key driver for moving to an entirely new location for a shared service center. However, the reality is that there are many staff people who can and want to make the change to operating in the dynamic new marketplace. The value of corporate history and an understanding of the past cannot be underestimated. It is critical to know what has gone on before trying to recreate the future. Green field service operations will say that the one downside is having people who neither have history nor know how the business runs.

In at least two-thirds of cases, the people are not the problem. They are operating the way managers have always asked them to. Managers now have to ask for a new way of operating, showing:

✦ sensitivity and responsiveness to the needs of customers;

✦ willingness and ability to aquire new skills continuously;

✦ acceptance of personal responsibility for the results of actions;

✦ application of business disciplines and measures to all activities.

When executives of shared services say staff don't understand, the question is, "What are you going to do about it?" Education is a major component in any successful culture change and it has to start from the very beginning. People need to understand why the company is moving to shared services and there should be no sugar-coating of the truth. If demand falls, there will be implications. Perversely, there is nothing like the prospect of future unemployment should the new business fail. This is not a goal, and management has to make sure they are supporting people in their personal development and helping them to succeed. People also need the benefit of the education and understanding of what the executive went through to adopt the idea in the first place.

TRAINING CLIENTS TO LOVE US

One of the favorite myths around is that you can train and educate clients to learn how great the corporate staff functions really are. It is true that there have to be communication processes in place to help line managers and staff in the business units understand what will be different. This is not the same as training them how to be a good client. Prior to the introduction of shared services, staff groups often floated the idea of this kind of training as an answer to getting the love and respect they desire. Unfortunately, there is no known training program that results in undying love and affection for a staff group, only loyal clients who keep coming back because they are getting great service.

Clients generally love shared services anyway. Finally, they get to decide what they want, how they want it and when. Changing the culture begins the moment shared services is announced and clients realize that they are going to have the opportunity to move into a service relationship where they are treated as clients. This is the good shoe. The other shoe drops when they realize they now have increased accountability for their purchasing decisions. If a manager orders a report from finance, there will be a charge for the report. Nothing is free. One must think before buying. This is a major cultural change in accountability.

Having explored some of the myths about executing shared services strategy, it must be said that the change is risky, thrilling and frightening all at the same time. It is a little bit like working the trapeze without a net, especially for the staff groups within shared services. Staff people have to think about whether what they are doing adds value to the client or not. External consultants understand this dynamic since their revenue picture is directly tied to their perceived value. It is a new culture for internal staff groups.

CRITICAL ACTIVITIES TO ENSURE THE SUCCESS OF SHARED SERVICES

Since the implementation takes about 12–18 months, here are some of the critical activities required to help get shared services up and running. More importantly, these activities will help shared services endure.

When people understand the logic, when people get a chance to explore issues and dilemmas, to confront fears openly and talk with their peers, it makes it easier to move forward.

SHELL SERVICES INTERNATIONAL

Dennis Wymore, Management Consulting Group

The hardest thing for corporate staff people to learn is the humility it takes to earn a service relationship, to not take clients for granted.

The internal relationship is fragile and it is hard for staff people to focus on what the customer needs, not what we want them to want. It takes people who are secure and not afraid of risk. It does take real skill to engage clients.

TABLE 10.2   Building blocks for the staff in shared services

Element	People
Executive quarterly planning sessions	To help the top management team maintain momentum in the implementation; to bring issues for resolution; to pool important client information
Bi-annual management forums	To develop new leadership skills for managers and supervisors in how to run a client-centered business
Staff meetings × ten	To maintain momentum, keep communication channels wide open; to encourage problem resolution
Intranet and newsletters	A living history of issues and actions from senior management and management forums
Townhall meetings	Critical mass of shared service staff and management in relationship and project management; raise the bar of professionalism
Staff development	To provide a foundation of skills and competencies in relationship and project management; raise the bar of professionalism
Performance management	Redesign performance management and compensation to reflect at least 50% of the job tied to customer expectations and real outcomes
Rewards and recognition	New rewards and recognition deliberately tied to "new behaviors;" make rewards highly visible
A distinct identity or brand	A flag or trademark with which both staff and customers can identify and relate to positively because it is synonymous with quality service

Executive planning sessions

BC Hydro, which is an extremely well-run utility in Canada, has one of the country's largest multi-functional shared services groups. In operation since 1996, the scope is wide and includes all of finance, information technology, facilities, supply, and human resources. David Harrison, the CFO and senior vice president in charge of shared services, was very diligent during initial implementation: *first,* he insisted on quarterly executive planning sessions with all his direct reports in shared services; *second,* he decided to invest in management forums with about 90 of the management staff directly involved in running shared service units. These two actions alone played an essential part in shifting the culture. Historically, staff groups like finance and supply services never met because they saw nothing in common. So these actions were worth a million words!

The executive planning sessions served as an important touchstone to bring to light issues of concern from staff, to raise thorny issues on pricing or service quality, to discuss difficult client relationships. These management planning sessions always ended with concrete action planning that would advance and further the implementation of shared services. The regularity of and dedication to this kind of planning sent a clear signal to the staff that the top leadership team was indeed committed to making shared services a success.

Management forums

The leadership challenges during the implementation of shared services are significant and it is essential to work with the management team on its own. It does have a significant role in shaping how shared services will run and operate on a day to day basis. Managers have to help themselves and their people look at the organization through a new set of lenses. They have to see what the clients are seeing. It is also important to acknowledge and let managers air their own very real concerns about the impact of shared services and to do that away from their staff. This bringing together of managers therefore is a pivotal element in building a cross-functional service culture and getting people away from the narrow discipline approach. Middle management has been much maligned over the past few years with searing testimonials about them being major blockers and impediments to organizational change. Luckily the tide is turning and the value of middle management is once again on the ascent due to the realization of their contribution as integrators and managers of operations. Middle managers will actually make shared services work if the organization pays attention to their concerns and helps them to work on the positive elements. No longer on trial for being seen as a redundant layer, managers are the key to long-term success. Once they are part of the solution and given the opportunity to figure out how to make shared services work, managers have a job in assisting employees to see the up-side about working in an environment where business is earned and reputations rise or fall based on client satisfaction.

One of the best ways for executives to get managers started on the pathway to staff commitment is to design a session in the management forums that has them tasked with the following:

✦ to decide as managers in shared services how best to build staff commitment;

✦ to identify the processes and initiatives which should be developed to achieve this.

This forces managers to take responsibility and accountability for designing mechanisms which will result in improved staff understanding and commitment and keeps the lines clear between the executive role and the management role. Executives have to ensure that good management is in place, not do the job of the manager. Finally, it is critical to let the managers define what they need from the executive in order to succeed in their role. Typical responses include, "Support us with funding to do a good job of building staff commitment, support us when we want to manage poor performance, support us when we stumble and make mistakes, as we try to learn how to put shared services in place." The forums also serve as legitimate problem solving sessions. Here are some of the typical questions raised:

✦ What do we do if clients refuse to pay for our services?

✦ What do we do if clients change their requirements mid-way through projects?

These questions are part of any professional services firm's daily ritual, but for staff groups it is a whole new way of thinking about their work and they need time to chew over some of these pithy problems.

Newsletters and Intranet

As a way of maintaining continuity and leveraging the investments in forums of this nature, newsletters and bulletins that go out to staff need to be posted on a company Intranet. This is an excellent way of keeping shared services fresh and on everyone's mind. These kinds of communication tools do take a lot of care and feeding. People think once they put something up on the Intranet, the job is done. The point is to ensure the site is kept up to date and that it provides for real two-way interactive communication. Action items from the quarterly executive planning sessions and any management forums should be posted and distributed so that the whole staff group can see the forward motion.

Staff meetings

Managers are the ones who must help staff to succeed in the enterprise model. The best method for achieving culture change is to multiply exponentially the number of staff meetings during shared service implementation. Plan on frequent and longer staff meetings during the first twelve to eighteen months. Vary the type of agenda and style of meeting. Bring in outside speakers on the topic of shared services, bring in facilitators who can raise the issues and concerns, keep the discussion going. Social change or organizational change doesn't come from people at the top making announcements. It happens over time which is why the business of staff meetings and communications needs to be multiplied to a factor of ten times normal over the whole implementation period.

If managers and executives are guilty of one thing during culture change, it is the one big bang theory, notoriously referred to as the launch or kick-off. This method places high energy and enthusiasm on a one shot basis at the outset of the shared service announcements followed by a long and hollow silence for the rest of the time. Given that one of the major goals of shared services is to improve service, staff are the critical mass who shape the overall service mindset.

Building staff commitment: what will happen to me?

There will be a lot of unease within the staff ranks. Quite frankly, this strategy of moving to a full business model is a considerable change of rules for people. One day, a mandated staff function, the next day a services company. For people at the lower ranks in an organization, it can feel hopelessly out of control. After all, they had no real input into the decision and, in fact, believe that they are powerless to make the strategy successful.

The real question on people's minds during change is simply, "What will happen to me?" So although it is important to paint the bigger picture for staff and to help them understand what shared services is and what it will mean, managers need to tackle the big question directly. Since the move to a free market model means that clients now have considerable control over the destiny of the staff groups, the answer is likely to be, "We don't know." One thing for sure is never to sugar-coat the truth or dance around the issue of potential layoffs if business falls dramatically. It is so perplexing that many managers and executives

Ultimately, there is a great fear of telling people what they already know

have such a hard time being candid and telling the truth. Ultimately, there is a great fear of telling people what they already know. By the time the staff meetings start to roll out, people have figured out the impact of moving to shared services and have made the leap in logic that comes from a former life of mandated free services, to a business model where clients will have choice over the volume and type of products they receive.

Cynics argue that managers and executives are somehow deliberately out to shadow the truth from people. In actual fact, it is more likely out of wanting to shield people from bad news, a sort of quaint paternalism. It is far better to acknowledge openly that there may be reductions of staff and there may be certain functions over time that will not be retained in-house due to the inability to be competitive. These kinds of messages although not reassuring do set the tone for the new way of doing business and are an integral beginning.

There is no place for euphemism or ambivalence. Communication has to be clear, precise and from the top. The talk has to be action and people, not maybes and resources, and it has to be seen to come from the most senior levels of management. As Peter Block said in his book, *Stewardship*, "We need commitment from people when we can no longer offer them much security." Managers need to set the tone for staff to get involved and engaged in the business of improving service delivery and reducing costs. Their survival will literally depend on it so it is far better to get the message out on the table and up front.

Townhall: in person or video conference

The townhall idea is simply to get as many people as you can physically into one room or in one place through the use of video conferencing technology. Townhall meetings are an excellent vehicle for mobilizing energy and helping staff to build confidence by discovering that other people are just as concerned as they are about the future. This does a lot to build team spirit and to break down the barriers between functions and between the hierarchy. Managers, vice presidents and staff all finding out about shared services in one place at one time.

Staff development

Successful shared service organizations invest heavily in staff development to raise the bar for service quality and to help people develop positive skills for managing their client relationships. People in shared services generally need assistance in the areas listed in Table 10.3 depending on the nature of their work.

These skills do not have to be developed overnight but should form part of an overall curriculum designed to improve the professionalism and capability of internal shared service staff. Companies have got to see this development as an investment in their people and see it as one of the costs of doing business.

TABLE 10.3 Help for shared services staff	
Service centers for processing	**Professional and advisory services**
✓ service relationships	✓ relationship management
✓ problem solving	✓ consulting skills
✓ conflict resolution	✓ project management
✓ financial management	✓ financial management
✓ negotiating skills	✓ negotiating skills

Performance management and rewards

There is an old saying, "What gets measured, gets done." It is true that measures and performance management systems need to be revised to reflect the new service environment. However, there is a tendency to overcomplicate performance systems and create gigantic multi-layered, matrixed competency frameworks. Great for consultants who have to spend years training people how to understand them! If you have been around organizations long enough, you will no doubt recognize the complexity of competency-based performance management systems; elaborate schemes and layers of complicated ratings all meshing together into an apparent development plan. It is worse than reading instructions on how to program a VCR.

The point of any performance management system is simply to help individuals understand what is important in their job. Basically, people need to know what is expected of them and they need to get rewarded when they meet expectations. In shared services, the key shift is away from insular thinking and self-imposed standards of quality to total commitment in satisfying client expectations. A simple one-page form can do the trick provided that clients really do evaluate the quality. In other words, good old-fashioned performance management can work because it is how managers spend their time that really tells staff what is important. If there is no discernible change from corporate business as usual, they will know that shared services is just another one of those programs to wait out. If on the other hand they see managers and executives spending time with internal clients, going out to see clients in their locations, staff will quickly pick up the new service attitude. Jim Kouzes and Barry Posner, in their wide-ranging research on leadership practices, presented the idea, "You can't lead from a seated position. You can write a report, you can read a letter but you cannot actually lead anything unless you get up on your feet and go somewhere." In shared services, it better be going physically or psychologically to where the clients are operating.

Primary and secondary strategies for shifting the culture

Dr. Edgar Schein is one of the founding fathers of culture change and changing performance. His work illustrates that some strategies are more powerful than others when it comes to shifting performance and that the main focus of leaders should be on the primary strategies before worrying too much about the secondary ones.

Performance systems for shared services need to be redesigned to include an evaluation of service from the clients' perspective. Saying client satisfaction is important, and then getting measured for meeting budget targets, is too often the case. Schein's basic premise is that what managers and leaders do every day is what signals to staff what is really important. The secondary strategies are useful but not ideally the place to start.

TABLE 10.4   Applying Schein to shared services

Primary strategies	Secondary strategies
What leaders pay attention to, measure and control on a regular basis: % of performance appraisal based on client satisfaction	Organizational design and structure of shared services
How leaders react to critical incidents and organizational crises: how client disasters are handled	Shared service systems, technology and processes
Observed criteria by which leaders allocate scarce resources: money spent to improve client service	Design of physical space, façades and buildings including green field site
Deliberate role modeling, teaching, coaching: how much time managers spend with clients	
Observed criteria by which leaders allocate rewards and status: what gets rewarded in shared services	Formal statements of organizational philosophy, values and creed
Observed criteria by which leaders recruit, promote, retire and excommunicate organizational members: who gets ahead and who doesn't	

One of the critical incidents for any organization is budget preparation and approval. Reg Milley, the senior vice president of corporate services at Husky Oil, is in the process of moving to a shared services model. He was perplexed as to how to convince his staff functions to think and act pragmatically about budget requirements. He was steeling himself for the traditional pleading for more budget dollars. In most organizations, staff people traditionally spend time arguing and cajoling for a bigger slice of budget funds. With the advent of shared services he has noticed a difference. Staff come forward and say, "I think I can do with less this year, I think I can save money by doing this and that." Radically different than the past!

As has been discussed earlier, one of the biggest signals an organization can send about what is important is in the selection process. Who rises and who gets sidelined is one of the most powerful messages for what is now going to be important. In one organization, there had been a somewhat arrogant vice president of finance who was known for running a tight, iron-fisted fiefdom where finance acted like it ran the show. Service orientation was not in the skill set, nor did it seem to be valued. When the organization went to shared services, the vice president was removed and an outsider was brought in from a sales and marketing background. The organization got the message loudly. One of the senior managers in this organization said, "It reminds me of an ancient saying – shoot one monkey, scare thousands. It worked. We got the message about service."

Although organizational design, structure and systems are important, they are not the immediate focus to transmit culture change. Better to work on improving the service culture before designing elaborate pricing models and sophisticated service level agreements. One company we know has spent the last year behind closed doors, working up all the detailed arrangements about how shared services will succeed following a spectacular launch that painted an optimistic, brave new land for the clients. The clients meanwhile have seen nothing different and are quite jaded since, from their perspective, nothing has changed. A betting person would be willing to wager that either the strategy will fail or that corporate staff functions will be seeing some outsourcing pressure in the next year.

When shared services fail, it can usually be traced to an inordinate amount of attention on the mechanics and a failure to deal with the large or cultural issues

So to effect the culture change required, it is wise to invest heavily in the first twelve to eighteen months in helping people in the new shared services group engage in the successful running of the new enterprise. Mission and value statements are useful as a tool but they are not a replacement for the leadership group setting a tone for good service and spending real money to develop professional skills in relationship management. Service slogans on mugs and t-shirts are all right too but they alone do not change behaviors or embed new values on how to treat clients. Offering staff the opportunity for training and development in service management is a better way to get the values in place. Creating project teams where people are given the challenge of figuring out how to deliver services at half the current price may be one of the many dilemmas facing staff groups. Project teams like this are an excellent way of training people to think differently. Having the guts and courage to rethink the services and how best to deliver them may be second nature to entrepreneurs but for corporate staff people who have spent a lifetime in a bureaucracy, it is an incredible leap.

The reward for staff as one forward-thinking union executive put it is, "We may get to keep our job." Brutally honest, he was really trying to get union members to realize that the business of meeting client expectations is very serious stuff. Informal and formal rewards do work to keep the momentum and to signal explicitly what is desirable and by omission, what is not valued. Employees who consistently demonstrate a dedication to service should be openly recognized, as should those employees who make a difference by streamlining and cutting costs without sacrificing value. Staff functions, especially in the finance area and in areas of supply management, are not notorious for their ability to celebrate achievements in any kind of openly festive and showy manner. When finance and supply functions enter into the service enterprise model, there is a need to signal a major shift. Plaques, gifts, pins and awards need to be part of the way of doing business. Financial analyst of the year! Property manager of the month!

As John Ashurst, a frequent conference presenter on shared services, put it, the only thing that really counts is building a culture of service and relationships. This from the man who at the outset of designing and implementing shared services claimed that price would be the largest issue to focus on and that clients would never want their services because they would be priced too high. Initially skeptical of focusing on strong service relationships, he is now the biggest advocate for working at the soft stuff. He has noticed that the culture is different now, that when he walks around, he hears a different conversation than in the old corporate staff days. People are talking about their clients, about their clients' issues and business problems and how they need to reduce the costs of their services. He enthusiastically shows everyone his new performance management system that links everyone to the success of shared services. The word *culture* is part of his vocabulary and the key to effective execution of shared services, as he will tell anyone who asks him.

Chapter 11

EVOLVING THE SHARED
SERVICES BUSINESS

*Thousands of ordinary men and women boarded ships, vision in
hand, as they set sail under terrible conditions for Southeastern
Australia between 1851 and 1855. The hardships and difficulties
diminished at the obsession with the image of shining gold!*

If there is one persistent idea, image or desire that shared service
groups should have in mind, it is the fact that what has been created
here is a business, a business that hopefully is obsessed with client service and satisfaction. This picture has to be firmly planted in shared
services like the image of shining gold for those brave explorers. This
vision has to help staff become obstinate, persistent and even bloody-
minded in their relentless pursuit of hard-won respect from clients. The
pursuit is a never-ending journey. There is never any final destination
when you can sit back and say, "I have done the job, it is over, shared
services really works and clients are now finally satisfied." If somebody
wants to turn a bureaucracy into a business, they will have to give
themselves an awfully big "to do" list. Here is what a leader in shared
services might want to say to themselves.

"I need us to have a common vision about our core business and
what we want to be known for in the minds of the clients. I need us to
face the fact that we do have external competitors who want our internal staff business. I need us to place clients' needs first, ahead of our
own. I need to think of clients as market segments and create a value
proposition through different products and services. I need us to have a
marketing plan and to follow through on it. I need everyone in shared
services to think of themselves as being in the sales business. I need us
to start really loving and appreciating our clients. Yes, that's right, really

caring about our clients enough to want their loyalty. No more taking each other for granted. They are our future and so I want us to have the kind of relationship that is based on mutual respect and trust. I know you're thinking of some of those clients right now and the idea that you have to care about them is probably making you want to run in the opposite direction, but come back. If we don't put this fundamental issue on track, we're doomed to failure."

Anyone who has built a successful business started with a vision. Whether they wrote it down formally or not doesn't matter. What does matter is that somebody had an idea for a business and had a dream about doing things better or doing something new and innovative. A vision is about putting the stake in the ground. Go to any company website. Right there you'll see how the company articulates what business it is in, what it stands for, what it can do for you and why it can serve you better than any competitor. In less than 30 seconds, the company has captured your interest. These people are in business! So why should it be any different for shared services? It's a service business too, isn't it?

All shared service groups need a common vision. This vision is not necessarily going to ever be communicated to the clients, but rather is a rallying force for the internal staff of the shared services organization. Anyone who has ever been on the receiving end of a vision that they had no hand in creating can often be cynical. So generally speaking, it is critical to have as wide an involvement as possible. The real power of vision is to take action that supports the vision, otherwise it is just a bunch of words on a piece of paper.

Clients of shared services will really get what it's all about not when you tell them your vision but when they actually perceive the benefit from services that meet their needs at a quality, cost and timeliness that is better than other sources. This may be because the accounts receivable group is able to process incoming payments faster and more accurately so the next sale can be made without delay. Or, as the legal advisor, you have invested time up front with your business people to understand what makes the business tick and can now turn around contracts that make sense and achieve the business purpose faster.

A VISION FOR SHARED SERVICES

Creating a service vision is not about writing a slogan that can be laminated on to a t-shirt or coffee mug. That might come later. Rather it is the articulation, clearly and succinctly, of what the business is, what you stand for and how you want to be known by your internal clients, *those ones you are going to treat with the utmost respect.* External consultants and suppliers are usually very good at what we call the thirty second elevator speech. When someone leans over to you and says, "What is it you do anyway?" you should be able to answer without pulling out a big long strategic plan or set of overhead slides. Good visions are relatively succinct – they are held in memory and can be recited by heart. They have been thought about and discussed in great detail by the shared services team prior to seeing daylight. When vision works, it is because shared service leaders actually use it to guide their decisions, both long and short term. It is not a document hidden in a drawer that gets shown once a year at budget planning time.

Procter and Gamble's Global Business Services Center has done a lot of work on vision and you can see how it is trying to position itself with its internal customers as well as what values it is bringing to the party. Procter and Gamble's vision of "Nobody one does it better" provides an excellent example of a customer-oriented statement because it focuses on what the new shared services group wanted customers to be saying about it in the future (see Figure 11.1). No shared services business could ever expect a greater compliment.

You did not have to be in the room when this vision was created to understand its meaning. It is really great example because it is clear to an outsider exactly what they are trying to achieve and how they are going to try to influence the organization that shared services makes sense! The point of vision is to articulate a point out in the future, a final destination, one that is not necessarily achievable today.

A vision should articulate a point out in the future, a final destination

To understand the idea of vision, imagine that you are holding an elastic band, one finger at each end. Stretch the elastic band as far as it will go without snapping. Feel the spring and tension. This is what vision should do. It should be enough of a stretch that it creates energy and positive tension in trying to achieve the vision while not so stretched out there that it is impossible to achieve. Being number one in

FIGURE 11.1   The vision of Procter and Gamble's Global Business Service Center

"NO ONE DOES IT BETTER!"

"We are # 1 in the business of delighting customers with innovative value-added business services by leveraging the power of one."
- ❑ we are one organization
- ❑ with one culture
- ❑ using one global system
- ❑ where every single person makes a difference
- ❑ creating a defect-free culture with no re-work
- ❑ with individual responsibility and accountability

the universe is an example of too much of a stretch for most shared service groups and so it can become a target of cynicism. Now let the elastic band go loose. This is what happens when vision is simply an articulation of what is done today. This is when vision is stated as, "Continue to provide clients with the same good old service as today." It is flacid and without energy. So for vision to work in shared services, it has to be a stretch from today but not an impossible goal. Proctor and Gamble has not said zero defects, it has wisely chosen instead to say a zero defect culture.

Vision is not new but it still works

There is nothing new about vision. The context for vision in shared services is that it is a positive experience after the analysis and design phase and can act as an important rallying cry for a new shared service organization. As Joe Corry from the Ashland Company says, "Shared services is not like turning on a light. It takes time to build the culture."

This vision from the Ashland Company is deceptively simple while posing quite a stretch to meet customer needs (see Figure 11.2). The positioning of this group is obviously designed at the overall outcome of business advantage for the corporation as a whole. Once shared services was set up, Joe found that clients kept demanding more and more, that their expectations were rising dramatically. It is a living example of the saying, "Good performance is punishing." The better the service, the more they wanted! The more they wanted, the more the shared service group had to make sure it wasn't promising what it couldn't deliver. Ashland's shared services group has been so successful that environment, health and safety and logistics are scheduled to be included.

For those who think vision is wishy-washy and airy-fairy, think again. Someone better be thinking about how to answer the question of

FIGURE 11.2　Ashland Company's shared service vision

ASHLAND COMPANY, Rotterdam
Joe Corry – Dir. of Shared Services

"Provide business solutions that consistently meet customer needs and provide them with a competitive advantage."

- ❏ cash management
- ❏ accounts payable
- ❏ legal
- ❏ information technology
- ❏ accounts receivable
- ❏ legal and management reporting
- ❏ human resources

what business you are in and what you want to stand for. Actually, everyone in shared services better be thinking about how to answer this question. Staff functions won't survive on historical merit in a shared services environment. Just like any other business, they have to prove value for money and differentiate themselves from the competitors.

The ABB Group has one of the largest shared service groups worldwide and is a recognized leader in making the strategy work. Their revenues are in the $100 to 1,000 million range and their scope is fairly wide. All support service centers operate as profit centers. At ABB, services that are mandated are accounting and payroll. All other services are voluntary and so they must compete for market share within the organization. Given the need to operate as profit centers, and the fight to maintain market share, their vision clearly articulates this pressure by positioning themselves as equally competitive with third party suppliers.

To achieve this simple but elegant vision, the shared support service group plans on making productivity a key measure of success. It believes that cost savings alone are not sufficient. Its pledge is to deliver 10% improvement in productivity and price year on year as a way of achieving the vision.

Another recognized leader in shared services and now part of the BP group, Amoco probably has had more press on shared services than it ever wanted. The sheer size and scope of Amoco's shared service group in the US warranted attention, weighing in at services worth $1.4 billion, including 17 different corporate service groups and 8,000 staff in

FIGURE 11.3   ABB's shared service vision

> **ABB, Group**
> **Bertil Wrethag – President, Support Services**
>
> *"Our vision is to be competitive with external services in quality and price."*
>
> ❑ 36 shared service centers around the world; 3,000 –4,000 people; 17 different countries
>
> ❑ office services
>
> ❑ training and development
>
> ❑ competency development
>
> ❑ consulting services, purchasing
>
> ❑ logistics
>
> ❑ health care
>
> ❑ information technology

shared services. At one point, the number of requests for information on shared services was so great that the company supposedly had to put someone in charge just to manage inquiries (see Figure 11.4).

The story of cost reduction at Amoco Canada is equally compelling. Wayne Bester, the director of shared services, talks about the relentless drive to take costs down. This is evident in the company's vision.

Wayne talks about the pride it takes in its remarkable achievement of driving costs from $113.5 million down to $80 million for these corporate services over a period of approximately four years. He believes shared services is a sustainable strategy. After all, he points out that outsourcing is a tougher decision for most corporations. It involves real money. Amoco Canada has found that a common vision and strategy is essential to make shared services work.

The Post Office in London, England, has a vision to help its internal services close the gap between themselves and external competitors. They are on a vision to prove that their prices are lower than external competitors, that the value is as good as their competitors, and that they can respond positively to changes.

THE POST OFFICE, UNITED KINGDOM

Malcom Kitchener, Managing Director, Services Group

We can help our internal service lead the market by proving that we add unique value over and above our external suppliers.

The vision of the internal market is to maximize the competitive advantage of the Post Office. These internal services play a key role in keeping our operation running smoothly.

FIGURE 11.4   BP Amoco's shared service vision

BP AMOCO, Canada
Wayne Bester - General Manager

"Becoming a world-class supplier of services, adding value through:

maintaining and deploying appropriate skill sets, competencies and business processes to meet customers' current requirements at lowest total cost and anticipating future requirements to create competitive advantage."

❑ accounting business services	❑ analytical services (labs)
❑ auditing	❑ engineering and construction
❑ employee health and safety	❑ government relations
❑ facilities and services	❑ human resources
❑ law	❑ public and government affairs
❑ purchasing	❑ tax

We are new and improved

Most organizations in shared services want to have a unique and distinctive culture, one that is clearly different than the old central service groups. Shared services is a chance to dream of a new vision as to how the business can operate, both with its customers and with its own people. Many shared service groups are trying out flatter models, less management, and more of a team approach where the internal client and customers are everyone's responsibility. Perhaps, this is a chance to get it right. The opportunity is there at least to start on a new foot. Vision is one of the tools for evolving corporate service groups into businesses. Even where shared service groups are offering mandated services such as payroll, travel and expense reporting or disbursements, there is still a requirement to help the new group position itself as a valued supplier. A helpful way to begin defining a vision is to use the following questions as a guideline:

+ How do we want to describe our shared services business?
+ What do we want to be known for by our clients?

The idea is to get as many shared services staff as possible involved in defining the overall vision. Get people to write answers to these two questions in twenty-five words or less and guaranteed there will be the making of a compelling vision. After all, the question that is really on clients' minds is this: What are you in shared services going to do that will make me or my business faster, better, more profitable, easier and/or save me money? To get perspective on the power of vision and being able to articulate clearly what you stand for, consider the vision statements in figure 11.5 from third party suppliers. Recognize that these businesses are your future competitors, whether you like it or not.

These two outsourced suppliers are probably the largest in their field; their visions are obviously working. So dream a little, create your vision and work at turning it into reality. As someone once said, "The future is not what it used to be and as a matter of fact the past doesn't seem to be getting much better either!" Wishful thinking about how it was in the days when improving functional expertise was what really seemed to matter will not help define your dream of a client-focused future. Your vision will set the direction, will provide a sense of purpose and will enable you to define what exactly you must deliver to cause your clients to work with you. Without a vision, you will simply lack the focus and drive to compete effectively for your clients' business.

FIGURE 11.5   Vision statements from third party suppliers

IBM GLOBAL SERVICES:

People who think. People who do.

Largest IT service provider in the world with more than 465 strategic outsourcing contracts.

IBM Global Services is people. Strategists. Problem-solvers. Implementors. Over 100,000 worldwide who have worked in all kinds of industries. People who understand how technology can solve real business problems, or take advantage of new opportunities. People who help you make sense of technology, who work with you, making sure the solution you want is the solution you get.

GELCO INFORMATION NETWORK:

A complete outsourced solution for travel expense management.

We offer a complete outsourced travel expense management solution that empowers companies.

Get quick administrative relief and cost savings of up to 75% with our proven processing infrastructure.

Get dedicated ongoing traveler and solution support with Gelco's experienced help desk and customer service department.

TRANSLATING VISION INTO ACTION

To make vision concrete in shared services, there are a number of things that need to be done:

✦ identify and segment client and customer groups;

✦ understand client expectations: their needs and wants;

✦ design and package service offerings to meet unique requirements.

Not all clients and customers want the same level and kinds of services. This is the big shift away from centralization where central groups decided on the products with little or no consultation with their clients. The new world means developing mechanisms to find out what clusters or groups of clients want from the shared service group. The really essential ingredient is understanding what they will value. Some clients will choose speed over 100% accuracy! Some clients will choose higher priced services if they believe they will be an asset to their business. Shared service groups should unbundle products and services and offer differentiated levels of service. For example, if clients want and are willing to pay for mail delivery services twice a day rather than once, they should have that option. If clients prefer face-to-face advisory services and are willing to pay for them, give them the option. If clients want recruiting services instead of organizational development, provide them with what they want.

> Robert A. Clausen Solutia, Inc.

Without a clear understanding of the business unit strategies and priorities, too often you will do a great job of providing the wrong services.

One of the most important tasks of the shared services leader says Clausen is to realign staff services. Defining what value means to the business is not as simple as it sounds. It may mean lower costs, or it may mean increased quality and speed.

The value proposition will be different within the various client groups and will reflect their unique needs. The transmission group in a gas or electric utility will have radically different needs than the marketing and sales group. The mobility business in telecommunications will expect a certain style of working that is unique to the dynamics of a sector in an explosive growth mode as compared to the more traditional land line part of the business. The challenge for shared service groups is to try to meet these perhaps contradictory needs. One wants lowest cost, one wants speed of response!

The shape of offerings might be quite different than they are today because what clients value may not be what you thought they would. Often, there is a need to cull products and reshape offerings and redesign new services. Too many businesses have gone bust by trying to please everybody all the time. Shared services is certainly not about offering what you think clients should have or what you want to deliver. One communications group in a large computer company wanted to do the fun stuff like the annual report and sales materials. It turned out that the clients wanted to use top external advertising and print houses but meanwhile were crying out for newsletters and help in executive presentation materials. Shared services solves this kind of mismatch. Some people in shared services might need to make a choice about staying with the company or leaving if they are not interested or inclined to deliver only those products and services that clients want and are willing to pay for.

Quality of products/services = Quality of the service relationship

Clients are not wrong

In a marketplace and advanced marketplace model, clients are not ever really wrong. They may have unrealistic expectations, they may need to be educated, they may need to be provided with a range of options, but essentially they are not wrong. In the old bureaucratic mindset, clients were treated to a large extent just the way you would expect with any captive audience. The vision articulated at the beginning of the chapter is one that demonstrates a fundamental respect and appreciation for the clients' business. In this way, shared service groups do have to work on developing a culture that sees clients as the *raison d'être*, not as a necessary impediment.

RELIANT ENERGY

Waters Davis, Senior VP, Shared Services

Most people who start in shared services do not come from an environment where you win or lose clients.

One of the biggest challenges for shared service leaders is how to motivate employees to be aggressive about customer service. How can they anticipate client needs? How can they go from order-taker to value-added partner? We have worked hard to educate our people that any change in service level or cost affects the business unit's bottom line.

This raises the proposition then of shared service groups having to think like marketers in a competitive environment. The marketplace is not always kind and gentle. It takes a ruthless desire to know what is going on in your clients' minds and to be intelligent about what is going on around you. This is not about creating fancy marketing brochures. It unfortunately is harder than that, it is about earning the business and thinking like a business.

All external and internal staff consultants share two fantasies. Fantasy one goes like this. The phone rings and the client at the other end breathlessly says, "I want you, I need you, I hear you're great, money is no object and when can you start?" Fantasy number two also begins with a phone call. "I am looking at your brochure, the logos and graphics are great, the typeface is fantastic, you must be awfully good given the expense you went to for these materials. When can you start?" At a personal level, we all secretly desire to be loved and wanted, respected and sought after, whether we are inside or outside the corporation. Too bad it doesn't happen by idly sitting back and waiting. Secondly, it is a cardinal mistake to think fancy marketing brochures will get clients to want to do business with the new and improved shared service groups. No one buys consulting services because the graphics are great.

MARKETING ACTIVITIES FOR SHARED SERVICES GROUPS

The kind of marketing activities that are appropriate to shared services are the following:

1   Developing external and internal market intelligence.
2   Relationship management as a role and an activity.
3   Refining image of shared services groups.
4   Heightened professionalism in communications.

1 External and internal market intelligence

External

It is the responsibility and accountability of shared service groups to develop a running body of market intelligence that includes knowledge about competitors, benchmarks, how internal prices stack up against external prices for similar services. As Waters Davis at Reliant Energy says, "If you do not manage your clients, they will manage you." This means a need to have good intelligence at your fingertips. It is the shared service provider who should be quoting prices from competitors and explaining to clients what the differences are between the outsourcer and the internal shared service group.

The concept of competitors is a hard one for most staff groups to grasp in a practical way other than the usual moaning and complaining about consultants running rampant in any organization, at any time, scooping up all the good work. Senior shared services staff should take the time to understand who their real competitors are in the external marketplace. These are the consultants or vendors which line managers regularly use if they have any choice or power to go outside or around the internal groups. It is worth the time to profile the strengths and weaknesses of the competitors and compare them to your own. In one shared services organization, each senior manager took one competitor and produced a short profile which was evaluated against their own organization. This gave the management team in shared services valuable information that they could turn around and use to plan for improvements. It also pointed out some weaknesses in their internal capability.

Internal

Internal groups do have some key advantages over external consultants and third party suppliers, that is if they choose to use them. Shared service groups have open access to business plans, strategies, performance targets and just about any other kind of information that is within the walls of the company. Most internal staff groups fail at leveraging this one key advantage over external suppliers. To do the job of leveraging inside intelligence will mean creating mechanisms to enable formal information sharing and creating a climate where informal networking is greatly encouraged. People complain about how difficult this is in big companies but global consulting companies realize the power of collective market intelligence and build webs of information across hundreds of office sites around the world. There are common databases that consultants can access worldwide. Surfing their own Intranet, individual consultants can see who else has experience with the same or similar kinds of clients, the type of problem they are experiencing, or knows of a product that might work for a given situation. Knowing people would need an incentive to input data, there are bonuses for individual consultants based on the number of times they feed local market intelligence into the website.

Market intelligence is important in building credibility and reputation with clients but it is only a piece of the story. Leaders of shared services have to help the organization develop a nose for intelligence and a mechanism to do something with the data once it has been found. This need to keep up with the market both inside and outside should be one of the key performance deliverables for any shared services group.

2 Relationship management as a role and an activity

The whole concept of building client relationships in a corporate environment is often met with an audible gasp by traditional corporate staff managers. They confuse relationship building with selling which is usually met with a fair amount of resistance. Staff and managers in shared services can even get resentful over the idea that actively building relationships is a part of the new reality. Their cynicism boils over as they snort derisively and ask if this will mean having to take clients out to lunch for martinis and expensive food. Maybe in the movies, but anyone in the relationship business knows the job is just a little bit more complicated and a lot more hard work than sitting in fancy restaurants, helping the client choose between the grilled tuna or the roast leg of lamb.

Relationship building is influencing, understanding and responding to client needs

Relationship building is influencing, understanding and responding to client needs, not a lesson in schmoozing. Clients need convincing that something is really different here, that the people in shared services are going to put clients front and square of everything they do. The challenge is getting internal service groups committed to client satisfaction, no matter what it takes.

We are not advocating a sales and marketing function for the shared services group unless there is intent to market services commercially to the external marketplace. As a matter of fact, shared service groups have had bad experiences when they have tried to create a sales type function. It just doesn't work and this includes spending a load of money on expensive brochures designed to advertise services. It is earned every time someone in shared services does a good job at service. Overall, good service is built on good relationships. As Ian Gordon said in the introduction to his book *Relationship Marketing*, "The fundamental thesis is that relationships are the only real asset to any enterprise."[1] In shared services, this means creating new positions that are focused on building and maintaining relationships with major business unit clients at a senior level. The term relationship manager has emerged as a formal way to ensure the building of relationships is taken seriously.

> *The credibility of shared services will be based on clients perceiving good service and this happens one client interaction at a time*

Relationship management as a formal role

There are generally two schools of thought when it comes to having a formal relationship management role or not: one says yes and the other says maybe. The idea behind a formal role for relationship management in shared services comes from the idea that there is too much work to be done in running a day to day services group. Unless there is a formal role set aside to manage relationships with the executives of the business units, it simply won't happen despite good intentions.

LOCKHEED MARTIN

Fran Bengtson, Business Development Manager

You have to have someone to do the relationship work, someone without a stake, someone independent, who has done shared services before and knows what to expect.

Our centers are up and running full blast. The service managers have their plates full and several balls in the air, doing reengineering, changing systems, and handling migrations. We have learned that you have to listen very carefully in this culture, to get the requirements right. That takes time so you need someone whose job it is to take care of client relationships.

There are obvious benefits for shared service groups which want to create a separate relationship management or client services role since it provides one overall point of contact whose main job is to maintain positive relationships with the business units.

The role of a relationship manager is to do the following:

+ act as the overall face to the client, not the only face;
+ have a clear understanding of the business partner's business and priorities;
+ monitor satisfaction and progress of ongoing work and projects;
+ high level problem resolution;
+ act as a catalyst for improvement within the shared services group;
+ ensure clear, open, ongoing communications between both groups;
+ develop a strategy for influencing the overall service-mindedness and relationship management capabilities within shared services.

The function is like that of a senior partner in a consulting or law firm, who has regular contact with the executive who contracted for the services and works to ensure that he or she has a clear understanding of what is keeping the business unit executives up at night. What is on their mind? What are they concerned about and how can I help? This role is also essential to monitor overall satisfaction with service delivery for both regular day-to-day operations and any projects currently under way. For example, there may be several financial type projects under way in any business unit at any given time. The relationship manager would be a common touchstone to get a general picture of how things are going. Where problems are identified, the relationship manager has a responsibility to get them solved even though he or she has no direct control over the resources.

This concept of accountability without control is what makes this position so exciting and so tough. Relationship managers should be measured on overall satisfaction with services just like sales people who are measured on sales volumes even though there are many variables out of their control. For example, if a shared services group puts a relationship management function in place, it should be measured at the end of the year on the overall client satisfaction, assuming there is such an annual kind of survey. If there isn't, then there better be one. This is the only way the relationship management function will meaningfully operate as a catalyst for change and for improvement. Otherwise, the role is pretty fuzzy and hard to measure.

Ontario Hydro, in Canada, had one of the largest shared services organizations globally until the company was recently split into two separate companies due to deregulation and impending competition. John O'Connor was in a relationship management function and he had responsibility for about two-thirds of the major client groupings. Half of his compensation was based on overall client satisfaction with the shared services group. In this role, he had to help managers solve problems that had been identified in his meetings with executives of the business units. He admits the role takes diplomacy and tenacity when trying to get people who are not in your direct control to resolve service issues.

The role then of relationship manager can also be to ensure clear and ongoing communications between clients and shared service groups. This may mean relationship managers acting as facilitators to resolve relationship issues in the short term. In the long term, it is essential that the relationship management function be tagged with the responsibility for developing the shared service organization's capability in relationship management.

Some organizations create a multi-functional relationship manager who looks after several shared service functions. This can be beneficial to the clients. Fewer meetings to deal with corporate staff problems and satisfaction issues. There are also more opportunities for cross-marketing if required. Consulting firms cross-sell all the time. The downside is that the bigger the scope of functions for the relationship manager, the less knowledgeable he becomes for real problem resolution.

Relationship management as part of the shared services manager's job

Many shared service groups are embedding relationship management in the existing manager's role instead of creating a separate role. In other words, the manager of disbursements is also the relationship manager. To do this well, managers need to be provided with development in building relationships and to recognize that this is a major part of their job, not something to do off the side of the desk from time to time.

A relationship manager by function on the other hand offers a lot more depth and identity with the functional discipline. In shared services for systems and technology groups, this role is an important strategic tool in helping business units make wise technology investments. Synergies are much more possible with a good relationship management function whereby business units can tap into solutions that may already have been developed. This saves money and time for business units eager and under pressure to get to market quickly with new products.

Relationship management as an activity

The relationship management role is designed to formalize client relationships for shared service organizations. It does not preclude informal relationship building that has to be a way of life in day-to-day business. Networking is essential and not only for people charged with relationship management. Relationship management is also an activity. Jokes aside about the power of doing business on a golf course or on a sailboat, there is a lot to be said for being able to get to know clients informally and outside the corporate bricks and mortar. Building relationships is an interactive experience so finding ways to connect with clients should be part of the new assignment. Staff groups should seek opportunities to participate in conferences and developments that are about the business of the client. Too often staff groups spend their time with each other in the same old conferences, preaching to the converted.

LEVI STRAUSS AND COMPANY

Gordon Shank, Chief Marketing Officer

Staff groups have to learn to become disciples of their industry, not their own discipline.

Far too often staff are accused of being not in the business, therefore somehow losing about 30 IQ points instantaneously. We all need to be in the business. This is the relationship we have in common.

For shared service groups which operate globally, the chance for face-to-face networking and informal relationship building might be severely limited. However, the advent of technology and e-mail provides us with new opportunities for building relationships. Video conferencing and the good old basic telephone are still sound tools for making connections with clients and their businesses.

3 Image of shared services groups

The challenge for shared service groups is to create a specific brand identity and image that is built around the service image and what shared services wants to be known for. For people who think this is insubstantial, just consider how an organization such as Intel has built a worldwide reputation and brand loyalty for something called a "pentium processor" inside a computer. Most people don't even know what a processor actually does in their computer, just that pentium ones are apparently really good and we all ought to have one.

Why bother trying to impress the client, after all we both work for the same company. Executives, increasingly exposed to external consultants and other service providers, are consciously and unconsciously comparing the differences. For staff groups which whine about the unfairness of comparing their own middle managers with senior partners from slick vendors, our advice is to get with the program.

For internal staff groups, there is sometimes an unconscious attitude of complacency

4 Heightened professionalism in communications

Every time someone from shared services gives a presentation, the client is forming an impression, good, bad or ugly, about the quality of service. It might not be a bad idea to form a logo and identity for shared services, even though this might seem a bit over the top for some traditionalists. The reality is that this kind of branding can be a powerful tool in raising the bar of professionalism. Too often, there is a complacency about internal presentations and meetings. In a study done for a very large financial company, clients of the systems group were asked to define the difference in their minds between external technology suppliers and the internal group. One of the glaring differences in the clients' minds was what they called the degree of professionalism exuded by externals as compared to internals. They saw internals from their own shared service group arriving late for meetings, no agenda sent out ahead of time, no attention to aesthetics in their presentations. They saw externals taking great care and attention with polished and planned presentations. They found that external consultants respected the clients' time pressure and knew how to manage time appropriately inside the meetings. This kind of basic attention to detail can easily be duplicated internally. How many shared service groups consciously plan for presentations that include a formal introduction of who they are, what they do and what they stand for?

The major point is that shared service groups need to develop an obsession for operating as a professional business and this means paying attention to the details. A new vision and identity that is based on earning credibility and building client loyalty is essential. There is a business video used in leadership training, based on the work of Jim Kouzes and Barry Posner who wrote the book *The Leadership Challenge*, about the power of identity. One of the managers profiled in the video took over the mailroom at Berkeley University. In a very short period of time, he managed to instill life and passion into an area through his vision of the mail being the lifeblood of the university. He managed to change the identity of mailroom from a nothing service buried somewhere in the basement to "the lifeblood of the university." He sold everyone on the idea that mail was important and that the people in the mailroom really cared about the service relationships. This kind of leadership is required to help people be obsessed with service and to value what they do every hour, every day in the business of serving clients. This obsession will result in client loyalty because clients are always going to be loyal when they know they are respected and appreciated.

NOTES

1 Ian Gordon, (1998) Relationship Marketing

Chapter 12

MEASURING AND
EVALUATING SUCCESS

All great civilizations built up treasuries of the lustrous metal, reserving golden objects for their most important rituals. So valuable was gold that the Egyptians reserved its use for Pharaohs only

S ome things are so sacred that it is impossible to quantify their value, or so goes the old cliché. Important ideas do not always add up neatly into lines and figures. At the end of the day, it may be hard to pinpoint exactly and precisely what it is that makes something feel valuable. Or, that the benefits are so truly profound that the mere act of measurement cannot in any way capture what has really gone on. Any team or group that has been through a significant change process would find it hard to select the one or two things which evaluate how it came to pass, what it was in the final moment that could be summed up as the point of it all. Value in some ways is in the eye of the beholder. There was no need for ancient Egyptian society to come up with a precise measure for gold. Its value was made obvious by allowing only pharaohs to use it. In essence, measurement is simply a method for ascribing value. Shared service groups need to find ways to affix value to what has been accomplished. They have an obligation to prove the worth of the idea for ever and ever. Measurement is not a one shot deal.

THE BURDEN OF PROOF

Measuring the value of shared services is essential, it is the burden of proof. Measures are presented to demonstrate that the case for action has, indeed, lived up to its expectations, that the strategy has resulted

193

in some kind of value to the organization! For organizations which made a business case citing the merits and benefits, measures are the connection between what was promised and what has actually been delivered. Whether in the eye of the beholder or not, measurement is necessary to demonstrate, unequivocally, that shared services has resulted in something better than before. Beyond this proof is the fact that shared service groups must commit to the ongoing pursuit of measuring their value. What is effective today may not be good enough for tomorrow. At any point in time, shared service groups should be able to report on their effectiveness. This means putting a comprehensive set of measures in place. But what kind of measures should these be?

Obviously, there is a desire to find measures that are objective and irrefutable; as though in a court of law, the evidence is presented logically, without flaw. Information that speaks for itself. On the other hand, one of the fundamental measures that has to be present is client and customer evaluation of the services, which by its very nature is subjective. Clients aren't tested for their aptitude in being clients before they score their satisfaction with shared services. They evaluate shared services using whatever subjective and anecdotal information is in their heads at the time. The biggest shift for most shared service groups is the dawning realization that quite simply, the key group to evaluate services is in fact the clients and customers. Granted, they are not the only measure. Shared service groups will also have to answer the question, "Did we achieve the savings that were promised?"

So there is no question that measurement is essential. The dilemma is in choosing what kind of measures, how many measures and what kind of processes to measure. It is an accepted truism that what gets measured, gets done. Equally, companies need to be careful that what they are measuring is what they want done. In one company, call center operators were measured for handling the maximum number of calls. The company got what it wanted all right: brief, curt, get the customer off this line as soon as possible service. Another classic is measuring the

What gets measured, gets done

number of grievances as a supposed sign of a good labor relations climate. The lower the number, the better the labor relations climate! In one organization, the senior managers relinquished their control and authority, caved in on all issues, just to avoid getting a grievance. The company did not really get what it was hoping for because the measure was fundamentally wrong. The most common measurement error is to focus narrowly on costs and on adherence to the budget, sometimes at the expense of rich opportunities. The central point being overall that any one measure is likely not to suffice.

All in all, it is a balance of measures that will provide the right picture. This is why the balanced scorecard approach, made famous by Kaplan and Norton of Harvard Business School, is receiving so much attention.[1] The scorecard approach means that shared services has to be connected directly to the overall corporate or organizational direction and that there is a certain level of consistency among performance measures.

THE BALANCED SCORECARD

The balanced scorecard provides a strategic focus to performance measurement that goes beyond the traditional focus on financial data. It emphasizes that financial and non-financial measures must be part of the information system for employees at all levels of the organization. The balanced scorecard methodology establishes objectives and measures performance from four fundamental perspectives.

In the context of shared services, the four measures include the way internal clients and customers evaluate the services, the extent to which shared services is able to demonstrate innovation and value, the ultimate financial returns, and finally the detailed internal productivity metrics for running the operation (see Figure 12.1). These four measures then in balance provide a comprehensive picture revealing how the shared services group is operating. The advantages of the balanced scorecard approach is the ability to take one entity and look at it from four distinct angles. Bjarnie Anderson from Mobil Business Resources Corporation finds balanced scorecard information a key tool for communicating shared service priorities, plans and the vision for success. The performance data then is not only essential to demonstrate the effectiveness of the operation, it can be used as a way of generating dialogue with clients about future improvements.

Ultimately, measurement data is good only if it translates into action. It should not be a means in and of itself. The data has to be communicated to staff within shared services, to clients and customers, to

FIGURE 12.1   The balanced scorecard

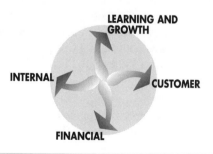

the executive of the organization if it is to have any real worth. The shared services group has to be committed to acting on the data if there is to be any long-term credibility for the process. No matter how good the measurement system, it is only as good as the people who use it.

WHAT INTERNAL CLIENTS WANT

Customer metrics assess the level of satisfaction that internal clients have with the services they are receiving and enable the shared services group to adjust as required to meet their changing needs and requirements. This scorecard measure is only as good as the clients who provide input to the evaluation, which raises the next question: which clients should assess this element of the balanced scorecard?

Who assesses the customer scorecard?

The answer is that there are multiple levels of clients and customers: from senior and middle management all the way across and down to actual users of the services. The person who calls the help desk in information technology, the employee who wants to know if they have benefits cover, the shipping clerk who wants to check an invoice, the manager who signed the service level agreement. It is the collective picture from clients and users that will ultimately provide the picture of client satisfaction and score shared services on this dimension.

The old central groups often operated as if the CEO was the client. This in essence short changes the clients, who end up on the

---

PETER BLOCK

Author of *Flawless Consulting and Stewardship*

Staff groups should be judged on feedback that includes lower levels. CEOs should stop using staff as personal advisors. The CEO is not the client of the staff group. If the staff leader spends more than 20% of the time serving the top, they are wasting the corporation's money.

When companies outsource staff groups, they ultimately believe they are not getting enough value from the current internal group. Companies should deal with this lack of value directly. Better to improve the quality of in-house groups than express their low esteem by treating them as a commodity that can be bought cheaper down the street.

receiving end of poor and unresponsive service. Staff groups which operate as upwardly serving see no real need to take the time necessarily to be client-oriented. Shared service groups have to be different. They have to take responsibility for getting wide client satisfaction data. Moving to shared services means that client satisfaction data is no longer optional, it is essential to send the message that this is not centralization. Clients are a fundamental part of judging the success.

The United Kingdom Post Office describes the various levels of clients it will be seeking feedback from and in what area. Table 12.1 defines the kind of feedback required from senior managers, contract managers and end users.

This model provides an excellent overview of the different kinds of inputs required from various levels of client. The hard and concrete measurement data has to come from the contract manager and user level. This is directly tied to the service level agreement. It is the determination of how well the shared services group has lived up to its part of the bargain. Service level agreements will vary greatly across the functions and across companies. Hopefully, they are simple enough to be practical and therefore can be used to evaluate easily how well the shared service group has performed. But

TABLE 12.1 Shared services feedback required from the Post Office, United Kingdom

Type of customer	Feedback required
Senior clients: direction setters	Provide information on new customer requirements and evolving future needs. They provide overall information on what the internal suppliers need to do to deliver the desired results.
Contract managers	Provide information about how well the internal supplier is meeting the terms of the current service level agreement and how well shared services is listening to customer comments and suggestions.
End users	Should provide information about how happy end users of the services are. This information supplements information provided by contract managers and may pick up new issues not sufficiently covered by the service level agreement.

what are some of the characteristics that clients expect from staff groups? What are the qualities that clients look for in determining value for money?

How clients evaluate service

There are some fundamental needs and expectations contract managers and users have of staff services. One of the principal themes to emerge from the quality movement is that clients have two kinds of quality

Quality of products/services = Quality of the service relationship

expectations, both of equal value. The products and services have to be good and so does the service relationship. In other words, an organization with superior products but poor relationships isn't a winner and vice versa, great relationships with inferior products is not a sustainable value proposition.

The challenge for leaders within shared services is to work simultaneously on both sides of the equation. It makes sense. A systems group might pride itself on having great hardware and super infrastructure but if client relationships are strained, it still runs the risk of being outsourced because fundamentally clients want and need both elements: good products and good relationships. Figure 12.2 presents a framework for assessing client expectations.

FIGURE 12.2   Framework showing the balance that needs to be present for client satisfaction

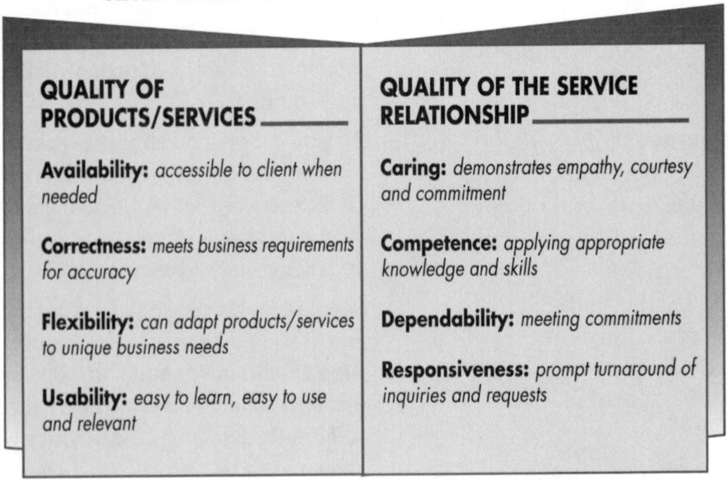

QUALITY OF PRODUCTS/SERVICES	QUALITY OF THE SERVICE RELATIONSHIP
Availability: accessible to client when needed	**Caring:** demonstrates empathy, courtesy and commitment
Correctness: meets business requirements for accuracy	**Competence:** applying appropriate knowledge and skills
Flexibility: can adapt products/services to unique business needs	**Dependability:** meeting commitments
Usability: easy to learn, easy to use and relevant	**Responsiveness:** prompt turnaround of inquiries and requests

A QUALITY FRAMEWORK

Measuring the quality of the product/service

Availability

On the product and services side, clients are looking for availability and access to services. One of the winning propositions for service centers is the opportunity to extend business hours and therefore access. Clients work different hours, sometimes in different countries, and they want to be able to access services when they need them, not when the service center happens to be open. Staff groups which are insular, which design their services around what works best for them, always receive poor marks for service. There are staff service groups today which are still trying to operate in a nine to five mode or even worse, there are still staff groups which close their operation for half a day to catch up on filing and paperwork. This does not do wonders for client satisfaction – at the end of the day, clients don't rate staff groups well because their filing is immaculate. Technology can be an enabler to access, especially for service centers that allow self-service, either through interactive voice response or by directly getting data and answers for themselves.

Correctness

There is no question that all service groups must work on accuracy. When clients get information that is not accurate or correct, they begin to mistrust the unit and eventually try to find ways to go around the unit. Accurate information is essential. Just ask anyone in payroll or human resources how critical accuracy is to developing a smooth client relationship. This is a fundamental and basic need for any kind of staff work. Many a staff group fails at positioning itself at a senior and strategic level in its organization because the basics are not well done. David Ulrich, the author of *Human Resource Champions*, and an outspoken advocate for human resource groups to position themselves as value-added strategic partners to the business units, told a great story at a major conference in Toronto. Apparently, a chief executive officer was invited to speak to the entire senior human resources community in his organization. The conference was aptly titled Strategic Partners or something like that. The CEO got up to the podium, looked out at the crowd and said, "I was going to talk to you today about strategic partnership but instead, I am putting my speech aside and want to tell you what just happened this morning." He then went on to describe the fact that they had been trying to recruit a very senior person to come and take over a key portfolio. They found the right person and made an offer. The potential recruit had phoned the CEO that very morning, concerned and taken aback at the salary offer. The offer letter had a wrong salary number, it might have even dropped an all-important zero. The point of the story, the CEO said, was this, "Don't come and tell me you want to be strategic partners if you can't even get the basics right." So the basics are important in all staff functions and it takes a lot of internal discipline with well-trained staff to ensure a high degree of accuracy and correctness.

Flexibility

There is a delicate balancing act in shared services on the subject of flexibility. Service centers and consolidation often means a move to standardizing processes which seems to fly directly in the face of flexibility. Yet clients need flexibility so that services can be adapted to local country or business needs. Although consistency is critical for the overall company, clients want flexibility, not consistency, as a rule. Clients need to be able to adapt and modify services to meet local cultural needs. For example, one human resources group had instituted a 360 degree feedback performance system. Some countries and cultures found this idea shocking and completely antithetical to what was considered proper. The very idea of subordinates evaluating their leaders was not acceptable. So the issue is how to help that country modify or adapt the performance system to work effectively, not to ram it down their throats telling them this is the standard and it's going to be good for them.

The subject of flexibility is always controversial because there are usually a few dogmatic souls who want to insist that one size fits all. Failure to allow for clients being able to adapt and modify services is a recipe for client dissatisfaction. Client dissatisfaction with shared services will ultimately be one step towards its dismantling.

Usability

Usability relates to the fact that clients have to be able to use products and services in their own context. Take the business of advice which is a key product for all staff organizations. Clients have to be able to apply the advice, it has to be simple to understand and simple to make work. Ease of use then is a critical element to client satisfaction.

Time after time, good systems or good ideas go down the drain because clients just can't work with them or find it too difficult to do. Shared service units might find the system great for their own needs but if clients find it cumbersome, then it will go unused. One finance group had a ridiculously complicated business case process. You had to be a finance brain to figure out how to work with the process. Finance thought it was brilliant. Clients did not.

These dimensions of product and service quality are generally what clients want and a shared services group won't be very wrong if it pays attention to these factors. Assuming good products and services then, clients also have expectations about the relationship.

Measuring the quality of the service relationship

Caring

Although clients may not use the word caring to describe how they want to be dealt with, the sub-text of empathy, courtesy and commitment is what they want. These words describe what people generally feel they did not get with centralized services. In the old bureaucracy, staff people often had little empathy for clients, preferring instead to lecture clients when refusing them service. Clients wanting a manual check would often be read the riot act before being told they weren't going to get it.

When a shared services group is good at the caring dimension, it means that all staff do have a genuine respect for what the client is going through and is committed to helping them. This kind of commitment comes through by phone, by electronic mail, and any time someone contacts anyone from the center. It is palpable from the moment you call someone whether or not the person at the other end really cares or not. You can't fake empathy and you can't disguise courtesy. Some service people answer the phone with exasperation, as though the clients are interrupting them.

Competence

Evaluation of service from any organization has a lot to do with how competence of the people who work there is perceived. Credibility is an essential component to the service relationship. If I perceive that people have the right skills and knowledge and know how to apply them, I am inclined to think well of them and want to use them. You don't need to force people to use services if the people involved are seen as highly competent.

Competence in the professional services area is even more critical. Skills have to be up to date. Riding on old knowledge and ancient models does not engender confidence with clients. They want to know that the people know what is happening in the outside world, hence the intense interest in best practices. Staff professionals who want to earn competence credits should make sure they are perceived to be experts in the areas of service being offered. For example, if finance wants to interest clients in risk management, there have to be skilled people who actually know how to do it. If facilities wants to position itself as knowing how to design the office space of the future, clients want confidence that the people are competent in this area. Clients do not generally appreciate being a guinea pig. "Gee, I've never actually done a successful implementation of an integrated system, but I am anxious to give it a try with you."

For newly formed shared service groups, this is one dimension to pay a lot of attention to. There is likely to be a requirement for a major investment in training and development. In some cases, there will be a need to bring in outside talent to shore up the expertise. Wise shared service groups will learn to bring in external consultants themselves so they can learn from them rather than trying to fight it and do everything themselves even when they do not have the credibility.

Dependability

When clients learn over time that their service unit will deliver *what* they said they would, *when* they said they would, they will form a long and loyal attachment. Another word for dependability is reliability. This dimension is one of the cornerstones to a foundation of trust in the client relationship. Trust is eroded when service units don't deliver on their promises. Fancy mission or vision statements quickly become hollow when actions do not meet the words.

External consultants know the power of repeat business. Getting the first piece of work is important but it is the second piece of work that means the beginning of loyalty and that the service has been good enough to warrant a second project. Internal staff groups need to know the power from being counted on and delivering no matter what the circumstances. Excuses for non-delivery or non-performance are proverbially worth a dime a dozen. You don't get too many chances when there is failure to deliver. Excuses sound lame especially when there is a pattern of not meeting commitments.

Responsiveness

The ability to project a responsive approach has a lot to do with attitude. When clients call for assistance, they can sense whether the service person realizes their urgency. It is true that clients may have unrealistic expectations for a turnaround to their requests but the fact of the matter is a service provider has only two choices. Either find a way to close the gap and give clients turnaround the way they expect or find a way to reshape their expectations. If I expect instant answers and it takes generally a few hours to get back to me, the longer I have this unmet expectation, the worse I perceive the service. Gaps that are unchecked or not openly discussed lead to an erosion of the service relationship.

Many service groups fail to find out what expectations their clients have for turnaround and will swear up and down that one day is great service for a credit check or two months is reasonable to get a job evaluation done. It's only great if the client thinks it's great. This is the basic truth of service.

Service is only great if the client thinks it's great

The service relationship is at least half the key to client satisfaction. A trusting relationship is formed when service groups are able to score successfully in these dimensions. Reliant Energy has a rigorous set of performance evaluation criteria for rating client-focused attributes.[2]

Client-focused performance at Reliant Energy:

✦ develops effective working relationships and partnerships with clients and external parties;

✦ adds value through understanding and satisfying client expectations by applying business strategies and staying abreast of the marketplace;

✦ willingly takes responsibility for decisions, actions and results achieved;

✦ understands key business drivers, the competitive environment, and the relationship between cost benefits and the profitability of the business units.

So although evaluation by clients is certainly at the heart of measuring satisfaction with shared services, there are other metrics that round out the balanced scorecard for shared service effectiveness.

LEARNING AND GROWTH METRICS

The learning and growth perspective focuses on the organization's people and infrastructure. This measure provides a focus on what the organization is doing continually to innovate and add value to the enterprise. For shared services organizations, this represents a commitment to continual development of new skills and capabilities that will enable the organization to enhance service quality and operational efficiency. The organization needs to evolve into a dynamic customer-focused culture that anticipates and develops services that will contribute to overall enterprise performance. Learning and growth measures need to also take into account the climate of the organization and its openness to change, risk taking and entrepreneurial spirit: all factors predictive of the organization's ability to move forward and be a sustainable operation. The business of leveraging intellectual capital is emerging as a hot new area for measurement. In essence, this measure tries in some way to get a

firm hold on a worthwhile but abstract concept, simply known as the amount of learning that has taken place and can be counted on as retained value. The logic and merit of such a measure is not in question. There is still not agreement, however, on what exactly constitutes retained learning value. Maybe there doesn't have to be. Maybe the ultimate point is to ensure that there is some kind of measure of climate, learning and innovation.

The most common measure of climate would simply be some kind of survey of employees from shared services that asks directly about learning and innovation on the job. This is not necessarily a true objective measure but rather a subjective attempt to capture perceived value. The work in intellectual capital is evolving in such a way that companies are actually trying to define outcome measures such as the number of successful patents, or the number of new products to market, as a tangible sign of leveraged value.

Whether this element of the scorecard is measured precisely is really not the question. The principal theme is to ensure that the shared service organization looks beyond the traditional measures of quality, cost and customer satisfaction and attempts to measure the impact of shared services *vis-à-vis* its value to the enterprise as a whole.

FINANCIAL METRICS: COSTS AND COST SAVINGS

Financial metrics indicate the ultimate results that the business provides to its stakeholders in terms of value added, productivity and long-term contribution. For a shared services organization on full cost recovery there is a basic need to determine costs against revenue. If costs exceed revenues the two options are to reduce those costs or increase the price of services. For most shared services operations the latter is not the preferred option. Financial metrics include actual monthly and year-to-date expense tracking as well as calculations of the cost per transaction, per report or per call.

INTERNAL METRICS: PRODUCTIVITY AND PRODUCT PERFORMANCE

This element of the scorecard relates to the fact that each kind of staff service business has its own internal set of measurement criteria related to its processes and unique products and services. For example, there are standard measures of productivity for accounts payable.

FIGURE 12.3 Kraft Foods' metric for the shared services accounts payable function

- disbursements processed and distributed
- headcount
- invoices per processor
- phone response time
- phone calls and customer types
- rejection percentage and type
- exceptions by type
- exceptions outstanding
- exceptions – average days
- post audits
- 100% audits
- duplicate payments
- account payable balances

More detailed process-based metrics will enable the shared services organization to predict potential areas of decreasing or increasing productivity. The results provide the basis for making decisions on the need for process improvements or alternative cost reduction strategies. Figure 12.3 illustrates the nature of metrics used by Kraft Foods to measure the performance of its shared services accounts payable processes.

Overall then the balanced scorecard provides a good balance of external and internally focused metrics for determining the effectiveness of shared services. The combination of data is what shared service groups require to report their value to the organization and to assess how well the promises are being delivered. No discussion of measurement can be complete, however, without attempting to describe how to measure or what methodology to use in collecting the data.

CUSTOMER METRICS

Customer data can be gathered using some kind of survey methodology in combination with focus groups or interviews with selected groups of clients. There is no way other than surveying clients directly for their input. Generally, a combination of methods yields the best results. Surveys are good for providing a level of quantitative measure since scales and numbers provide the opportunity to come up with succinct measures of satisfaction. For example, clients can rate shared services as five out of seven in the area of responsiveness. On the other hand, interviews provide qualitative and anecdotal information that is often essential to capture the spirit of the service being delivered.

Internal growth can be measured again with an employee type of survey designed to gauge the degree that learning is being leveraged in the organization. Although not perfect, it is certainly preferable to doing nothing.

Financial data is usually a straight analysis of actuals against fore-casts. This can be done internally and without client involvement.

Finally, internal metrics will have to be gathered on an ongoing basis with measurement tools built into the day-to-day operations.

SPECIAL CHALLENGES FOR MARKETPLACE AND ADVANCED MARKETPLACE MODELS

For shared service groups that place their internal professional and advisory services into an open marketplace where these services are voluntary and groups must earn their way or stay away, there are some unique challenges. In essence, these staff groups then are inter-nal consulting groups competing against external consultants for the same business. Services typically include systems consulting, organi-zational development, management consulting, financial advice, logistics consulting.

In a study done for one of the largest companies in Canada, clients of the systems group were interviewed and surveyed to determine what they wanted from their internal systems consultants. One of the framing questions used was to ask business clients what they valued from external consultants. We then asked how they compared external to internal consultants from their own organizations. At the time, there were a few executives from the systems organization who did not agree with asking anything about external consultants. One execu-tive hotly announced, "The business partners have no right to compare us to externals, they shouldn't do it." To which we replied that clients do, in fact, make comparisons and rather than argue whether this was right or not, it was far better to find out what they valued and what they perceived the internal group to lack. Although the context of the staff group happened to be an information systems group, these consulting practices are every bit as relevant to other staff groups. Here is what clients value in external consultants that internal consultants can take to heart.

How clients measure the value of external consultants

This original list was developed through open-ended questions asking what clients value. These elements were a result of the most common themes. A year later, clients were resurveyed and asked to rank the fol-lowing performance areas for consulting practices. Here is the ranking with number one being the most important performance area and six being the least important performance area:

1 Global and business literacy;

2 Urgency and accountability;

3 Professional communication skills;

4 Innovative problem solving;

5 Superior project management leadership;

6 Relationship building.

The business clients confirmed that they do, in fact, make comparisons all the time between their internal group and the external consulting community. They pointed out that over the past few years, they have had considerable exposure to outside consultants and therefore have heightened expectations and concerns over the service being provided by the internal community. Here are some of the comments under each of the categories:

Global and business literacy
External consultants bring superior knowledge of the outside business world and expert knowledge; they seem to grasp business issues quickly; they are able to tap into a database of solutions instead of recreating the wheel every time; they bring a real value for money orientation.

This behavior contrasted with that of the internal systems consultants who were generally seen to focus too narrowly on the technology solution rather than the business solution and seemed to have a vested interest in building the technology rather than utilizing what has already been developed. In general, the internals were criticized for jumping into the technology conversation too early and did not seem to appreciate or know much about the business issues and environment.

Urgency and accountability
Externals take responsibility and accountability for driving the process; they are fast and deliver to expected pace without making excuses why they can't do something; they have a sense of urgency and act as if I am the only client; external consultants are relentless, they force us to work as hard as they do.

The contrast to internal consultants had a lot to do with speed from the internal group which was perceived as taking too long to deliver. This relates to a need to improve and streamline internal processes, to fast track projects when and where required. On the other hand, business clients did like the fact that externals managed clients' time well, that externals demanded them to work hard and fulfill their role. This is one area that externals have over internals. Business clients seem to pay more attention when they have to put real dollars out on the table. External consultants are also better at being candid about what clients have to do in order to get value from consulting dollars.

Professional communication skills

External consultants are strong presenters, they talk the business language, actively listen and don't presume anything; they are enthusiastic; they tell the truth and are able to confront us when we are wrong; the communication is professional, frequent and thorough; they are open-minded and extremely neutral.

Who would have thought that professional communication skills would be ranked so highly? Clients really appreciate the professionalism in communications, both presentations as well as preparation for meetings and status reviews. External consultants were seen to be extremely polished in their presentations, obviously having taken the time to design and prepare ahead of time. Externals were seen as enthusiastic as opposed to internal consultants who were seen as more complacent, taking the situation a little more in their stride, a little more for granted.

The area of surprise for internal consultants is that clients actually appreciate being told the truth and like the candor from external consultants even though they may not like the message. Externals were seen as being open-minded and neutral which helped clients to receive the truth without feeling threatened.

Innovative problem solving

External consultants are able to get to the heart of the problem. They ask the right questions; they are flexible in their problem solving ability and can adapt quickly to new information; they work with us as opposed to going away and solving problems for us; externals relentlessly probe for issues and requirements before looking at solutions.

Clients related that they were under enormous pressure and were therefore looking to their staff groups for a high degree of innovative thinking and problem solving. Basically, they found external consultants more willing to try a range of solutions, whereas internal consultants tended to be more traditional in approach. They like being engaged to problem solve jointly rather than be served a solution on the plate; they did not mind the amount of involvement in the front end where the issues and requirements need full exploration.

Superior project management leadership

Externals seem to know how to get the right expertise at the right time. They seem to be able to draw the right resources in when needed and can therefore leverage their skills and expertise; they are consistent in their approach, they are organized and well-prepared and have a professional approach to project management; externals are perfectionists in follow-through; they pay attention to detail without burdening me unnecessarily with details.

These comments relate to the ideal of a dynamic environment where resources can be applied on a just-in-time basis whenever clients may need them. This kind of flexibility then is what internal staff groups will have to build if they are to simulate a consulting company. The issues around organizational skills and being well prepared relate to how clients perceive they are being managed. Clients pointed to basics like sending an agenda out ahead of time so that they could be prepared, a practice they did not find all the time with internal consultants. In other words, external consultants looked and acted more organized, which in turn engendered a spirit of confidence that they knew what they were doing. Lastly, and this is more so with executive level clients, external consultants followed through but did not burden clients with all the details. Knowing when and when not to provide detail is essential in order for clients to respect and trust consultants.

Relationship building

External consultants value the building of relationships and trust with us; they work hard at establishing their credibility by publicizing their capability; they demonstrate respect for the flux of business issues and know the pressures in our environment; their empathy towards our business drivers is most evident.

It was curious why this element came last especially when you consider the earlier framework for evaluating quality whereby relationships and product service excellence were equally weighted. Looking deeper, a few working theories surfaced. Clients do see its value and although ranked sixth, it is very important. Secondly, the real issue is that if you look at what clients actually said in the other categories, issues around the service relationship are embedded. For example, under business literacy, clients were really speaking about credibility when they said external consultants understand the business and can talk our language. When they talk about active listening as an essential characteristic in professional communication skills, they are talking about empathy, one of the four elements to a service relationship. It is likely that clients do not pick out the term relationship management in and of itself as something that has value as compared to other issues.

WHAT INTERNAL SHARED SERVICES CONSULTANTS MUST DO TO SUCCEED

Overall, the lesson for shared service groups which include professional advisory services is that these practices can and need to be built into the picture for internal consultants. Shared service groups will need to invest training and development dollars to raise the capability in these areas. This is achievable. These practices can be learned and performed by internals as well as they can by externals. It will just take concentrated efforts and a will to drive the internal staff group to this level of professionalism.

Internal consulting groups need to do the following:

+ stay up to date and contemporary with skills and capability;

+ ensure there is money to buy outside talent and learn from it;

+ learn the business language and motivations of clients;

+ provide products and services clients want, not what you think they ought to have;

+ learn the consulting process and become masters at consulting skills;

+ crave and seek constant feedback, formal and informal;

+ understand if clients would choose an outside supplier and why;

+ help people in staff consulting groups leave, if they find themselves constantly complaining about the clients and wishing they were something else;

+ raise the bar of professionalism in communication skills;

+ work with external consultants rather than against them.

HUMAN RESOURCES CHAMPIONS

David Ulrich, Author

CEOs and executives have to ensure they are providing their staff groups with funding so they can access and develop their own expertise.

Organizations will hold on to their internal staff groups provided they are able to create a culture and identity for the company or offer their organization unique competitive advantage by having deep expertise. This is why executives must understand and commit to the investment required to develop deep expertise.

The need for constant self-evaluation and external evaluation is a requirement in shared services. Feedback has to be seen as valuable or maybe even sacred to ensure that the value of shared services is realized.

NOTES

1 Norton and Kaplan, The Balanced Scorecard

2 Houston Industries Conference Board Report Number 1210-98-CH

Chapter 13

FAST FORWARD

The theater crowd sits in hushed silence as the show Mining for Corporate Gold *comes to its close, the narrator revealing the final act to be about the future. The film suddenly explodes as if someone has pressed the fast forward button, so shapes and images blur, streaks of color fly across the screen, sounds squeak intermittently and the audience tries to grasp the last part of the story as it flashes past them. The film flutters and jolts to a final stop. The house lights come on. The usher walks on to the stage and asks the group what they thought they just saw, what did they make of the future. People sit there, thinking, and then one by one the audience begins to tell their version of the story of the future. It is clear that certain patterns and shapes begin to appear. Some sharper and more pronounced than others. Some audience members get impatient and press for the one common and right answer, one coherent picture. Others shrug, content to dabble in the muted grey areas and select certain images here and there at will, playing with ideas and weighing possibilities. They discuss the irony of their lack of agreement on the future and how one person's hero was another one's villain. They laugh at how despite all this, certain fundamental messages came through loud and clear.*

Universally, the audience saw the delivery of staff work as a patchwork quilt, some parts done inside organizations, some parts outside, but the stitches basically invisible to line managers who don't really care where the services come from as long as they receive good service. Shared services is one of those shapes in the future that will be a permanent fixture. Costs and improved service arguments are too compelling to ignore. Old notions about uniqueness and needing local control are wearing thin. Even in the most geographically distinct region in the world, companies are moving to pan-European organizations in their core businesses, making shared services a logical companion.

Government and the public sector know that shared services is a workable solution to their problem of insufficient funding. Courageous leaders are starting to think about what would be involved in reducing the enormous duplication of staff work currently in practice. They know in their hearts that this is one corporate strategy that will translate well once they have figured out how to make it happen within the politically sensitive environment.

Outsourcing is a piece of the future but will be more carefully executed on a case by case basis as more of the bad news hits the press on less than stellar performance and higher than expected costs. Wise and careful selection though will ensure that organizations find the right suppliers to offer first-class services. The heroes of outsourcing will be those suppliers who only do outsourcing for a living, in a narrow and specific area such as travel and expense reporting or network services, and make it their business to be number one at what they do. There will also be failures in outsourcing which will cause organizations to backsource these same functions. The ones which fail will do so because they have not thought out their business strategies very well; they do not have first-class processes in place or they have underestimated the challenge of running a large-scale operation. The winners in outsourcing options will emerge as brand names. Right now they are an anonymous group known only in narrow circles. Tomorrow, they will have distinct identities and strong brand name recognition as all world-class companies do.

Multi-functional consulting companies which promote outsourcing options and then offer outsourcing services will begin to fray at the seams, getting so big that they will have a hard time holding their gigantic businesses together. These companies will begin to split again, away from one gigantic monolith into thinner, deeper areas of specialty. Outsourcing divisions will likely be spun out so they can concentrate on being the best in that field. The professional practice parts of the giant consulting companies will up the pressure to seize internal professional staff work and claim it for their own. The push is already on to take back audit and internal risk functions. They are in for a harder ride than in the last decade as smart companies drive for better bargains, insist on lower rates, and are wiser about holding consultants accountable for claims made during the sales pitch process. Global sourcing means a careful watch on mega-consulting companies charging exorbitant rates for the same system that has already been paid for, as though every piece of work is customized when it is the same stuff, often with a new cover.

Chief executive officers are seen to show increasing attention to staff work and to insist on relevance, value and cost effectiveness. They want to know what their staff groups are doing to get ready for the future. They are also seen talking to the operating executives about the need to get over their concern for control and to stop wasting time and energy on work that is simply not core to their business. Forget payables, focus on market share!

RICHARD HAYS

Author of *Internal Service Excellence*

The CEO needs to understand the opportunity that exists from demanding change from their staff groups.

Staff operations which have reconfigured report a 31% improvement in costs and an astounding 45% improvement in service levels. There are not many other opportunities where you get gains like this.

Staff groups are seen in two camps. The larger group is seen leading the charge, enthusiastic about covering new territory, energetically marching forward, even whistling as they walk through the wind, sun and rain. The other smaller group is huddled with their heads down as if they are trying to wait out some storm.

The audience admits to a strong identity with the larger group. Although tough hiking lays ahead, it almost looks like fun.

SHARED SERVICES AS PART OF THE FUTURE

Shared services is one of those shapes in the future that look to be a permanent fixture even if the form changes. The costs are too compelling to ignore for both the private and public sector. This is real money going to the real bottom line. It is precious government funding going to public programs. Chief executive officers and public sector executives need to wake up and demand that their staff groups adopt a code of permanent and ruthless self-examination. Sharing has to be more than a spiritual and co-operative notion. Capturing synergies is not about sitting around in a room brainstorming how we might work better together, it is much sharper than that. Shared services has sticking power because the strategy works on both lowering costs and improving service in a range of corporate and organizational scenarios. It works for companies which are shrinking in scope and want to reign in operating costs. It works for companies which are reporting a flat line of growth and want to make sure operating costs don't rise unexpectedly. It probably works best of all when clients are poised for explosive growth as an intelligent alternative to growing overheads to meet demand. When Sun Microsystems realized it was on the brink of a steep growth curve, it selected shared services not because of any problem today but to avoid problems in the future. This was a smart and proactive stance. Faced with a 25% growth curve, finance chose shared services as a pre-emptive strike to counter-attack the normal strategy of simply growing to meet demand.

FIGURE 13.1   A continuum of shared services models

BASIC	MARKETPLACE	ADVANCED MARKETPLACE	INDEPENDENT BUSINESS
• Consolidation of transactional/ administrative work • Focus on economies of scale • Services charged out to recover fully loaded costs • Objective to reduce costs and standardize processes	• Includes professional and advisory services • Separation of governance and service functions • Services charged out to recover fully loaded costs • Objective to reduce costs and improve service quality	• Client choice of supplier • Market based pricing • Possible external sales if surplus capacity • Objective to provide clients choice of most cost effective supplier	• Separate business entity • Profit is retained • Multiple organizations as clients • Objective to generate revenue and profits for service company

The public sector is perhaps one of the biggest arenas for shared services to flourish. Governments have to respond creatively to their budget crises. Often feeling misunderstood, public sector and not-for-profit organizations find the application of corporate thinking out of step with their own reality. In many cases, this is likely to be true, since the demands and constraints of doing work in the public eye with myriad competing stakeholders and agendas is different than a business driven more singularly by profit and shareholder value. The one area that both profit and not-for-profit groups have in common is internal corporate functions. Staff work in the public sector is pretty similar to staff work in the corporate environment. Although the work of the public sector is different in that education, health care services, social agencies, tourism, all have very unique properties compared to cars, electricity and pharmaceuticals, staff work is staff work. Although the requirement for more rigorous processes is a given due to the magnitude of public scrutiny, the fundamental needs from corporate staff groups are the same as in the private sector.

Shared services offers government a chance to reduce operating costs and better leverage expertise without taking a negative hit on the program side. In fact, government and public sector agencies which are not actively pursuing shared services can be seen as irresponsible. There is no rationale for the amount of duplication inherent in staff functions across ministries and state government units. Failure to capture the synergies and opportunities from shared services is morally reprehensible.

PAN-EUROPEAN COMPANIES MEAN PAN-EUROPEAN SHARED SERVICES

Global companies are increasingly looking to the idea of a pan-European model, one entity covering all of Europe, despite the protests of individual country managers and operating businesses. Historically, global companies have created power structures dominated and driven by individual country managers. Titans in their own land, these country managers often worked against each other, building up their own resources, sheltering costs and generally not looking at the business as a whole. Trying to counter the natural tendencies of self-preservation first, companies have ended up with a patchwork of matrix reporting relationships, none of which is particularly effective in helping country managers think enterprise-wide.

The drive for change is not as much internal as it is external. Global customers and dealers are demanding the answer to why different practices, including pricing, could exist between France and Italy. Customers are not static and they no longer stay in the confines of one local region. They want to see an integrated holistic package from the same company.

Internally, companies are worried about the fragmentation of their brand and identity across countries and are looking for a more consistent image. New product launches require a single launch pad, not myriad different approaches. Running a business as a unique entity in each country is slowly diminishing and is being replaced with a pan-European model. It is true that American companies tend to minimize the differences across European countries and often underestimate the challenge of creating a single European entity. The American business approach is clearly a bottom line focus which is making shared services the logical strategy of choice. Hence the emergence of pan-European shared service centers. Economies of scale are far too compelling to ignore.

A BUSINESS IN A MARKETPLACE

The marketplace model of shared services is the place where the most radical and fundamental new thinking has emerged. Putting internal services into a business model where products and services are provided at costs the clients are willing to pay is a radical departure from a staid bureaucracy that is internally focused and internally driven. The future picture here is less clear. A powerful image, but one that not many staff groups are keen to consider, except for a few bold and courageous ones who are willing to put themselves on the line and offer clients choice.

PETER BLOCK

Author of *Flawless Consulting and Stewardship*

Staff groups have to give up their protected class role.

Staff groups have to become more self-supporting, have to see themselves in an open marketplace.

Without client choice, these models are no more than centralization. Allowing choice of supplier is an opportunity to put the proverbial "money where the mouth is" for staff groups and to create accountability for providing value. The size and investment for staff groups then become directly proportional to client demand and perception of value. The size and price tag for staff groups will only be as large as clients want them, no more, no less.

In a recent survey we conducted, the predominance of client choice was minimal in shared service organizations, with less than 20% of companies actually providing for real choice (see figure 13.2). Although intellectually appealing, the concept of choice for service is not exactly a groundswell movement.

This is partially due to the fact that most shared service organizations follow the basic model which is a consolidation of transactional mandated services. For example, payroll is usually a mandated shared

FIGURE 13.2   Client choice

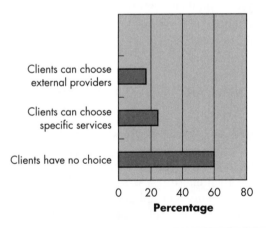

service due to the infrastructure and embedded costs to run such a system. This is not a service that any company or government would want local units to begin outsourcing on a piecemeal basis. Having said that, the provision of choice is still minimal. Unfortunately, staff groups seem to lack the courage to put themselves on the line and be compared to external providers.

SHELL INTERNATIONAL SERVICES

You are a victim of where you come from!

Traditional staff people want continuity and security and are therefore fearful of choice. The rest of us love the thrill that comes with choice. We are energized and excited. We have more freedom and impact than we ever did.

THE IMAGE OF INTERNAL CHARGING

Charge-back for services is a fleeting glimpse at the future picture. It is a necessary but interim tool for a few years to facilitate the fundamental and radical change in mindset of the people in staff groups. Like the golden rule in Monopoly™ it is not recommended passing "go" until you implement charge-back for a period of time. Staff groups have to be forced to work without a safety net, they have to start from the ground up and figure out how much their services actually cost and whether anyone would buy them for that price. This is the basic formula for business: goods and services at prices customers are willing to pay. Naysayers who frown on internal charge-back and call it funny money are just plain wrong. Charging for services is an explicit symbol for the understanding of value. Most staff groups cannot go from bureaucrats to service providers without this major step. Chief executive officers and heads of business units should insist on charge-back to help the shared service group succeed, even if it means parking private assumptions about this practice. In the long term, a simpler method may be more appropriate. What is essential is that business units understand what they are getting and how much it would cost them.

Judging from the survey results listed in figure 13.3, a lot of shared service organizations do have some form of billing although a minority still allocate overhead rates. Without charging for services, it is pretty difficult to show an explicit shift from corporate bureaucracy to a business mindset, where clients will have greater control over what services they want, based at least partially on what they cost. Charging for services is not a petty issue. It is a critical tool for leaders of shared

FIGURE 13.3 Client billing

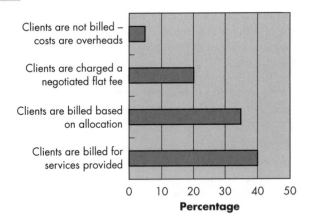

services to shape a brand new outlook and for getting people to accept that nothing can be taken for granted any longer. There are many critics lined up along the wall taking potshots at the practice of charge-back but we believe it is absolutely essential to make shared services successful. After a few years working with shared services, it may be acceptable to dismantle the practice provided that costs are still monitored and benchmarked with external practices.

THE LIBERALIZATION AND RESETTLEMENT OF GOVERNANCE

Organizations ensure governance through corporate policy. John Carver, the renowned author and expert on board and governance, says that because policies permeate and dominate all aspects of organizational life, they present the most powerful lever for the exercise of leadership. "Leadership through explicit policies offers the opportunity to think big and to lead others to think big."[1] For the critics of shared services, policy is always brought forward as the sacrificial lamb for why giving clients choice won't work and why the whole idea of operating as a business is rife with problems. Shared services does not mean anarchy, it does not mean the absence of meaningful governance. Leaders of staff groups have to help executives and boards shape important policy and help them think big. It does not mean though that the people who define and enforce policy are the same ones who provide service. The wearing of two hats for staffers is flawed from the beginning. How can anyone really provide service while also being the company law-enforcer? This dual and conflicting role has to be seen as the root cause of much of what is wrong with staff groups. Chief executive officers and heads of business units have to wake up and see how impossible a role this is for their internal staff groups. It puts them into a love-hate relationship with their internal clients. Staff groups should be liberated from policy enforcement by being allowed internally to separate the two kinds of services.

The Ontario government of Canada is leading a revolution in the public sector for shared services and it is doing it right. Its blueprint and design is impeccable because it has factored in both governance and services but in a completely separate fashion. The public sector is good at policy and although business likes to pretend government isn't good at anything, it is not true. Government people know all about policy, it is one of their core competencies. When they do policy, it has far-reaching impacts on voters, taxpayers, lobbyists and constituents. Policy is a big deal in the public sector. Ask any public official who has been exposed in the media for failure either to have policy in place or to ensure it was obeyed. Staff functions need policy to govern but the design of shared services will be flawed if governance is not separated from the services.

WHOSE POLICY IS IT ANYWAY?

Corporate policies should not be owned by staff functions; they are a line management responsibility. When an executive team adopts a policy of standardization for computer acquisition, it is done from a governance perspective as a way of legitimately minimizing risk and overburdened costs. It is not information technology's policy, it is line management's. Failure to comply should be placed squarely at the feet of line management. In practice many CEOs and executives are only too happy to hang its staff groups out to dry by feigning ignorance or failing to monitor their own executives and staff. It is much easier to blame finance for its annoying capital allocation process than admit that it is, in fact, a line management policy designed to protect shareholder value and fiscal responsibility. As Vipin Suri, the former head of one of the largest shared services groups in North America, says, "It is not the responsibility of shared service groups to make sure that line managers are doing their job."

Let the chief information officer do the policy and policing while the technology service group provides service, hopefully with the two physically and organizationally separated, to make it clear within the company who is doing what and to whom. This thinking is exciting. Staff groups in the service role get to concentrate on the clients and their needs without the baggage that comes from constantly telling people they can't have something they want.

The domain of accountability for policy compliance is one area where line management has generally failed. If not, why then do most business units still insist on the disbursements group checking the expense accounts for violation of policy? Or human resources checking if the business unit has headcount approval to hire a new staff member? Or the information technology group for catching purchases of unauthorized software? Perhaps over time, it is due to the fact that many large public and private bureaucracies have created so many policies that it would take a brain with a photographic memory to recall what they are and where. The fact is there are usually too many policies in a company. It was Ricardo Semler, the author of *Maverick,* who raised the ire of many a corporate audience when he spoke about the philosophy and values at his manufacturing company Semco in São Paulo, Brazil. Too much policy according to Semler strips out important qualities such as thought, judgement and common sense. Mind you, corporate audiences used to go wild at the level of democracy his company practiced, like people setting their own salaries and no corporate policy on travel. The only caveat was that they had to be prepared to defend their decisions on salary and first-class travel arrangements to their peers. The company even eliminated the traditional security hut and replaced it with a sign that simply said, "Please make sure as you leave that you are not inadvertently taking anything that does not belong to you." When pinned against the wall by angry conference participants as to the statistics on loss and theft after the experiment, Ricardo would shrug and say, "I don't know and I don't care. On average probably 2–3% of employees steal so why would I subject 97% of employees to a daily ritual of humiliation?" Conventional thinking on policy does need to be challenged since much of policy has been designed for the minuscule percentage of the population who will behave badly. The fewer the policies, the better!

The marketplace model for shared services will work as long as a few key policies are in place and the company has adequately placed a governance role in the corporate headquarters as well as worked at increasing line accountability for adhering to policy. It is not a matter of either/or, it is both. Staff groups which throw up the tired excuses for not moving to shared services because of the need for policy and consistency should listen to themselves. They are basically saying that line management can't be trusted. They are really saying that line managers are too stupid to figure out what is right.

INDEPENDENT BUSINESS

Whether shared service groups can turn themselves into businesses, or whether they even ought to try, is unclear. Although organizations are often selectively trying to market particular services externally, not many are following the full independent business model like the Royal Dutch/Shell Group. Shell Services International Inc. (USA), is confident the company can create a viable enterprise given its infrastructure and know-how worldwide. It sees the idea of core business processes as a shrinking definition with opportunities for its organization to provide world-class capabilities at reduced costs.

Watching executives debate the idea of letting their staff groups become separate business entities outside the corporation is an interesting study in values. Clearly, there are those executives who fundamentally do not see the point of spending any time and energy in helping staff groups create a business that is not core to the enterprise. They are impatient with the idea and negative about even spending time on the subject. Other executives clearly see the upside potential for revenue and believe that the business idea is a good one. These executives are confident that their own processes are so good that there will be an eager and willing market for them. Secretly a few executives delight in the idea that staff will have to prove their mettle by competing on an equal footing in the outside marketplace. There are two schools of thought on the independent business model. One theory holds the possibility that large shared service businesses such as these will emerge on the horizon as the new outsourcers, competing with existing suppliers and consultants for a piece of the lucrative pie. The other theory is less optimistic with a view that predicts business difficulty for a company within a company whose energy and motivation will be all but absorbed by serving its own organization. The question on people's minds is how much spare capacity will the shared services company really have after it has effectively served the internal clients of the original organization?

So this picture is a little less clear although it blurs nicely into outsourcing as companies find themselves bombarded with new opportunities and alternative delivery systems.

OUTSOURCING'S RISE AND FALL

Like a silver bullet screaming across the screen, outsourcing is definitely in the future. As someone wryly quipped at a conference, "If outsourcing is the answer, I want to know what the question is." Apparently, the question has to do with lower costs in some cases, and higher costs in others. In a study done by the Corporate Leadership Council, costs were shown to be higher post outsourcing on some occasions while lower on others. The answer lies in a case by case approach. Caution will be thrown to the wind if companies are not seriously smart about why they want to outsource and what they are giving up in the act.

ROYAL BANK FINANCIAL GROUP

John Cleghorn, Chairman and CEO

We believe the functions that should remain internal are those that have unique value, are proprietary, strategically important, exploit economics of scale, can be proven to perform cost effectively or are comparable with value to outside vendors.

There is no question that we are increasingly looking hard at our internal operations. We are exploring a range of models including co-sourcing as opposed to pure outsourcing. For example, we have recently formed an alliance with S1 Technologies to develop Internet banking technology.

Too many suppliers are rushing into the outsourcing craze to make a buck when they haven't really taken the time to create outstanding processes. This will be a problem for them and ultimately a problem for the companies which have happily tossed their basket of staff stuff over the wall. Once functions are outsourced, it would take considerable investment to bring them back inside should the outsourcer fail to live up to expectations.

On the other hand, staff groups should not be lulled into a false sense of security. The most common form of resistance to outsourcing is completely illogical. Staff groups claim that outsourced suppliers cannot possibly figure out the unique culture and practices of their company. Think again, suppliers have figured out how to learn about numerous cultures and processes because they make a living out of serving multiple groups of clients.

Many internal staff groups have the opportunity and are well positioned to take advantage of this chance to drive value and change. They have a head start over the outsiders, consultants and contractors who want the work, that is if they choose to exercise their power.

Backsourcing

No strategy or idea is complete until it is neatly coined into a term. Backsourcing has already emerged to describe the practice of taking a function previously outsourced and bringing it back home. An article in the

---

ROSABETH MOSS KANTER

Author and Harvard Business Professor

Contractors are quickly learning how to embed themselves deeply into their client's strategies and business processes.

Staff groups will be outsourced if they cannot provide strategic value which means contributing to the company's core competence, innovating to help the company create new business concepts. Technically, this would be hard to get from an outside contractor, but times are changing.

Wall Street Journal recently revealed the gravy train on which the likes of International Business Machines, Electronic Data Systems Corporation and Arthur Andersen have been hitching a ride, valued at more than $80 billion in 1998. Lam Truong, vice president of based chip maker LSI Logic Corp, knows from personal experience about backsourcing, having made the decision to terminate the company's outsourcing contract for information technology services.[3] He now claims a 35% cost saving from taking it back in-house but does not universally dismiss outsourcing, seeing it instead as a selective strategy for goods and services when needed, not as wholesale long-term contracts with huge dollars attached. Backsourcing will grow as outsourcing continues to explode in growth.

THE CONSULTING IMPLOSION

There is a John Cleese scene in a Monty Python film where a man sits down at a table groaning with food and eats non-stop sumptuous and grand portions, blowing up bigger and bigger in front of our very eyes. Someone delicately offers the man in his blown-up state a tiny chocolate mint, but he repeatedly claims not to be able to take one more morsel. He finally relents, slips the tiny mint into his mouth, only to find it was indeed the final straw, at which point he explodes. Consulting companies may be expanding their repertoire too much.

Out on the horizon loom new giants eager for a bigger slice of internal staff pie served up juicy and hot. Consulting companies that are multi-disciplined and multi-functional are growing in revenue at unprecedented rates and have recently been merging with a fever. Big will be a problem in the long term. Who is to say that consulting companies know how to run huge businesses just because they advise them on a regular basis?

A sword is beginning to dangle over consulting firms as clients and technology are increasingly pressuring for lower fees.[4] James O'Shea and Charles Madigan's book *Dangerous Company,* a tantalizing read on the spoils of consultants, poses the question, "How much is professional advice worth?" The book describes in horror how companies have not only spent millions of dollars, or in the case of AT&T, a half a billion dollars, on consulting fees but in some cases, companies have actually been ruined by the advice. Up until now, there has never been any real accountability for the advice-giving business. Given the number of creeping and silent lawsuits against consulting companies, it is likely that there will be new requirements for conduct, with companies insisting that claims pitched in the sales cycle actually do come true. The fees themselves also have to be questioned. US consulting fees for partners and top talent run easily in the range of $5,000 per day. That translates to about $625.00 for every consulting hour. Companies will have to become smarter about the use of consultants and insist on accountability and value for these kinds of rates. Rates will fall for professional consulting services. Executives will increasingly negotiate for better prices and challenge conventional notions about consulting rates.

Knowledge and expertise is at the heart of professional service firms and although consulting companies have long held the claim that they are able to attract new talent and savvy graduates, the reality is quite different. Consulting companies are hunting for an increasingly smaller pool of talent as new graduates are choosing to go to smaller start-up firms, often for an equity stake. David H. Maister, leading author on professional service firms, predicted ten years ago that consulting companies would be facing a 25% shrinkage in their non-partner labor force and he was right. As he says, consulting companies are referring to this as the battle for talent. The scarcity of resources is already here and unless consulting companies dedicate time and money to nurturing and developing a positive culture for their culture for their knowledge staff, they will have trouble meeting demand.

Companies should watch for this and make sure they are not leaving themselves open to this vulnerability. The supply may exist now for professional staff services but how prepared is the company in case there is such a shortage? To hedge their bets, smart companies will make sure they actively attract and retain top staff talent.

GUNN PARTNERS

Bob Gunn

Companies should develop their own capability to improve staff work. It is too valuable to leave up to outsiders.

Investing in staff groups is a worthwhile effort. CEOs have to help staff groups by consciously working with the executive to insist on collaboration amongst line and staff groups.

Curtain call: messages to the CEO

As the curtain closes on the show, we sit there wishing there had been more previews because a number of audience members are looking forward to seeing what the new kids on the block will be doing with their staff groups. These are the burgeoning new high technology companies, denim and technology woven in cyberspace. These companies are growing at unprecedented rates and have the opportunity not to make the mistakes of their forefathers and mothers.

PSINet Inc.

David N. Kunkel, Executive VP General Counsel

We believe we are the Internet. We outsource functions wherever possible: legal, financial, MIS, HR to name a few. We don't have time to work out a hierarchy so we rely on key providers of services and people. It doesn't matter to us where the services are physically located. We communicate from around the world daily.

The CEOs leave, thinking there was more to the show than they had banked on, and make a mental note to bring up the subject of staff functions at the next corporate meeting. Chief financial officers are proud that everyone knows how shared services came to be born from their own discipline and that the cost savings are too big to ignore any longer. Information technology executives are glad to see how powerful the application of technology can be in transforming staff work into value work and are thinking how they could separate their governance role from their services role but they do cede it is a good idea. Human resources executives are glad to see the CEOs engaged in staff work and want to make sure that they keep it high on the agenda. They too ponder the fundamental dilemma of having governance meshed in with their service role and start to think about how to change it. Supply executives know they are part of the future and can see beyond shared services on a function by function basis. They are dreaming of maps that include the entire supply chain process. Marketing executives know that they are different but are beginning to see how line management in reality just might see them as another staff group. They are glad that the show focused on the need for dramatically better client service and that it wasn't all focused on numbers, costs and technology. They see how they could help staff groups do a better job of marketing themselves.

Some of the consultants and outsourcing suppliers seem to be walking out in a bit of a huff, vowing to go to a different movie next time, one that clearly had themselves featured only as heroes. The executives from government and the not-for-profit companies are pretty animated as they look at the potential for shared services in the public sector, seeing that for once this business strategy was tailor-made for them. Finally, line managers decide the show wasn't bad and they are thinking about how they can get their own organizations to do a better job on the policy stuff and how they really do have to work better with the staff groups. They do, however, make a date to see the action film down the street called Where the Rubber Hits the Road. They figure they'll invite a few of the staff groups so they can get in on the action and see what it is like to live life in the fast lane.

Notes

1 John Carver, (1990), Boards that Make a Difference
2 The Conference Board, January 1999
3 Kevin Delaney, *Wall Street Journal,* reprinted in *The Globe and Mail,* 17 May 1999
4 James O'Shea and Charles Madigan, 1997

BIBLIOGRAPHY

Banister, Gaurdie (1999) *The strategic value of outsourcing.*

Proceedings: LaJolla, CA: The Conference Board.

The 1999 Strategic Outsourcing Conference – "Optimizing the value of outsourcing."

Bell, Chip R. (1994) *Customers as partners.* San Francisco, CA: Berrett-Koehler Publishers Inc.

Bengston, Fran (1998) *Creating a high service level environment.*

Proceedings: Vancouver, BC: ICM Conference – Implementing a shared services strategy.

Bester, Wayne (1998) *Using Metrics and Measurements in the Development of Shared Services.*

Proceedings: Vancouver, BC: ICM (International Communications for Management) Conference – Implementing a shared services strategy.

Block, Peter (1993) Flawless Consulting and *Stewardship.* San Francisco, CA: Berrett-Koehler Publishers Inc.

Bragg, Steven M. (1998) *Outsourcing.* New York, NY: John Wiley & Sons Inc. Publishers.

Carver, John (1990) *Boards that make a difference.* San Francisco, CA: Jossey Bass Inc. Publishers.

Collins, James and Porras, Jerry I. (1994) *Built to last.* New York, NY: HarperCollins Publishers.

Cooke, Robert S. (1997) *Getting senior level buy-in and executive level sponsorship: building consensus with the stakeholder.*

Proceedings: Toronto, Ontario: Institute for International Research Conference – Shared services program for your organization.

— (1997) *Getting executive buy-in.*

Proceedings: Victoria, BC: Royal Roads University Conference for Graduate Students in Leadership.

— (1999) *Planning for success.*

Proceedings: Chicago, ILL: ICM Conference – Strategies for quality enhancement and cost reduction.

— and Quinn, Barbara E. "The executive team is an oxymoron." *Proceedings:* Victoria, BC: Executive Team Planning Session for Forest Renewal BC.

Davis, Waters (1996) "Shared services: a business perspective." *Proceedings:* Toronto, ON: International Quality and Productivity Center Conference on Shared Services.

Delaney, Kevin (1999) "Outsourcing takes a back seat to backsourcing." *The Globe and Mail,* 17 May 1999.

Gordon, Ian (1998) *Relationship marketing,* Ontario, John Wiley & Sons.

Greaver, Maurice F. II (1999) *Strategic outsourcing.* New York, AMACOM, AMA Publishers.

Hays, Richard (1996) *Internal service excellence: a manager's guide to building world-class internal service unit performance.* Summit Executive Press.

Huhn, Stephen (1999) *"Negotiating the contract/defining the relationship."* *Proceedings:* LaJolla, CA: The Conference Board. The 1999 Strategic Outsourcing Conference: "Optimizing the value of outsourcing."

Kaplan, Robert S. and Norton, David P. (1996) *The balanced scorecard: translating strategy into action.* Harvard Business School Press.

Kearney, Tim (1997) Recognizing the organizational challenges surrounding the implementation of new processes in your shared services environment.

Kellogg, David (1998) "The development of a pan-european greenfield site: the case of whirlpool." *Proceedings:* Toronto, ON: ICM (International Communications for Management) Conference – Implementing a shared services strategy.

Kercher, Lee (1999) "Making the outsourcing decision". *Proceedings:* LaJolla, CA: The Conference Board. The 1999 Strategic Outsourcing Conference: "Optimizing the value of outsourcing."

Keuzes, James M. Posner, Bury Z. and Peters, Tom, *The Leadership Challenge: How to Keep Getting Extraordinary Things Done in Organizations,* Jossey-Bass Management Series.

Kris, Andrew (1999) "Shared services and the impact on company staff." *Proceedings:* Brussels, Belgium. IQPC Ltd Conference: "Transforming internal staff and support functions."

Kris, Andrew (1998) "Internal marketing of shared services: a necessity not a luxury." *Proceedings:* Rotterdam, The Netherlands. IQPC Ltd. *Conference:* "Achieving cost effectiveness and service excellence in the energy industry."

Lewis, Jim and Hart, Charles (1998) *Goldpanning.* Surrey. B.C.: Heritage House Publishing Company Ltd.

Maister, David H. (1993) New York, Free Press Paperbacks. Simon & Schuster Publishers.

O'Shea, James and Madigan, Charles (1997) *Dangerous company.* New York, Random House Publishers.

Peters, Thomas and Waterman, Robert H. (1988) *In search of excellence: lessons from America's best run companies.* Warner Books.

Pinchot, Gifford and Elizabeth (1994) *The end of bureaucracy and the rise of the intelligent organization.* San Francisco, CA: Berrett-Koehler Publishers Inc.

Quinn, Barbara E and Robert S. Cooke (1999) "Adopting and Implementing Shared Services. Management Accounting Guideline" Hamilton, ON: The Society of Management Accountants of Canada.

Quinn, Barbara E. (1998) "From corporate bureaucracy to shared services." *Proceedings:* Toronto, ON: ICM Conference – Implementing a shared services strategy.

Quinn, Barbara E. (1999) "What is shared services and why." *Proceedings:* Toronto, ON: CMA Canada Annual Conference for The Canadian Academic Accounting Association.

Quinn, James Bryan (1992) *Intelligent enterprise,* New York, The Free Press, Simon & Schuster Inc.

Rahaim, Joseph W. (1999) "Shared service trends, Ernst & Young LLP." *Proceedings:* Chicago, ILL: ICM Conference: "Strategies for quality enhancement and cost reduction."

Schein, Edgar H. (1992) *Organizational culture and leadership.* San Francisco, CA: Jossey Bass Inc. Publishers.

Schulman, D., Dunleavy, J., Harmer, M. and Lusk, J. (1999) *Shared services.* New York, John Wiley & Sons.

Semler, Ricardo, (1993) *Maverick.* New York, Warner Books Publishers.

Swiggum, David (1997) "Shared services: from cost centers to market driven teams." *Proceedings:* Toronto, ON: The Canadian Institute Conference on Shared Services.

Ulrich, David (1997) *Human Resource Champions: The Next Agenda for Adding Value and Delivering Results,* Harvard Business School Press.

Young, David and Kay Dirk Ullmann (1998) *Benchmarking corporate headquarters staff,* Ashridge Strategic Management Centre, England.

The Drucker Foundation (1996) *The leader of the future.* San Francisco, CA: Jossey Bass Inc. Publishers.

___ (1998) "Shared services: achieving higher levels of performance." The Conference Board Report. New York: Report Number 1210-98-CH.

INDEX